PRAGMATISM AS POST-POSTMODERNISM

PRAGMATISM AS
POST-POSTMODERNISM

Lessons from John Dewey

LARRY A. HICKMAN

FORDHAM UNIVERSITY PRESS   NEW YORK   2007

Library of Congress Cataloging-in-Publication Data

Hickman, Larry A., 1942–
   Pragmatism as post-postmodernism : lessons from John Dewey / Larry A. Hickman.—1st ed.
      p.   cm.—(American philosophy series)
   Includes bibliographical references and index.
   ISBN 978-0-8232-2841-6 (cloth : alk. paper)—
   ISBN 978-0-8232-2842-3 (pbk. : alk. paper)
      1. Pragmatism.   2. Dewey, John, 1859–1952.
   3. Postmodernism.   I. Title.   II. Series.
   B832.H53   2007
   191—dc22

                                                    2007045726

Printed in the United States of America
09 08 07 5 4 3 2 1
First edition

Contents

{ *v* }

Part 4. Classical Pragmatism

Preface and Acknowledgments

For the most part, the essays in this volume were written with the aim of extending the reach of John Dewey's insights into areas where they have so far had little or no recognition. The underlying claim is that his work still offers much that is fresh, and that when properly understood, it is capable of making important contributions to contemporary philosophical debates.

Following the practice advised by the fifteenth edition of the *Chicago Manual of Style* (section 8.85), I have capitalized Pragmatism and its cognates throughout "to distinguish them from the generic words used in everyday speech." I have done the same for Instrumentalism and its cognates.

References to John Dewey's works are to the standard (print) edition, *The Collected Works of John Dewey, 1882–1953*, edited by. Jo Ann Boydston (Carbondale: Southern Illinois University Press, 1969–1991) and published in three series as *The Early Works* (EW), *The Middle Works* (MW), and *The Later Works* (LW). These designations are followed by volume and page number. "LW 2.235," for example, refers to *The Later Works*, volume 2, page 235. An electronic edition, based on the print edition, is available from the InteLex Corporation, Charlottesville, Virginia. The electronic edition preserves the line and page breaks of the print edition.

Special thanks are due to James Downhour for the diligence and patience that he brought to the preparation of the typescript for this volume. Special thanks, also, to the entire staff of the Center for Dewey Studies: James Downhour, Barbara Levine, Michael McNally,

Paula McNally, Karen Mylan, and Harriet Simon for the energy and care they bring to the task of collecting and editing the research materials that make volumes of this type possible.

During the final stages of the preparation of this volume, I received the sad news that Richard Rorty had passed away. In several of the following chapters I have taken issue with Rorty's reading of Dewey, and even argued that his version of neopragmatism did not always avail itself of the full range of philosophical tools that the classical Pragmatists offered us.

Nevertheless, I think it important to point out that during the last quarter of the twentieth century American Pragmatism broadly conceived, as a way of thinking about the complex problems and prospects of human life, had no more dedicated champion than Richard Rorty. If there is to be a Rorty biography, I hope it will tell the story of his many efforts to place Dewey's books in places where they were greatly needed. For more than twenty years, Richard Rorty was a dedicated supporter and friend of the Center for Dewey Studies. He will be missed.

PRAGMATISM AS POST-POSTMODERNISM

INTRODUCTION

P hilosophy in America is enjoying a period of unprecedented pluralism. The gradual erosion of the hegemony of Anglo-American
analytic philosophy that began in the late 1970s has created enlarged
spaces for new interests, new ideas, and new debates. New research
programs in French postmodernism, phenomenology, Frankfurt
School Critical Theory, Heidegger studies, analytic philosophy, neopragmatism, and classical Pragmatism are now happily (and energeti-
cally) engaging, challenging, and informing one another. New fields
such as the philosophy of technology, environmental philosophy,
biomedical ethics, feminist philosophy, and the philosophy of geogra-
phy—to name but a few—have established themselves as legitimate
participants in the great philosophical debates of our time.

The essays in this volume are offered as a contribution to these
ongoing debates. They are premised on the conviction that the inno-
vations of the founding Pragmatists—introduced and refined over
some eighty years, from Charles Peirce's *Popular Science Monthly*

publications of the 1870s until the final essay John Dewey published before his death in 1952—have still not been sufficiently understood or appropriated by contemporary philosophers.

I. Postmodernism

Chapter 1, "Classical Pragmatism: Waiting at the End of the Road," identifies some of the main advances of French-inspired postmodernist philosophers over their modernist predecessors. But it also documents the fact that well over a half century before the term "postmodernism" came into currency as a philosophical idea, classical Pragmatism had already adopted most of those advances, including antifoundationalism and a deflationary attitude toward traditional metaphysics that amounted to a rejection of what Jean-François Lyotard would later call a "grand narrative." From the vantage point of classical Pragmatism, however, postmodernism continues to suffer from two great difficulties that the Pragmatists had already resolved: how to account for and use objectivity; and how to terminate processes of infinite self-referentiality, redescription, and reinterpretation in ways that can produce reliable platforms for action. The founding Pragmatists are thus presented as "waiting at the end of the road"—to use Richard Rorty's felicitous phrase—that postmodern philosophy is traveling. It is in this sense that I cast classical Pragmatism as a form of post–postmodernism.

These matters receive further development in the next two chapters. Chapter 2, "Pragmatism, Postmodernism, and Global Citizenship," argues that some of the key ideas of the classical Pragmatists are ideally suited for application to problems of knowledge and valuation that are related to defining and promoting global citizenship. For one thing, Pragmatism claims to discover a strain of human commonality that trumps the postmodernist emphasis on difference and discontinuity. For another, when classical Pragmatism's mature theory of truth is coupled with its moderate version of cultural relativism, the more skeptical postmodernist version known as cognitive relativism is undercut. On the surface, cognitive relativism might appear to oppose ideas and practices that militate against global citizenship by allowing that no standpoint is uniquely privileged above all others, thus leveling the cross-cultural playing field and fostering pluralism. The actual consequences of cognitive relativism have been the opposite: Postmodernist relativism has in fact been used to provide cover for various forms of religious fundamentalism and racist politics, including the Hindu fundamentalist defense of the caste system in India and the racist programs of the political Right in France. Pragmatism, on the other hand, by holding that there are objective results of inquiry in the social sciences as well as in the physical sciences, would not provide cover to oppressive ideas. Even though these results may not have been universali*zed*, they are nevertheless universal*izable* in ways that provide firm platforms for the development of global citizenship at the same time that they honor cultural pluralism.

Chapter 3, "Classical Pragmatism, Postmodernism, and Neopragmatism," continues the discussion of Pragmatism and postmodernism begun in the two previous chapters by examining the postmodernist themes that have been taken up and woven into some forms of neopragmatism, such as the one advanced by Rorty. I argue that Rorty's neopragmatism differs from Dewey's classical Pragmatism in several important ways—ways that reveal neopragmatism's debt to postmodernism. Whereas Dewey honored the distinct roles that the arts and the sciences can play in social reconstruction, for example, Rorty tends to alternate between blurring that distinction, on the one hand, and maintaining the distinction but privileging literature over the technosciences, on the other. It also appears that the type of relativism found in neopragmatism—a type that is also found in the writings of some postmodernists—does not allow us to hope for anything more solid than personal and cultural preferences. Neopragmatism of this variety thus appears to be an attempt to displace classical Pragmatism's thick program of active experimental analysis and social reconstruction with thinner projects that present hoping and coping as the best available outcome.

II. Technology

In the next four chapters I turn to a discussion of some of the major themes in the philosophy of technology. Chapter 4, "Classical Pragmatism and Communicative Action: Jürgen Habermas," presents a Deweyan critique of the work of Jürgen Habermas. Despite his important contributions as a major public intellectual, from the vantage point of his Pragmatist critics Habermas's project appears to rest on an unstable dualism of strategic action versus communicative action. In the view of his Pragmatist critics, Habermas's project places so much weight on the noninstrumentalist side of the breach that it consequently fails to give experimentation its proper place in human doing and making. Dewey's project, in contrast, being richer and more flexible than Habermas's, avoids some of its pitfalls by avoiding its explicit dualism as well as the quasi-transcendentalism nested within it. I close this chapter with an invitation to Habermas to engage Dewey's work more systematically.

Chapter 5, "From Critical Theory to Pragmatism: Andrew Feenberg," engages one of the most insightful and productive philosophers of technology working today. I present the trajectory of Andrew Feenberg's career as moving away from the Critical Theory of his teacher, Herbert Marcuse, toward the critique of technology advanced by Dewey. I argue that in *Questioning Technology* Feenberg follows Dewey on several important points: he moves from an essentialist to a functionalist understanding of technology; he develops a vigorous form of social constructivism; he rejects a Heideggerian type of romanticism in favor of a naturalized technology; he rejects the Critical Theorists' notion of technology as ideology; he accepts the idea that the project of Enlightenment rationality is not as much of a threat as the Critical Theorists had imagined; he proposes the idea that technical decisions are made within a network of competing factors in which one weighs various desired ends against one another; he warns against the reification of the results of inquiry as if they had existed prior to inquiry (Dewey's "philosophic fallacy"); and he recasts technology in a way that bridges the traditional split between artifacts and social relations. In all this, I suggest, Feenberg's progress toward a Pragmatic reading of the philosophy of technology is the right move at the right time.

Chapter 6, "A Neo-Heideggerian Critique of Technology: Albert Borgmann," continues a conversation that I have had with Albert Borgmann for some fifteen years. Borgmann's books, including *Technology and the Character of Contemporary Life, Across the Postmodern Divide*, and *Holding On to Reality*, advance what is arguably one of the best neo-Heideggerian critiques of technology currently available. Whereas Borgmann's arguments against hyperconsumerism and commodification are unassailable, I suggest that his project suffers from the same sort of dualism that has plagued the projects of the first and second generations of the Critical Theorists. For both Borgmann and Heidegger, technology tends to distract us from the great embodiments of meaning. For both Borgmann and Heidegger, technology has been responsible for a diaspora of focal things and practices. For both Borgmann and Heidegger, the vacuity of technology provides the grounds for a negative kind of hope, for an opening or clearing where focal things can once more be clearly and purposefully engaged. To his credit, however, Borgmann also parts company with Heidegger on a number of points, including Heidegger's apparent desire to return to a kind of pretechnological romanticism and (of course) Heidegger's disastrous social and political ideas. Borgmann attempts to introduce an agenda of social and political reform that is in many ways quite salutary. Nevertheless, to Borgmann's Pragmatist critics he appears to be enmeshed in a fatal dualism and an uncritical acceptance of what he terms "ultimate concerns."

Chapter 7, "Doing and Making in a Democracy: John Dewey" goes beyond the oblique presentations of Dewey's critique of technology presented in the previous three chapters. In this chapter I present Dewey's critique directly. I present his reading of the history of philosophical treatments of technology and his proposals for "naturalizing" technology, that is, locating it in a realm that is neither supernatural nor extranatural and in which the only telic elements are the natural ends of objects, individuals, and events, all of which in turn may become means to further ends. Dewey rejected the notion that technology is no more than applied science and argued that technology is prior to science historically and functionally. In Dewey's view, technology can form a buffer between the forces of antiscience and science and function as a means by which science can be appropriated by the scientifically uninformed. He had little sympathy for those who attack technology in the name of humanism for usurping a place that is more legitimately held by abstract moral precepts. For Dewey, unlike Heidegger and the first- and second-generation Critical Theorists, technology was never the problem. Instead, he thought that what is called for in a world of constant change is intelligence, especially as it is exhibited in democratic practices. What is called for is no more or less than determined and systematic inquiry into our tools and techniques, or in his words, technology.

III. The Environment

The two essays in this section locate Dewey's work within the past and present of environmental philosophy. Chapter 8, "Nature as Culture: John Dewey and Aldo Leopold," argues that Dewey's environmental naturalism allows him to accept and defend the central tenets of Leopold's land ethic without the appeal to an idealized, nonhuman nature that occasionally surfaces within Leopold's work. I argue that Leopold's attempt to provide a foundation for his ethic by that means is the least workable and the least defensible feature of his otherwise excellent project. Dewey's alternative locates itself in the thick of current debates regarding the relations between human beings and nonhuman nature. It offers the promise of continuing insights within this arena of human experience.

Chapter 9, "Green Pragmatism: Reals without Realism, Ideals without Idealism," builds on the material presented in the previous chapter. I discuss the relevance of Dewey's ideas to more recent philosophical debates among environmental philosophers such as Bryan Norton, Holmes Ralston III, J. Baird Callicott, and Michael Zimmerman. I argue that Dewey's work anticipated some of the central concepts of the work of Callicott and Norton, such as source versus locus of value and felt versus considered values. On the other hand, Dewey's Pragmatism stands in sharp contrast to Ralston's idealism and some of the mystic strains encountered in the work of Zimmerman. I suggest that a careful reading of Dewey's 1909 essay "Nature and Its Good: A Conversation" provides an interesting and informative foil against which to read the works of these four environmental philosophers and serves as a wedge by means of which Dewey is able to enter into their conversation. When taken with the 1896 essay "Evolution and Ethics," it bears witness to Dewey's concern, almost a century ago, with matters that today we term environmental.

IV. Classical Pragmatism

The final section comprises six essays devoted to some of the central ideas and figures of classical Pragmatism. Chapter 10, "What Was Dewey's Magic Number?" probes the substructure of Dewey's philosophical method. Taking my cue from Abraham Kaplan, who once suggested that Dewey's "magic number" was two, I suggest that he thought more basically in terms of threes, even though the titles of Dewey's books—such as *Experience and Nature*, *The School and Society*, and *Human Nature and Conduct*—and his goal of reconstructing disparate elements into new wholes might support Kaplan's thesis. Some of his cases seem to be inspired by Hegel's dialectic, while others recall Peirce's categories, especially as they are related to Peirce's method of fixing belief. In order to make my case, I discuss Dewey's treatments of three areas of philosophical interest: the arts, ethics, and inquiry.

Chapter 11, "Cultivating a Common Faith: Dewey's Religion," takes up the highly controversial matter of Dewey's analysis of religious belief. Dewey argued that there is no such thing as religion in general—that there is nothing that all religions qua religions have in common. Moreover, given the wide variety of the world's religions, he argued, and given differences in cultural background and temperament, how is it possible to choose a religion from among them? What sort of criteria are available? Rejecting claims that ideals must be grounded in absolutes, justified by objects and events that transcend experience, or warranted by history or tradition, Dewey invites us to exhibit a particular type of religious faith. This religious faith—this common faith—would be one that takes experience seriously as a source of values, that tests values and ideals experimentally, and that honors the religious qualities of experiences of many types, including aesthetic, ethical, scientific, and educational types. It is this religious attitude that Dewey thinks can drive, inform, and refresh religious institutions. It is this common faith that can insure the continuing relevance of religious institutions in a changing world and provide a platform for their cooperation on matters that transcend narrow sectarian interest.

Chapter 12, "Beyond the Epistemology Industry: Dewey's Theory of Inquiry," presents a succinct overview of Dewey's theory of inquiry. I discuss his criticisms of what he termed the "epistemology industry" and his notion of warranted assertibility. Topics discussed in this essay include Dewey's idea of inquiry as organic and instrumental behavior, the role of the a priori in inquiry, the relation of common sense and science, the status of logical objects, the nature and function of abstraction, the relation of matter and form in inquiry, the role of judgments in inquiry, propositions and their relations, and the social dimensions of inquiry. Dewey rejected the idea that logic, or the theory of inquiry, is a strictly formal discipline complete in itself and devoid of relevance to the affairs of public life.

Chapter 13, "The *Homo Faber* Debate in Dewey and Max Scheler," begins by identifying some of the significant personal and professional differences between Dewey and Max Scheler. One of these differences was that Dewey accepted the *homo faber* thesis as it had been advanced by Henri Bergson, according to which intelligence is the faculty of manufacturing artificial objects, especially tools to make other tools. Scheler, on the other hand, rejected what he regarded as the primary features of the *homo faber* thesis, namely that human beings can make signs and tools because they have a larger and more powerful cortex than other animals. Scheler opted instead for a "discontinuity thesis," according to which human life possesses a uniquely new characteristic best termed "spirit." Despite these and other differences, however, and despite Scheler's attacks on the Pragmatists, he and Dewey articulated remarkably similar views regarding the function of tools in intelligent adaptation. The fact that Dewey held a version of the *homo faber* thesis that Scheler rejected should not obscure their fundamental agreements regarding the issues that vitalize that thesis.

Chapter 14, "Productive Pragmatism: Habits as Artifacts in Peirce and Dewey," returns to a question that was central to the first section of this book: To what extent can we expect the outcome of inquiry to provide anything more than infinite processes of redescription and reinterpretation? Critics of the Pragmatists, including Bertrand Russell, Max Horkheimer, and Theodor Adorno, have accused Pragmatism of making action an end in itself. If this criticism were justified, then one of the key differences between classical Pragmatism and neopragmatism would evaporate. In this chapter I argue that neither Peirce nor Dewey thought that action—except incidentally—is the end of inquiry. The function of inquiry is instead the production of new artifacts, including new habits. It is true that early in his career Peirce held the view that there is an infinite continuum of signs, and that there is neither a first nor a last object that is not a sign of something further. But he eventually abandoned this view and began to write of logical interpretants that are "ultimate," "final," and "veritable." When Peirce's later doctrine of signs and Dewey's Instrumentalism are taken together, I argue, then it becomes clear that these versions of classical Pragmatism should not simply be termed "praxis" philosophies. They are philosophies of production.

PART ONE

POSTMODERNISM

ONE

CLASSICAL PRAGMATISM

Waiting at the End of the Road

I take as my point of departure the now famous remark by Richard Rorty, that when certain of the postmodernists reach the end of the road they are traveling they will find Dewey there waiting for them.[1] The precise text I have in mind is from the introduction to *The Consequences of Pragmatism.* It goes like this: "On my view, James and Dewey were not only waiting at the end of the dialectical road which analytic philosophy traveled, but are waiting at the end of the road which, for example, Foucault and Deleuze are currently traveling."[2]

I freely admit that when Rorty wrote this sentence he probably had something different in mind than what I will suggest here. That much is clear from his remarks on Foucault and Dewey several hundred pages later. He tells us there that the burden of his argument "is that we should see Dewey as having already gone the route Foucault is traveling, and as having arrived at the point Foucault is still trying to reach—the point at which we can make philosophical and historical ('genealogical') reflection useful to those, in Foucault's phrase, 'whose fight is located in the fine meshes of the webs of power.'"[3] Rorty fleshes this point out in an admirable manner when he writes that although Foucault's philosophy of language and his analysis of power relations seem new, Dewey anticipated both. Even further, he suggests that Foucault's "structures of power" are not much different from what Dewey described as "structures of culture."

Just taken as they stand, however, these remarks only allow us to conclude that Dewey is on the same road and has reached the same point that the others have traveled. In what sense is he, as Rorty put it, "waiting at the end of the road"? Rorty thinks that this is a matter of Dewey's superior vocabulary, which "allows room for unjustifiable hope, and an ungroundable but vital sense of human solidarity."[4]

In what follows I want to indicate some of the ways in which Dewey's version of Pragmatism can be viewed as having advanced beyond the positions held by some of the authors commonly identified as postmodernists. In other words, I will suggest that Dewey's Pragmatism can and should be viewed as a form of post-postmodernism. Of course I do not intend to argue that there is any sort of linear progress in philosophy, or that Dewey has somehow leapfrogged postmodernism. There are in fact several important senses in which Dewey is a postmodern thinker. Kwame Anthony Appiah and James Livingston, among others, have called attention to elements of postmodernism in Dewey's thought, and Livingston has even identified some of those elements as already well formed during the first decades of the twentieth century.[5] What I intend to do instead is identify some of the problems postmodernism leaves unresolved, and then indicate how I think Dewey had already dealt with them early in the twentieth century. It is in this sense that I am terming his variety of Pragmatism post-postmodernism. To put matters another way, it is postmodernism without some of its problems. To put this in some sort of perspective, however, it would probably be good to say something about how I understand the term postmodernism.[6]

What precisely is postmodern about postmodernism? Precision is difficult here, since the term is notoriously slippery. Elizabeth Deeds

Ermarth, who has written an admirable book on the subject,[7] has even gone as far as to suggest that the word may not function so much as a term of reference as a way to "hold open a space for that which exceeds expression."[8] Postmodernism does refer to specific ideas, although they must be stated negatively. It is fair to say that postmodernism rejects some of the key assumptions, methods, and conclusions of the period from Descartes to Hegel and beyond. In doing so, of course, it also rejects many of the assumptions, methods, and conclusions of the philosophical tradition going all the way back to Plato and Aristotle. In Appiah's book, this involves the rejection of foundationalism and other forms of epistemological exclusivism, the rejection of metaphysical realism and other forms of ontological exclusivism, and the celebration of such figures as Nietzsche and Dewey.[9]

Ermarth has provided us with what is probably one of the best summary statements of the movement, if indeed that is what we wish to call it. She suggests that postmodernism can be recognized by two key assumptions. "First, the assumption that there is no common denominator—in 'nature' or 'God' or 'the future'—that guarantees either the One-ness of the world or the possibility of neutral or objective thought. Second, the assumption that all human systems operate like language, being self-reflexive rather than referential systems—systems of differential function which are powerful but finite, and which construct and maintain meaning and value."[10]

I find it extremely helpful that she is keen to differentiate postmodernism from its near relative, deconstruction. The latter, she argues, often gets caught up in its own circularity because of its preoccupation with what a text is not, rather than what it is. On the other hand, postmodernism is characterized by its positive efforts to construct meaning in the absence of transcendent value and to find ways of acting in the absence of absolute truth. Despite the fact that some may find this view controversial, I hope that I will be allowed to stipulate it and move on.[11]

While Ermarth provides a tight characterization of what the varieties of postmodernism have in common, Appiah offers a similarly precise characterization of how they differ by discipline. In technical philosophy, as I have already indicated, Appiah thinks that postmodernism involves the rejection of epistemological and ontological exclusivism and the celebration of such figures as Nietzsche and Dewey. In architecture, postmodernism rejects the exclusivism of function (the styles of Le Corbusier and Mies van der Rohe) in favor of playfulness and pastiche. Postmodernist architects would include the great Antonio Gaudí of Catalonia, as well as the less accomplished but equally playful designers of taco restaurants in the American Southwest that resemble giant sombreros. And then of course there is the incomparable postmodernist architecture of Las Vegas. A third type of postmodernism is encountered in literature, where, Appiah tells us, it is a reaction against the high seriousness of authors such as Marcel Proust, T. S. Eliot, and Virginia Woolf. This, I suppose, implies a turn toward the self-reflexive playfulness of authors such as James Joyce and Donald Barthelme. In addition, given the preoccupation of some French and American philosophers with the permutations of the trope, perhaps their work should be considered literary, rather than philosophical, postmodernism. Rorty, a neopragmatist trained in philosophy, was most recently a professor of comparative literature. Appiah finds a fourth type of postmodernism exhibited in political theory. In this case it rejects "scientific" Marxism and other monolithic enterprises and turns instead to a celebration of pluralism and perspectivism. The evolution of the Frankfurt School, to take one important example, supports Appiah's characterization of political postmodernism. First-generation Critical Theorists, such as Adorno, regarded technoscience as reified ideology, operating apart from and opposed to the activities of the lifeworld. Second-generation Critical Theorists, such as Habermas, focused on social problems of constitutionality and consensus-making. And their third-generation heirs, such as Feenberg and Axel Honneth, by regarding technoscience as embedded in society, thus concentrate on problems of globalization, pluralism, and multiculturalism. (See chapters 4 and 5.)

What all of this boils down to for Appiah is space: postmodernism is, in his view, "a new way of understanding the multiplication of distinctions that flows from the need to clear oneself a space; the need that drives the underlying dynamic of cultural modernity." "Modernism," he writes, "saw the economization of the world as the triumph of reason; postmodernism rejects that claim, allowing in the realm of theory the same multiplication of distinctions we see in the cultures it seeks to understand."[12] For Appiah, a close observer of modernism in the form of colonialism, postmodernism is culturally liberating. In fact, in various manifestations, postmodernism puts the individual front and center. As a system of communication, postmodernism is more or less the celebration of individual and group differences under an overarching communications superstructure that eventually replaces many of the functions of the nation-state, as Marshall McLuhan[13] described in great detail during the 1960s. In its commercial, and even in its educational, manifestations, it may well turn out to be what some entrepreneurs are now calling "mass customization"—the mass production of objects tailored to individual wants and needs.

At this point it seems appropriate to recall one of the best known statements of postmodernism: the well known remark by Lyotard. In his words, a crucial feature of "the postmodern condition" is the end of "the grand narrative." What does this mean? Even more to the point of the title of this chapter, what does it mean in terms of how we should understand Dewey's work? Does he avoid some of the problems that continue to plague postmodernism?

If the end of the grand narrative means recognition of the futility of attempts to build metaphysical systems such as those constructed by Hegel and Marx, systems that attempt to encompass everything, then Dewey was already a card-carrying postmodernist more than a century ago. In a letter to James Rowland Angell, dated May 10, 1893, for example, he wrote, "Metaphysics has had its day, and if the truths which Hegel saw cannot be stated as direct, practical truths, they are not true."[14] An indication of Dewey's disdain for systematic metaphysics, metaphysics-as-usual, can be found even in familiar remarks addressed to his wife, Alice. In 1891, two years before his "metaphysics has had its day" remark to Angell, Dewey wrote to Alice that he had been approached by a speculator at the Chicago Board of Trade, a certain Mr. Van Ostrand, who had been working on a philosophical "scheme." Van Ostrand had offered Dewey $100 to serve as a kind of philosophical consultant. (This was, by the way, no mean sum. We know that just eighteen months earlier Dewey's annual salary was $2,200.) "For the first time on record," he told Alice, "in our experience at least, metaphysics made the connexion with the objective world—. . . if there are many men like him in Chicago, I'll resign & go out there & hang up a sign 'Dr. Dewey, Metaphysical healer.' "[15]

In short, if Lyotard's remark about master narratives means that metaphysics-as-system-that-accounts-for-everything[16] is defunct, then Dewey was a postmodernist almost a century before Lyotard's famous dictum was published in 1979.   .

There is a second possible interpretation of Lyotard's remark. The end of the master narrative might be taken to mean that metaphysics *in any form* is impossible because it claims too much as a privileged position, that the varieties of human experience are at their most fundamental levels ungrounded and incommensurable. On this reading, the best that we can do is cope with that fact by constructing whatever solidarity we can in our roles as "ironists," in Rorty's term, that is, people who know that their brave front and best efforts may be futile. As Rorty puts it, "Liberals have come to expect philosophy to do a certain job—namely, answering questions like 'Why not be cruel?' and 'Why be kind?'—and they feel that any philosophy which refuses this assignment must be heartless. But that expectation is a result of a metaphysical upbringing. If we could get rid of the expectation, liberals would not ask ironist philosophy to do a job which it cannot do, and which it defines itself as unable to do."[17]

So this second possibility seems to reflect Rorty's version of the postmodernist distaste for metaphysics. If we accept this alternative, then Dewey was not a postmodernist, but held in fact a position that is much richer and goes well beyond that feckless view of matters. In other words, Dewey was a post-postmodernist.

Of course there is an irony that Rorty may not have fully appreciated. The positivism he dislikes and the postmodernism he apparently likes, share an interesting trait: they both hold the position that philosophy is incapable of addressing ethical issues such as the ones that Rorty raised in the passage just quoted. In the case of positivism it is because such issues are consigned to the jam-packed realm of everything that is noncognitive. In the case of Rortian postmodernism, it is because there is no adequate common denominator for human experience.) Bruno Latour is among the few thinkers who have noted this remarkable situation. In a 1993 interview, for example, he charged "much of postmodernism" with being scientistic: "They are not indignant at the ahuman dimension of technology— again they leave indignation to the moderns—no, they like it. They relish its completely naked, sleek, ahuman aspect. In other words, they accept the disenchantment argument, but they just take it as a positive feature instead of a negative one."[18]

How did Dewey go beyond postmodernism in this context? How did he resolve some of its core difficulties? Put simply, he argued that there is a commonality of human experience that can ultimately trump the compartmentalizing, hyperrelativistic tendencies latent in most forms of postmodernism. This view, which is a part of his evolutionary naturalism, is grounded in the empirical observations and experimental work of anthropologists and evolutionary biologists. For human beings inquiry is an essential component of communication, which can construct pluralistic links across otherwise isolated cultures and disciplines. Another important common feature humans share, Dewey contends, is our ability to do the type of cognitive, reconstructive work with respect to our environing conditions, including our social conditions, that allows us to *think in terms* of those common features.

This general cultural point is sharpened and called upon to do a prodigious amount of philosophical work in Dewey's famous remark about the role of philosophy as "liaison officer." In *Experience and Nature* he writes, "Thus philosophy as a critical organ becomes in effect a messenger, a liaison officer, making reciprocally intelligible voices speaking provincial tongues, and thereby enlarging as well as rectifying the meanings with which they are charged" (LW 1.306). This metaphor, by the way, has distinct advantages over some of its alternatives. It is more positive than getting flies out of fly bottles, it is more active than philosophy as *platzhalter,* and it is less imperious than philosophy as *platzfinder.* The first of these alternative metaphors, of course, we owe to Wittgenstein. The latter two we owe to Habermas, who accepts the first and rejects the second.

Dewey is thus a postmodernist in the sense that he rejects the notion that there is some foundation of certainty on which we can stand. He made that much clear early on, and put the matter to rest in his important little book *The Quest for Certainty.* But he is post-postmodernist in the sense that he reconstructed and put to work what the postmodernists had simply dismissed: a set of organic functions or activities that are natural to human beings as a group, that reveal their common evolution, and that can be employed as a part of the process of testing and securing desired ends. He argued, for example, that human communication, within which inquiry is embedded, is as natural an activity as chewing or walking.

If we fast-forward some thirty-two years past the "metaphysics is dead" remark that Dewey wrote to Angell and take the measure of his understanding of metaphysics in *Experience and Nature* (1925), then we find him criticizing both modernist and postmodernist conceptions. Whereas he had washed his hands of systematic metaphysics earlier in his career, he rejects the view that metaphysics should be abandoned altogether. His naturalism compels him to reconstruct the term and the enterprise for which it stands. He wants to break new ground. Of course there is still a postmodernist component to his efforts: he has jettisoned what philosophers from Plato to Hegel and beyond held dear, namely an "antecedent metaphysics of existence" (LW 1.49). This is without a doubt one of the features of his thought that has led Appiah to include him among postmodernists, or at least as having inspired postmodernists.

Put another way, if we take Ermarth's suggestion that for postmodernism "there is no common denominator—in 'nature' or 'God' or 'the future'—that guarantees either the One-ness of the world or the possibility of neutral or objective thought," then Dewey's naturalistic metaphysics goes beyond this skeptical claim to the more mature position that there are, after all, common features of human experience, among which are those he calls "the generic traits of existence." As for the matter of objectivity, Dewey's treatment is similar to that since advanced by Bruno Latour: objectivity means that something can be experimentally objected to within a community of inquiry, perhaps even one that is very broad indeed.

So we must read Dewey with care. To his attentive readers, it is clear he is not interested in merely exhuming the corpse of Enlightenment reason and giving it a new set of clothes. That critics as different as Bertrand Russell and Max Horkheimer accused him of doing something like this is a comment not about his work but about their careless reading of it. For all of his praise of Francis Bacon's experimentalism, Dewey is doing something much more interesting than merely restating, or even reinstating, modernism. He seems to be saying that once opponents of Enlightenment rationality tire, and once cultural criticism mires in irrelevant or divisive relativism, self-reflexivity that eclipses referentiality, or hopeless preoccupation with irony, then it will be time for a renewed attention to what he terms "the denotative method," that is, experimental attention to the pushes and pulls of existential affairs. Philosophy, having abandoned observation and experiment in favor of arcane stylistic felicities, will once again have to become more public, more vigorous. Philosophy will once again have to regain its footing by addressing some of the core problems of postmodernism.

Philosophy can remain relevant, indeed vigorous, as it employs what Dewey called "the denotative method." This denotation is, of course, not one of simple correspondence. It is rather experimental, reconstructive, and dialogical. The experiential or denotative method, Dewey writes,

> tells us that we must go behind the refinements and elaborations
> of reflective experience to the gross and compulsory things of our
> doings, enjoyments and sufferings—to the things that force us to
> labor, that satisfy needs, that surprise us with beauty, that compel
> obedience under penalty. A common divisor is a convenience,

and a greatest common divisor has the greatest degree of conve-
nience. But there is no reason for supposing that its intrinsic "reality" or truth is greater than that of the numbers it divides. The
objects of intellectual experience are the greatest common divisor
of the things of other modes; they have that remarkable value, but
to convert them into exclusive reality is the sure road to arbitrary
divisions and insoluble problems. (LW 1.375–76)

Dewey's post–postmodernist assessment of the human situation
will, I suggest, turn out to provide the advantage of objectivity without the disadvantages of inflexible modernist foundationalism and
disconnected, deracinated postmodernist topologies.

In order to see what is at stake, it may be helpful to understand
this dialectic between modernism and postmodernism as reflecting
the ancient struggle between classicism and romanticism. The classical position of the modernists—with its emphasis on foundationalism, essentialism, and realism—demands narrow discipline and thus
forecloses many of our options. The space it provides now seems
closed and cramped. But the romanticism of the postmodernists—
with its emphasis on uprootedness, narrativity, and nominalism—
tends to be short on discipline and thus promise what it cannot
deliver. The space it provides is so open that it is able to provide little
in the way of obstacle. It is within the arena where these two positions
come into conflict that we find some of Dewey's most fertile insights.

Dewey expands these ideas when he contrasts his post–
postmodernist metaphysics to the modernist metaphysics of fixity
and certainty only forty-seven pages into *Experience and Nature*. A
careful reader can also ascertain a response to those postmodernists
who argue that metaphysics *überhaupt*, including metaphysics as the
study of the generic traits of existence, is now defunct.

> We live in a world which is an impressive and irresistible mixture
> of sufficiencies, tight completenesses, order, recurrences which
> make possible prediction and control, and singularities, ambigu-
> ities, uncertain possibilities, processes going on to consequences
> as yet indeterminate. They are mixed not mechanically but vitally
> like the wheat and tares of the parable. We may recognize them

separately but we cannot divide them, for unlike wheat and tares they grow from the same root. Qualities have defects as necessary conditions of their excellencies; the instrumentalities of truth are the causes of error; change gives meaning to permanence and recurrence makes novelty possible. A world that was wholly risky would be a world in which adventure is impossible, and only a living world can include death. Such facts have been celebrated by thinkers like Heracleitus and Lao-tze; they have been greeted by theologians as furnishing occasions for exercise of divine grace; they have been elaborately formulated by various schools under a principle of relativity, so defined as to become itself final and absolute. They have rarely been frankly recognized as fundamentally significant for the formation of a naturalistic metaphysics. (LW 1.47)

Dewey then clarifies what he means by a naturalistic metaphysics, returning to the theme of communication, and thus inquiry, as natural functions of the human organism.

A naturalistic metaphysics is bound to consider reflection as itself a natural event occurring *within* nature because of traits of the latter. It is bound to inference from the empirical traits of thinking in precisely the same way as the sciences make inferences from the happening of suns, radio-activity, thunder-storms or any other natural event. Traits of reflection are as truly indicative or evidential of the traits of *other* things as are the traits of these events. (LW 1.62)

In short, we live in a world that is both precarious and stable. Ours is a world in which a certain amount of knowledge is necessary if we are to avoid disaster, and in which even more knowledge is required if we are to flourish. Common-sense knowledge, based on observation, and scientific knowledge, based on experimentation, are key ingredients in this mix, but they are not enough. The problem is that inquiry has proceeded over the centuries in ways that have left vestigial structures, cul-de-sacs, detritus, and other impediments to clear thinking. Once-valuable materials, now toxic, separate mind from body, subject from object, human beings from nature, individual

from society. Infelicitous remnants of dualistic metaphysical expedi-
tionary adventures continue to block the road to inquiry. In short,
there is a lot of junk that has been left rusting on the philosophical
landscape, some of it corrosive of thought.

One of the ways to clean up this polluted landscape is to develop a
sound philosophical ecology. Against the modernists, Dewey therefore proposes that we cease our attempts to attain certain knowledge
of Being in general, and proceed instead with an investigation of the
generic traits of existence. Against the postmodernists, he argues that
these traits are empirically available, that they are assumed by science,
and that they include such items as "structure and process, substance
and accident, matter and energy," to name a few (LW 1.67).

This, then, is the "special service" that Dewey thinks the study of
philosophy renders. At its most basic level, philosophy employs a set
of discipline-specific tools in its attempt to come to terms with lived
experience. But this enterprise often runs into difficulties. Our experiences are already "overlaid and saturated with the products of the
reflection of past generations and by-gone ages." We encounter the
many interpretations, classifications, and abstractions that Dewey
terms "prejudices" (he uses this term in its neutral sense). It is not
possible to go back and see how all these prejudices got established,
but we can use philosophical tools to criticize them and sort them
out. As Dewey puts it, "These incorporated results of past reflection,
welded into the genuine materials of first-hand experience, may become organs of enrichment if they are detected and reflected upon. If
they are not detected, they often obfuscate and distort. Clarification
and emancipation follow when they are detected and cast out; and
one great object of philosophy is to accomplish this task" (LW 1.40).

The prejudices that lie strewn all about us can either cause us to
stumble, endangering ourselves and others, or we can seek them out,
haul them in, melt them down, and recycle them as materials for fab-
ricating something more useful. The one thing we should not do,
however, is declare that metaphysics is at an end and retire to the
cocktail party or the library. The wreckage of modernist metaphysics
cannot be dismissed with a wave of the hand any more than can the

wreckage of past industrial excess. This is because there are still people attempting to negotiate a terrain that is littered with religious and philosophical junk. As long as it is accepted that the mind and the body are ontologically distinct, for example, then insurance companies will be able to claim rational grounds for insuring the health of the body while ignoring the health of the organism as a whole. And as long as it is accepted that human beings are bodies in which there dwells a literal, immortal soul, then many men and women will be tempted to neglect the pressing needs of the here and now even while attending to the putative prospects of the hereafter.[19]

It is in this connection that Dewey characterizes metaphysics as a "ground-map" of the province of criticism. On one interpretation this means that we need a map to find our way among potentially dangerous metaphysical entities so that we can avoid injuring ourselves. But we also need the map to find out what such things are covering up, what they conceal, thereby getting a better picture of the landscape. In a passage that is now quite famous, Dewey writes, "Qualitative individuality and constant relations, contingency and need, movement and arrest are common traits of all existence. This fact is source both of values and of their precariousness; both of immediate possession which is casual and of reflection which is a precondition of secure attainment and appropriation. Any theory that detects and defines these traits is therefore but a ground-map of the province of criticism, establishing base lines to be employed in more intricate triangulations" (LW 1.308–9).

Dewey's post–postmodernist metaphysics, then, constitutes an attempt to reconstruct that enterprise along naturalistic lines. In *Experience and Nature* he works out what he had tentatively advanced ten years earlier, in 1915, in his essay "The Subject Matter of Metaphysical Inquiry." He continues to eschew speculation about first and last things, he continues his attempt to undercut reliance on unwarranted hypostatized entities, and he treats inquiry into Being qua Being as a historical curiosity.

He also denies the claims of those who argue that there is no longer any place for metaphysics. He attempts to take account of the fact that the generic traits of existence are too complex to be the subject of common-sense observation and too general to be the subject of scientific experimentation. He expands on his claim that the generic traits are assumed by science. He locates his reconstructed metaphysics in the context of the live creature transacting business with its environing conditions.

Dewey's attack on modernist metaphysics thus provides an alternative to the claim of some postmodernists that metaphysics is at an end, as well as an alternative to the claim that philosophy no longer has anything interesting to say about cruelty or kindness, for example,[20] and an alternative to the claim that there is "no common denominator . . . that guarantees the One-ness of the world or the possibility of neutral or objective thought."[21] Dewey's post-postmodernism calls each of these positions to account.

There are no doubt those who will object that at the end of his life Dewey had a change of heart regarding the possibility of a naturalistic metaphysics. In an essay published in 1949, as he was approaching his birthday, Dewey announced that his attempts to reconstruct the term had failed. He promised never to use the word again in connection with his own position.

But that is not the full story. Dewey gave up the word, but not the enterprise. As for the enterprise, or what he had accomplished in terms of reconstructing the traditional discipline of metaphysics, he happily stood by that. And why? Simply because the point of recognizing generic traits, as he put it, "lies in their application in the conduct of life: that is, in their *moral* bearing provided *moral* be taken in its basic broad human sense" (LW 16.389). In other words, his reconstructed metaphysics—whatever it might come to be called—has a connection to the existential, which is to say objective, world that exhibits certain generic traits.

Returning once again to Lyotard's famous remark, there is a third interpretation. If the first interpretation has to do with the end of abstract metaphysical systems, and the second with the end of metaphysics generally, then the third might be understood to mean the end of the idea that the physical sciences are the models and measures for all other types of experience. In this sense it would signal the end of the positivist program advanced by philosophers such as Rudolf Carnap and Hans Reichenbach from the 1930s to the 1960s. Proponents of this view, in its most extreme form, held that, "all philosophy can be reduced either to the physical sciences or to lexicography," as one of the professors for whom I worked as a graduate student was still moved to tell his freshmen as late as 1965. But of course Dewey was postmodernist in this special sense as well. He was an ardent opponent of the positivists, rejecting their protocol sentences, their view of the nature of truth, and their various forms of reductionism and foundationalism.

Of the logical positivists Dewey wrote to Arthur F. Bentley, in a letter dated March 5, 1939, that "the profession seems to absolve them for responsibility for examining their own basic postulates—or finding out what they are."[22] On July 10, 1940, Max Otto wrote to Dewey, "I was talking with a number of students this morning who are here for summer school and have had courses in Positivism before they came. They wanted to know what illumination or help of any kind they were expected to get out of a study which they were assured [sic] demonstrated the meaninglessness of philosophy. I was not able to help them out. Perhaps you can help me out. If you do, I will pass the information on to them."[23]

Dewey responded, "It seems to be at least hopeful that the students reacted to Logical Positivism they [sic] way they did—of course there are a number always who like manipulating symbols, but who haven't had the energy or opportunity or skill to learn to do it in mathematics where at least it is something with a background & foreground. Im [sic] about convinced that most of this logistics is just *pseudo-*mathematics."[24]

In his revised introduction to *Experience and Nature,* written in 1949, Dewey's assessment of the positivists was even more acerbic. They assume, he wrote,

> that science as a total enterprise is inherently non-self-supportive,
> that it is necessarily incapable of supplying itself with whatever

"foundations" it may need and hence it is the task of the new type of rigoristic philosophers and their Logic to do for science what science cannot do for itself.

In view of the fly-blown condition of most of what passes as "logic" today there is something outright comical, rather than merely ironical, in the assumption that Logic is the author of and authority for the required foundations. This claim of competence is supposedly based on the fact that the new Logic is formulated in esoteric symbols which simulate, at least in form, the symbolism of mathematics. But the "foundations" of mathematics have undergone a radical, indeed, a revolutionary change. The old view that mathematical subject-matter is deduced from an ultimate set of self-evident or axiomatic truths has been supplanted by the view that the ultimates, the "foundations" of the mathematical enterprise are deliberately designed postulates. The method of postulation puts mathematical subject-matter beyond the need of any "foundation" supplied from without. The old view produced Kant. The ultra-moderns are, unwittingly, neo-Kantians of a very special and very peculiar sort. (LW 1.350)

These texts should provide sufficient evidence that Dewey viewed the brief reign of the logical positivists as one of modernism's final gasps, since new ways of thinking had already rendered their versions of foundationalism untenable. It was, of course, highly ironic that the positivists' criticism of traditional metaphysics tended to be buttressed by stripped down metaphysical positions of their own.

Nevertheless, Dewey refused to respond to the outsized claims of modernism as have some postmodernists. Take the claim by Ermarth, for example, that "all human systems operate like language, being self-reflexive rather than referential systems—systems of differential function which are powerful but finite, and which construct and maintain meaning and value."(See Ermarth, endnote 10) If not taken cautiously, this remark would be understood to disallow even the minimal referentiality that is required to account for the successes of common-sense inquiries, to say nothing of the experiments mounted by the natural sciences. In Dewey's post-postmodernism, scientific results are constructed, to be sure. But they are neither arbitrary nor are they constructed out of nothing.

If Dewey was postmodernist in his disdain for the modernist program of the positivists, as well as in developing his own version of constructivism, then he was anything but postmodernist in terms of his interest in logic and his commitment to working out a theory of living inquiry, of which his treatment of metaphysics was an integral part. I have trolled the works of Deleuze and Félix Guattari, Jacques Derrida, Roland Barthes, and even the master postmodernist Lyotard, in search of a comprehensive and coherent theory of inquiry. Nothing I have found approaches the treatment that Dewey gave the subject in his logic books of 1903, 1916, and 1938, and in the numerous published essays that served as sketches for, and clarifications of, those works.

Dewey developed his own moderate form of constructivism, then, and this is one of the senses in which he was a postmodernist. From a Pragmatist perspective, however, what seems to be missing in postmodernism, and what Dewey provides as a corrective, is a theory of experimental inquiry that takes its point of departure from real, felt existential affairs. And this analysis of the generic traits of existence is one of the areas in which Dewey's work shines brightly as what I have termed post-postmodernism.

TWO

PRAGMATISM, POSTMODERNISM, AND GLOBAL CITIZENSHIP

The founders of American Pragmatism proposed what they regarded as a radical alternative to the philosophical methods
and doctrines of their predecessors and contemporaries.[1] Although
their central ideas have been understood and applied in some quar-
ters, there remain other areas within which they have been neither
appreciated nor appropriated. One of the more pressing of these
areas locates a set of problems of knowledge and valuation related to
global citizenship. Classical American Pragmatism, because its methods are modeled on successes in the technosciences, offers a set of
tools for fostering global citizenship that are more effective than
some of its alternatives. First, Pragmatism claims to discover a strain
of human commonality that trumps the postmodernist emphasis on
difference and discontinuity. Second, when Pragmatism's theory of
truth is coupled with its moderate version of cultural relativism, the
more skeptical postmodernist version known as "cognitive" relativism is undercut.[2]

What is Global Citizenship?

There is scant agreement concerning what constitutes global citizenship, and even less regarding what constitutes "good" global citizenship. Onora O'Neill, for example, has reminded us that global citizenship has traditionally been understood as little more than citizenship in some nation-state or another that has various relationships with other nation-states.[3] Global citizenship, on this view, amounts to little more than efforts to influence the ways in which one's own national government interacts with the governments of other nation-states. Nation-states are thus viewed as both filters and buffers, isolating individuals from the possibility of direct participation as global citizens. To many traditionalists, any concept of global citizenship that expands the role of the individual beyond the limitations imposed by this model has been regarded as either incoherent or utopian.

Gradually, however, since the formation of the United Nations and its adoption of the *Universal Declaration of Human Rights* in 1948, this traditional picture has begun to change. During the last half century, new institutional frameworks such as agreements and regulatory mechanisms for trade, the environment, nuclear arms, terrorism, health issues, and travel have begun to emerge. Add to this a growing list of nongovernmental organizations (NGOs) as well as ad hoc interest groups capable of organizing themselves rapidly across political boundaries by means of electronic communication, and it becomes apparent that the era of the nation-state as we have known it is giving way to a new, more vigorously cosmopolitan milieu.

These changed and changing circumstances have had the effect of invigorating debates concerning the nature of global citizenship. Some critics of the traditional model have argued that the concept of global citizenship will have to be developed from within the current structure of nation-states. In this scenario, individual citizens of existing nation-states would work outward from existing conditions with a view to improving existing or emerging supranational institutions for international cooperation. In essence, they would form publics that would demand that their governments participate more actively in affairs of a global nature.

For other critics of the traditional model, however, this scenario is far from adequate. They have argued that a new cosmopolitanism will develop only to the extent that individuals educate themselves about considerations that transcend their own interests, those of their own nation-state, and even those of supernational institutions. Unlike the previous scenario, however, in which individual citizens would work solely, or for the most part, through their existing national institutions, in this model individual citizens would begin to leapfrog their national governments, as it were, by creating and participating in new publics of international scope. These new publics would arise from experienced needs, and, interacting with each other, pressure established organizational entities such as nation-states to satisfy those needs.[4] (At this time it is difficult to predict how these publics will be formed, and what form they will take since they have, by definition, not yet been formed. It may be, however, that currently existing NGOs and ad hoc interest groups, such as networks of peace activists organized by the Internet, can offer us some clues about what is to come.)

There is also an important overlapping question of whether global citizenship should be defined in terms of the traditional language of rights and obligations or characterized more broadly, for example, in terms of the formation of new democratic institutions and aspirations.

These issues are by any account complicated by the current trend toward globalization in its economic sense, with its increase of world trade and attendant expansion of the power of the World Bank, the International Monetary Fund, and multinational corporations. Even further complicating the situation is the current trend toward privatization of natural resources, including such basic items as water, as is now occurring, in some countries of South America.

In the introduction to their excellent collection of essays on the subject, Nigel Dower and John Williams invite us not to lose sight of the philosophical issues involved in discussions of the nature of global citizenship and the welter of problems and opportunities that we face during this transitional period of human history. They organize the philosophical aspects of this landscape in two components: ethical and citizenship. In their view, the ethical component includes issues such as how rights and obligations will be determined and what the core norms of global citizenship will be. This component would address issues such as economic and environmental justice, for example. The citizenship component, in their view, concerns issues such as whether, as they put it, "there is a plausible and substantive sense of 'citizen' in which it makes sense to say that we are global citizens."[5]

In what follows, I will attempt to frame the issue of how global citizenship can be fostered in terms of Dower and William's citizenship component. I will attempt to indicate some of the ways in which the core methods of classical American Pragmatism are relevant to creating and cultivating global citizens who can in turn be instrumental to the formation and sustenance of global publics. It will not be my aim to propose solutions to specific geopolitical and economic problems. Nor will I attempt to predict the types of global publics that will be formed or the mechanisms of their formation. Instead, I will apply some of the methods proposed by the founders of American Pragmatism to the issue, with a view to determining where those methods lead with respect to the education of the global citizen. In order to present these methods in as high relief as possible, I will first present them as succinctly as possible. I will then indicate some of the ways in which I believe them to be more effective than some of the methods and outlooks generally identified with postmodernism.

The Pragmatic Method

In his Lowell Lectures of 1907, William James offered Pragmatism as a radical alternative to what he termed "ultra-rationalist" tendencies in philosophy. Among these tendencies he listed the usual dogmatic suspects: overreliance on abstractions and verbal solutions, a priori reasoning, appeal to fixed principles and closed systems, and "pretended absolutes and origins."[6]

At first sight, James's proposal might have appeared to be just one more in a long line of offensives mounted by skeptics—moderate as well as not-so-moderate—against strongholds that have been occupied by the likes of scholastics, rationalists, and philosophical system-builders. But what James had in mind was far more radical than anything that his fellow empiricists had up to that point been able to put into play. His indictment of traditional rationalism also included a barely submerged indictment of traditional empiricism as well.

One of the striking things about James's proposal is that it did not anticipate or privilege any special result. It was offered as a method only—a ticket to ride to wherever the method went. Once the Pragmatic method was applied, James thought, it was sure to undercut some of the old philosophical antagonisms. In language that went even beyond the call of Jonathan Edwards for a return to "naked ideas" unencumbered by the dead weight of parasitic abstractions, James demanded that every word pay its own way—that it earn its living within the stream of experience. And he insisted that every theory be regarded as an instrument, as a tool for the remodeling of experience. In other words, the Pragmatic method would be flexible enough to allow for a wide range of viewpoints and activities, depending on individual temperament and context. But it would not accept just any applicant. Though they might live for a time on credit, ideas submitted to this test would eventually have to either pay their own bills or declare bankruptcy.

It is worth noting at this point that there is a significant difference between James's proposal for a working method that privileges no particular *result*, and the proposal issued by Lyotard and other postmodernists that no particular *narrative* or *standpoint* can or should be privileged. James's proposal possesses the virtues of what has been termed "the scientific method"[7] of inquiry (on which it is based): when it is properly applied, it does present a privileged method with respect to knowledge-getting, since it is experimental and therefore produces practical effects that are objective. It is self-correcting. Lyotard's postmodernist proposal, on the other hand, appears to be self-defeating: it must privilege its own announced narrative, namely, that no narrative is privileged. It is also important to keep in mind that Lyotard's book does in fact appear to privilege the domain of knowledge-getting. Its subtitle is "A Report on Knowledge."

Underscoring his claim that the Pragmatic method privileges no special result, James borrowed a metaphor from the Italian Pragmatist Giovanni Papini. The Pragmatic method would be like a corridor in a hotel, he said. Many rooms would open onto it, and inside those rooms there would be a wide variety of activities. Religionists as well as atheists would be found there and scientists as well as philosophers. Despite their differences, the occupants of the rooms would have one important thing in common: they would have to pass through the corridor—they would have to employ the Pragmatic method—to get in or out of their respective rooms.[8]

What James was suggesting, therefore, was that cultural, intellectual, and political differences, can in many cases be negotiated under the umbrella of the Pragmatic method. If his view is correct, we would therefore expect to find in it a tool for fostering global citizenship and its corollary, the formation of global publics.

But what, more specifically, is the Pragmatic method? Given that it privileges no particular result, what is it about that corridor that allows religionists and atheists to pass, as well as scientists and philosophers, but (presumably) not democrats and dictators, secularists and theocrats, and humanists and fundamentalists? This is a question that Pragmatism must answer if it is to pay its own way as a set of tools for fostering global citizenship.

The question is complicated by the fact that now, almost one hundred years after James's Lowell Lectures, and after a period during which it had precious few friends, Pragmatism appears to have become quite fashionable. Despite its current popularity (or perhaps because of it), however, the central tenets of Pragmatism have not yet been appropriated in some of the most important arenas of human life.

Stripped to its most muscular form, Pragmatism is a precise theory of meaning, truth, and inquiry, or perhaps better put, it is a closely related family of precise theories of meaning, truth, and inquiry.

Here is Peirce in 1878: "Consider what effects, that might conceivably have practical bearings we conceive the object of our conception to have. Then, our conception of these effects is the whole of our conception of the object."[9] Here is James, twenty years later, in 1898: "The effective meaning of any philosophic proposition can always be brought down to some particular consequence, in our future practical experience, whether active or passive; the point lying rather in the fact that the experience must be particular, than in the fact that it must be active."[10] And here is Dewey in 1938, sixty years after Peirce's statement: "The proper interpretation of 'pragmatic,' [involves] namely the function of consequences as necessary tests of the validity of propositions, *provided* these consequences are operationally instituted and are such as to resolve the specific problem evoking the operations" (LW 12.4).

Put succinctly, the Pragmatic theory of meaning insists that we treat the whole meaning of a concept not just in terms of its use in a language game, as Wittgenstein urged us to do, but in terms that are overtly experimental and behavioral and in ways that *transcend* particular language games: the meaning of a concept is the difference it will make within and for our future experience.

Another way of putting this is that the Pragmatic method is experimental at its core. Here is Peirce in 1906. "All Pragmatists will further agree that their method of ascertaining the meanings of words and concepts is no other than that experimental method by which all the successful sciences . . . have reached the degrees of certainty that are severally proper to them today."[11]

Applying Peirce's Pragmatic maxim, it seemed to James natural enough to conclude that since the word "truth" is not otiose, then it, too, must have a meaning.[12] Absorbing the best elements of both correspondence and coherence theories of truth (as well as rejecting their less defensible elements) and then adding a temporal dimension, James claimed that *"true ideas are those that we can assimilate, validate, corroborate, and verify. False ideas are those that we cannot."*[13]

Some who have read this remark have concluded that James equated truth with personal satisfaction, but Dewey understood the matter differently. James's real doctrine, he wrote, was, "A belief is true when it satisfies both personal needs and the requirements of objective things" (MW 4.112). In his most precise statement of the matter, Dewey *defined* truth as warranted assertibility.[14]

In a word, the Pragmatic theory of truth involves a robust form of experimentalism: it requires that we regard our ideas as true when they have both an objective basis (i.e., their warrant can be demonstrated before a candid world) and the capacity to resolve some type of objective difficulty (i.e., they are assertible under relevant conditions).

Pragmatism treats inquiry as a natural activity, that is, as intimately related to organic nature as the beating of a heart and the perches and flight of a bird. At the conscious level, inquiry takes its start in situations that are doubtful, from which it seeks to shape well defined problems. It then uses tools of all sorts, abstract as well as concrete, to form hypotheses which it tests in the very existential arena from which the motivating difficulty arose.

In sum, the Pragmatic account of inquiry is invariably situated with respect to specific circumstances. It arises from felt needs, employs both abstract and concrete tools, tests proposals in the laboratory of experience, and terminates in the resolution of the difficulties which occasioned that particular sequence of inquiry. In Dewey's book, logic is the theory of inquiry.

Pragmatism and Global Citizenship

What, then, can we say about the Pragmatic accounts of meaning, truth, and inquiry as they relate to the problems and prospects of global citizens and global publics?

First, the Pragmatic method claims an experimental basis for its emphasis on continuity and commonality, thus rejecting the claims of skeptics, racists, and others that the primary features of human life are difference, discontinuity and incommensurability.

Of course the Pragmatists did not deny that we experience disruptions and discontinuities. It is just that they thought that conjunctions and disjunctions are correlative within a broader context. In what can also be understood as an indictment of the postmodernist preoccupation with difference (or perhaps *différance*),[15] James criticized traditional empiricism for "leaving things permanently disjoined." (It should also be noted that he rejected "the fictitious agencies of union" that rationalists such as the absolute idealists of his time had sought to apply as a remedy).[16] He suggested that if we candidly examine our experiences, we will find that they exist in time, that they include overlapping elements, that they include transitions, and that their content is both disjunctive and conjunctive.[17] For his part, Dewey's theory of inquiry was heavily influenced by experiments that he and his colleagues at the University of Chicago conducted on neural stimulation and inhibition.[18]

For James and Dewey, in particular, the self is neither the subjective modernist self nor the fragmented and ineffectual self encountered in postmodernist literature. Instead, the Pragmatist self is an individual that exists as an individual only in relation to the connections and communities that enable it to do so. It is an agent within a nexus of thick social behaviorist morality, and thus within a nexus of thick social and political engagement. The Pragmatist self functions at its best when its activities are based on experimental methods and outcomes.

Further, because the aesthetic dimension of human experience plays such an important role within the Pragmatic account of inquiry, Dewey would doubtless have argued that aesthetic education will emerge as an essential component of global citizenship, that is, as individual selves prepare themselves for broader participation in the new global publics.

For Dewey, as for the other Pragmatists, perception is neither passive nor otiose. The new global citizens will be pressed to find ways of increasing their appreciation of aesthetic diversity of world cultures: the sounds of music, the rhythms of speech and gesture, the scents and flavors of cuisines, and the visual delights of cultural artifacts from clothing, to architecture, to arts and crafts, to literature. To the aesthetically educated citizen, all of these factors collaborate in delightful interchange and come together, contributing to a human commonality that is not fixed and finished, but emergent.

Seen from one end, therefore, the common features of the human nervous system, having evolved within a common natural environment, provide a platform from which aesthetic diversity can be appreciated and appropriated for productive purposes. Seen from the other end, disruptions and discontinuities are felt aesthetic phases of sequences of inquiry that are capable of producing enlarged conceptions of human commonality. Difference and discontinuity are thus neither primary nor ultimate, but inquirential phases or moments.

Pragmatists have argued that aesthetic education is doubly grounded. It is grounded within inquiry *into* aesthetic experience, and it is grounded within the aesthetic qualities *of* inquiry as a process. As to the first, it is worth recalling that Dewey used the term aesthetic in at least two senses: immediate, uninformed aesthetic delight; and aesthetic experience that has been experimentally reconstructed to sustain and secure the otherwise fleeting aesthetic values. It is the business of the arts to reconstruct such aesthetic moments and to secure and sustain them as aesthetic goods.

Second, Dewey and the other Pragmatists argued that all inquiry—even in rarified areas such as formal logic and mathematics—involves aesthetic experience. Inquiry begins with a *feeling* of unease or dissatisfaction. The inquirer feels the impact of colliding hypotheses, and concludes his or her work when the originating conditions—including the feeling of unease that began the inquiry—is replaced by a feeling of satisfaction. The tools of inquiry, including the aesthetic aspects of such things as blueprints, laboratory equipment, and even logical and mathematical notation, can stimulate inquiry and help bring it to a fruitful conclusion. In short, inquiry takes into account not only what the moderns regarded as primary qualities, but those that they regarded as secondary and tertiary as well.

The implications of a Pragmatist aesthetic theory for educating the new global citizen and providing the bases for the formation of global publics, therefore, can hardly be overestimated.

As I have already indicated, the Pragmatist call for enlarged and invigorated aesthetic experience does not entail dismissal or erasure of difference, but its incorporation into a thick, experimental, social behaviorist morality and politics. There can perhaps be no better example of this than Jane Addams's experiments at Hull House, especially during the 1890s. In her autobiography, *Twenty Years at Hull House*, Addams provided rich accounts of cases in which she and her colleagues first achieved a deepened appreciation and respect for difference, then developed that appreciation and respect in ways that both incorporated and transcended difference, thus creating new, vigorous communities. As Charlene Haddock Seigfried has reminded us, "The traits of Dewey's ideal democratic community—namely, that it is 'a mode of associated living, of conjoint communicated experience'—were actually instantiated at Hull House. It went beyond the merely physical and organic 'associated or joint activity [that] is a condition of the creation of a community' to embody the moral dimension necessary to a genuine community, namely, one that . . . is 'emotionally, intellectually, and consciously sustained.'"[19]

Pragmatists such as Jane Addams were thus deeply affected by the results of their experimental approach to the problems of building human communities. It should be recalled in this connection that Addams and Dewey were performing their experiments in Chicago under very difficult circumstances which included massive immigration of non-English-speakers, labor unrest, and ethnic and racial strife—in short, under the same sorts of conditions out of which the new global publics will have to be formed.

It might be objected that one of Dewey's most formidable experimental tools, his evolutionary naturalism, is itself a position that tends to undercut community, since it divides the supernaturalist from the naturalist and thus drives a wedge between individuals who would otherwise be capable of working together to form global publics. To this charge the Pragmatist response would be that James's Pragmatic hotel is able to provide rooms for the theist and the atheist, and it should be added, the naturalist and the supernaturalist as well. The Pragmatic method, Dewey reminded us, does not offer a method of determining whether god or gods *exist*. It is a method of examining the practical *consequences* of such beliefs. Since it is arguable that a majority of the world's population subscribes to some form of supernaturalist religious belief, this is of considerable consequence for global citizenship.

As a variety of naturalism, Pragmatism has no quarrel with supernaturalism or other religious beliefs per se. As variety of evolutionary naturalism, however, it does have a quarrel with nonnaturalist accounts such as the types of creationism that have been promoted by Christian fundamentalists as examples of good science and then urged upon school boards as an alternative to the teaching of objective, peer-reviewed biology and geology.

What this means in practice for the formation of global publics in these areas is that in terms of the Pragmatic method, naturalists and supernaturalists should be able to work together to form global publics. But their methods, as well as the methods of other publics, will have to be experimental ones of the type that are building the international space station, that discovered the double helix, and that invented social security—and not the methods of religious or political authority.

The application of the Pragmatic method to the education of global citizens would have consequences both significant and salutary. It would, for example, reveal the futility of Islamist attempts to return to a golden age of Arab science in which, as Seyyed Hossein Nasr has written, "*scientia*—human knowledge, is to be regarded as legitimate and noble only so long as it is subordinated to *sapientia*—Divine wisdom."[20] It would also encourage technoscientists in democratic societies such as the United States to be bolder and more candid, thus resisting attempts by their governments to co-opt and exploit the results of their research. In short, they would resist attempts to present political ideology in the guise of good technoscience.

As I write, this is a particularly worrisome problem in the United States, given the fact that the George W. Bush's administration has demonstrated a clear pattern of honoring ideological purity over the results of technoscientific experiments on such issues as global warming, arctic oil exploration (and even the effectiveness of condoms in preventing sexually transmitted diseases!).

As Dewey argued in *A Common Faith*, despite their other differences, human beings share many laudable ideals and goals. He urged that the Pragmatic method be employed to channel the idealism and enthusiasm that is found so abundantly within human communities—especially among the young—toward the securing of those common ideals and goals.

The Pragmatist emphasis on continuity and commonality thus stands in sharp contrast to the postmodernist claim that there is no underlying continuity of the self, as well as its emphasis on difference as a primary feature of human experience. As Ermarth put it, there is "no common denominator—in 'nature' or 'God' or 'the future'— that guarantees either the One-ness of the world or the possibility of neutral or objective thought."[21] Another has informed us that "now there are only differences."[22]

In short, Pragmatism provides tools for fostering global citizenship by indicating some of the ways in which global publics can be formed. It advances a rich account of aesthetic experience that includes accounts of inquiry *into* aesthetic goods as well as accounts of the aesthetic components *of* inquiry as it applies to areas of life in which the aesthetic is not the dominant concern. As demonstrated by Jane Addams's work at Hull House, its experimentalism finds ways of building communities even among the most diverse populations and under the most difficult of circumstances. Dewey's commitment to evolutionary naturalism stresses the commonalities which can serve as platforms on which global publics can be formed and from which they can be launched.

Second, the Pragmatic method has implications with regard to cultural conflict, and consequently the problem of relativism. Pragmatism, as I have characterized it, advances a moderate version of cultural relativism but rejects a stronger skeptical version known as cognitive relativism.

In accepting a moderate version of cultural relativism Pragmatism just honors the fact that what various cultures hold as good is much too rich and varied to be understood or judged in terms of one principle or one set of principles. In terms of the Pragmatic method, however, this should not be perceived as an effect of the poverty of the technosciences, but rather as an effect of the richness of human experience. As Dewey put it, there are areas of experience where knowing has no business.

Following Dewey's account of inquiry, Pragmatism holds that cultural difference per se is not an occasion that calls for inquiry, but only cultural difference that leads to a situation in which there are mutually exclusive claims about what is to be done. In other words, there are areas of experience where knowing does have business.

Cognitive relativism is one response to active cultural conflict. Here is how the author of an essay published in a 1996 issue of *Philosophical Forum* characterized this view: "The kind of relativism I wish to defend here is a very general form of cognitive relativism which takes as its object judgments in general . . . It is based on two theses: 1) The truth value of all judgments is relative to some particular standpoint (otherwise variously referred to as a theoretical framework, conceptual scheme, perspective, or point of view). 2) No standpoint is uniquely or supremely privileged over all others."[23]

How are we to understand these theses? If the first thesis simply states that all knowing is perspectival, then it is consistent with Pragmatism as its founders characterized it. Pragmatism emphasizes the situatedness of organisms within and as a part of their environments, and rejects the idea of an omniscient stance. Were this not the case, then human experience would be the poorer in terms of its aesthetic dimension and much else.

The second thesis is somewhat more complex than the first, but if it is taken to mean that with respect to judgments in the general sense all perspectives or standpoints are equally valuable, or even that they are equally valuable for the solution of specific problems at hand, then it is inconsistent with the experimental methods of classical Pragmatism.[24]

First, the founding Pragmatists rejected the idea that there is any such thing as judgments or knowledge in general. Second, they thought that, given a particular situation (which is, after all, what motivates inquiry in the first instance), some judgments are assertible with warrant and other judgments are not. It is not that the founding Pragmatists thought that every difficulty had a solution, either now or in the future. It is rather that they thought that objective inquiry, if pursued with sufficient vigor, usually tends to render some perspectives or standpoints tenable and others untenable.

This position follows from the strong commitment to experimentalism that is at the heart of Pragmatism. It is worth remembering in this connection that each of the founding Pragmatists had an intimate connection with experimental science from which he developed a rich notion of inquiry. For much of his career Peirce worked as a scientist for the U.S. Coast and Geodetic Survey. James taught medicine and experimental psychology at Harvard University. Dewey and his work-group at the University of Chicago organized and operated a laboratory of experimental psychology.

Although it is dangerous to impute motives, it is reasonable to conclude that the second thesis of cognitive relativism—that "no standpoint is uniquely or supremely privileged over all others"—is designed to function as an antidote to some of the ideas and practices that militate against global citizenship. An incomplete list of these ideas and practices would generally include racism, imperialism, and the like. More specifically, it would include efforts at ethnic cleansing, persecution of minorities on religious grounds, and so on. In other words, the cognitive relativist attempts to avoid being put in the position of deciding which of two conflicting cultural practices is superior to the other and so just allows that no standpoint is uniquely or supremely privileged over all others, thus, it would seem, undercutting the grounds for conflict.[25]

But matters are not so simple. It is one thing to hold the view that no standpoint is privileged over another and therefore that conflict has no legitimate basis, and quite another to be faced with the difficulties of resolving conflicts that are either threatened or already underway. In this connection, it is well worth remembering that one of the core features of Pragmatism is its perspectivism. But the Pragmatist's perspectivism is the result of limited access; it is not the result of intellectual promiscuity.

Dewey reminded us that novelty is a generic trait of existence, and therefore that as far as possible we should prepare ourselves for the unexpected. But he also reminded us that at any given time we have at our disposal a fund of well tested working tools. Even more importantly, we have the ability to develop new tools that are even more appropriate to emerging conditions than the ones we now possess. These tools can put perceived *values* to the test with a view to determining which of our alternatives can be sustained as the more valuable.

Put another way, one of the significant consequences of the Pragmatists' claim that ideas have consequences (that are operationally related to the situation or context from which they have come) is that not all ideas, not all standpoints, are equally valuable. This is not to deny that what is valued varies across cultures or even that conflicting statements may be equally valued. It is rather to hold that in many cases in which there are conflicts regarding what is to be valued, the Pragmatic method provides the tools by means of which we can determine which of the conflicting values can be demonstrated to be valuable.

In other words, Pragmatism holds that there *are* methods that are uniquely privileged if inquiry is to be undertaken (and it is worth noting that the second thesis of cognitive relativism appears to assume that inquiry is involved, since it is a thesis about judgments). The practice of good global citizenship dictates that we acknowledge this situation. In short, it is the experimentalism of the Pragmatists, not the skepticism of the cognitive relativist, that provides the better grounds for resolving differences that are rooted in conflicting cultural practices, and thereby providing the grounds for the formation of global publics.

It might be objected that the methods that have proven successful in the technosciences (for those are what are at issue) are privileged only conditionally, that is, only on the condition that some conflict needs to be resolved, but that knowledge is not thereby active everywhere within human experience. Fair enough: this was a point that Dewey made repeatedly and that served to distance his own view from scientism. Where there is no conflict, there is no need for inquiry. But global citizenship, like citizenship of less extensive scope, and global publics, like publics that operate on local, regional, and national political levels, are precisely responses to the fact of conflict–verbal as well as physical and possible as well as actual. Publics tend to be formed in response to the recognition of shared problems.

Dewey reminded us that citizenship involves acting in concert with others, and therefore requires that choices be made. A citizen is someone who has a part in making, as well as obeying, laws and regulations. If no method, perspective, or standpoint is any better than any other, or if there is no method of knowledge-getting that is any better than any other, then it is difficult to see how those choices can be other than local or arbitrary—or even worse, based entirely on self-interest. And as Peirce reminded us, the alternatives to the Pragmatic method are tenacity, authority, and a priori thinking.

Pragmatism can contribute to the development of global citizenship and global publics by advancing its central claims. Among these claims, as I have indicated, is an insistence that the meaning of a concept lies in its consequences for behavior, and therefore that when a judgment is true then it is one that "we can assimilate, validate, corroborate, and verify." Since true judgments are not only warranted but assertible, they are habits of action. Even though they are fallible, until they are successfully challenged they are nevertheless universalizable (as opposed to absolute or arbitrary). They constitute rules or habits of action, ready to be employed (even though possibly improved upon at some future date) when cultural conflicts arise.[26]

In short, contrary to the position of cognitive relativism, it is possible to have objective results of inquiry that are universalizable across national and cultural boundaries. (That the results are objective means that they can be publically objected to through a process of peer review, and that they are universalizable means that they are both warranted and assertible until they are successfully challenged.)

Global citizenship thus supports the experimental methods of the technosciences against political and religious attempts to undercut their methods and results.

Global citizenship demands educated persons—persons who engage issues and join with others to form publics that are global in terms of their interests and outreach. Because the goals of publics often conflict with one another, global citizenship will require a strong commitment to experimentalism. It is worth repeating in this connection that the Pragmatic hotel can accommodate the religionist and the atheist, but not the naturalist and the fundamentalist. This is because the primary method of fundamentalism, whether Christian, Muslim, or Native American, is the method of authority (including the varieties that privilege divine revelation, textual literalism, and oral tradition).[27] These and other types of fundamentalism have no mechanism for advancing their agenda short of appeals to authority or the application of psychological, physical, or political power. Because its methods are experimental, however, and because its emphasis is on what is assertible with warrant, Pragmatism offers a wealth of tools for overcoming such conflicts.

It is precisely for this reason that the Pragmatic hotel cannot accommodate the democrat and the dictator. The method of the former is experimental whereas the method of the latter is not: in dictatorships many voices, many sources of relevant information, are occluded or extinguished. It should also be noted that this result does not vitiate the claim that the Pragmatic method privileges no special result. That a result is not the outcome of the application of experimental methods does not mean that the result was excluded prior to the experiment.

In sum, the Pragmatists' accounts of meaning, truth, and inquiry, together with their commitment to human community and their moderate version of cultural relativism, can function as valuable tools for the fostering of global citizenship and the building of global publics. In order to highlight the effectiveness of these tools, I have contrasted them to the postmodernist commitment to cognitive relativism, with its consequent emphasis on difference, discontinuity, and incommensurability.

THREE

CLASSICAL PRAGMATISM, POSTMODERNISM, AND NEOPRAGMATISM

For those who are interested in coming to grips with the problems and prospects of our increasingly technological culture, classical Pragmatism appears to offer significant advantages over some currently popular versions of neopragmatism.[1] Whereas the experimentalist version of Pragmatism advanced by Dewey honored the distinct roles that the arts and the technosciences can play in, for example, social reconstruction, the neopragmatism of Rorty tends to alternate between blurring that distinction, on the one hand, and depicting technoscience as just one more of the literary arts, on the other. Moreover, whereas Dewey's version of Pragmatism emphasizes the objectivity of results achieved through application of what he termed "the denotative method," some versions of neopragmatism insist on the relativism of personal and cultural preferences. They thus attempt to displace classical Pragmatism's thick program of active experimental analysis and reconstruction with thinner projects that present hoping and coping as the best available outcome for progress.

There are a number of important differences between Dewey's classic version of Pragmatism, which he on various occasions termed "Instrumentalism" and "experimentalism," and more recent versions of Pragmatism collectively known as neopragmatism. Among those who have identified themselves (and been identified) with this recent version of Pragmatism are what might be termed "legal Pragmatists," such as Richard Posner, "literary Pragmatists," such as Stanley Fish, and others as well. Within the field of philosophy, however, neopragmatism has received its most eloquent expression in the work of Richard Rorty.

It is by now clear that Rorty has exerted an enormous influence on late-twentieth- and early-twenty-first-century philosophy. Two facts about his work stand out in high relief. First, his efforts have played a crucial role in the revival of interest in the classical Pragmatism of Peirce, James, Dewey, and George Herbert Mead. Rorty's 1979 presidential address to the Eastern Division of the American Philosophical Association, to which he gave the title "Pragmatism, Relativism, and Irrationalism," was at the time perceived as a dramatic intervention into the ordinary business of mainstream Anglo-American philosophy.[2] Today it can only be viewed as a watershed event, or better, a dredging operation that cleared away obstructions that had prevented mainstream philosophy from addressing what Dewey would today probably call the problems of men and women. The revival of American Pragmatism would probably have occurred in any event, since a new generation of philosophers was beginning to turn its attention to matters commonly termed "applied." But it can be said with confidence that Rorty's effort cleared the way for the current situation.

The second prominent fact is that Rorty constructs a novel type of Pragmatism that weaves together various strands of classical Pragmatism with themes from contemporary (primarily French) postmodernist philosophy.[3]

Rorty has not been shy about acknowledging this situation; he has in fact written extensively about the relations between classical Pragmatism and postmodernist thought. In general, it seems fair to say that he thinks that classical Pragmatism not only anticipated some of the problems that continue to vex postmodernist thought, but offered viable solutions for them as well. In 1982, for example, he wrote, "James and Dewey were not only waiting at the end of the dialectical road which analytic philosophy traveled, but are waiting at the end of the road which, for example, Foucault and Deleuze are currently traveling."[4] Elaborating on this theme later in the same book, he added, "We should see Dewey as having already gone the route Foucault is traveling, and as having arrived at the point Foucault is still trying to reach—the point at which we can make philosophical and historical ('genealogical') reflection useful to those, in Foucault's phrase, 'whose fight is located in the fine meshes of the webs of power.'"[5]

To the attentive reader, these passages might provoke the following question: what is there of postmodernism in Rorty's thought that is both worthwhile and that *cannot* be found within the classical Pragmatism of James and Dewey? A proper answer to this question will require a brief detour through some of the main points of modernist and postmodern thought.

Historian James Livingston provides a particularly helpful set of guideposts in this regard, so I will quote him at length. In Livingston's view, the Pragmatism of James and Dewey sanctions a personality that "seems both sensible and scandalous, both inevitable and impossible."[6] In Livingston's characterization, the practitioners of classical Pragmatism *are already* postmodernists in the sense that they

> do not believe that thoughts and things inhabit different ontological orders: they do not acknowledge an external or natural realm of objects, of things-in-themselves, which is ultimately impervious to, or fundamentally different than, thought or mind or consciousness. Accordingly they escape the structure of meanings built around the modern subjectivity, which presupposes the self's separation or cognitive distance from this reified realm of objects. More to the point, these theoreticians are not necessarily trapped between the epistemological extremes enabled by modern subjectivity—that is, between *romanticism*, which typically glorifies the "organic" or "subjective" inner self as against the "mechanical" or "objective" circumstances that constitute outward

existence; and *positivism*, which typically celebrates the increasing density of that external, thing like realm of objects and the evidence of progress toward the species' mastery of nature.[7]

Why does this situation appear to some as both "sensible and scandalous," both "inevitable and impossible"? Simply this: the classical Pragmatists were able to reclaim the continuities between mind and matter, facts and values, and, perhaps even more importantly, between past and present that had been disrupted in modernist thought, even while retaining and advancing a positive view of the technosciences. The classical Pragmatists argued that future possibilities can be assessed in the light of past events in ways that go beyond mere critique of, or resistance to, both choices made in the past and conditions currently in place. Classical Pragmatism thus introduces into the course of human events a type of thick social behaviorist morality—and thus a type of thick social and political engagement that is based on experimental methods, that rejects the traditional split between facts and values, and that is therefore unavailable to those working within the modernist model.

Although classical Pragmatism may legitimately be termed "postmodernism,"[8] then, it does not, as do some of the programs currently designated by that name, sanction radical forms of relativism such as those that have been termed "judgmental" or "cognitive" relativism. From the standpoint of classical Pragmatism, modernist models got locked up in a positivist outlook that apotheosized attempts by physical scientists and others to provide a philosophical basis for what they were doing. As a radical form of positivism, therefore, modernism consequently treated much of the cultural and moral life in reductive fashion either as straight-line instrumentalist or transcendentally based, or else as simply noncognitive. On the other side, from the standpoint of the classical Pragmatist, the accounts of the postmodernist thinkers have inverted this model, treating the proven methods of the physical sciences as if they were expressions of an infinitely self-reflexive nexus of literary descriptions and redescriptions which are tantamount to interminable discursive flights that do not offer the possibility of firm behavioral, referential perches.

On this postmodernist model cultural and moral life also is relativized and fragmented, since, as one postmodernist writer has put the matter, "The truth value of all judgments is relative to some particular standpoint (otherwise variously referred to as a theoretical framework, conceptual scheme, perspective, or point of view) [and] no standpoint is uniquely or supremely privileged over all others."[9]

In one sense, of course, this statement is trivially true. Putative absolutes are all relative to something or other. In a more important sense, however, if it were *nontrivially* true then it would be toothless because applicable only relative to the particular standpoint, theoretical framework, conceptual scheme, perspective, or point of view of its author. And in a still more important sense, if we accept the types of experimental naturalism and social behaviorism advanced by the classical Pragmatists, the statement is simply false. For one thing, it raises relativism to the level of an absolute. For another, its falsity can be demonstrated by various counterexamples such as can be found in the natural sciences. Among these are ones used by Dewey himself, for example, that pure tin melts at 232°C at 1 standard atmosphere. This is true in Dewey's sense of "warranted assertibility" and, save the fallibilist component built into the notion of warranted assertibility, it is not subject to endless redescription. Moreover, it is true whether we perform the experiment in Kansas City, Köln, Kandahar, or Paris.

Early on, then, during the last decades of the nineteenth and early decades of the twentieth centuries, long before the term "postmodern" had been coined, classical Pragmatism was by definition postmodernist. On one count it was postmodernist because it repudiated the various forms of dualism that had vitiated modernist thought. One need only revisit Peirce's essays "The Fixation of Belief" and "How to Make Our Ideas Clear," published in 1877 and 1878 respectively, to begin to get a sense of just how savage the classical Pragmatist critique of Cartesian modernism was.

In the place of modernism, classical Pragmatism advanced an account of human situatedness and engagement that stressed the objectivity that comes from responsibility for ongoing experimental involvement in the facts of a case. Perhaps even more important, however, classical Pragmatism stressed the real possibility that behavior can be changed, and that behavioral change can be expressed in both individual and institutional habits. To put this matter somewhat differently, classical Pragmatism is postmodern in the following senses. It rejects Cartesian and other types of attempts to provide ultimate foundations for knowledge claims, opting instead for a view of knowledge-getting that involves the construction and reconstruction of temporally differentiated platforms of action from which to construct further platforms, and so on indefinitely.

It rejects the spectator theory of knowledge, according to which true knowledge is constituted by an accurate internal representation of an external fact, electing instead a perspectival view of knowledge-getting that stresses themes currently associated with attempts to extend democratic participation and appreciation of cultural differences, or what Dewey termed "associated living."

It rejects the view that the sources of knowledge or the norms thereof are derived from locations that are outside of experience itself. In other words, both the transcendent accounts of supernaturalist theologies and various forms of Platonism, as well as Kantian accounts of knowledge-getting that depend upon a transcendental ego, are rejected in favor of an Instrumentalist/experimentalist account according to which norms, just as other types of tools, are developed in the course of experience as problems are encountered, articulated, and resolved.

It rejects the idea that human knowing can achieve absolute certainty, opting instead for versions of fallibilism according to which working hypotheses, rules of thumb, and even well proven instruments are open to revision under appropriate circumstances. And it rejects the possibility of the grand narrative, opting instead for situated, contexted attempts at piecemeal meliorism.

The central problems and issues of modern thought are thus thoroughly recast within the texts of classical Pragmatism. What Dewey termed "the quest for certainty," based ultimately on an obsession with skepticism that seems to have been the leitmotif of modernist thought, is rejected as unproductive. Its place is taken by confidence that the methods of problem solving—methods that have enjoyed their most spectacular successes in the natural sciences—constitute the best available means for knowledge-getting.

Modernist subjectivity is also recast. The self of classical Pragmatism is no longer isolated as a self-contained thinking entity—such as a transcendental ego—over against an external world of objects and (perhaps also) other thinking entities. The self of classical Pragmatism is instead an organic complex of impulses, abilities, habits, and behaviors that is deeply rooted in the natural history of the human organism and dependent on complex social environments for its growth and development. The self of classical Pragmatism is, nevertheless, not so decentered as to be elusive, as some postmodernist writers would have it.

In all this I have attempted to indicate how classical Pragmatism, from the 1870s onward, rejected the central claims of modern philosophy. This was not fruitless resistance, the shaking of a fist in the face of a dominant philosophical system. Classical Pragmatism replaced the modernist program with an alternative that was positive, detailed, and consistent.

If classical Pragmatism is postmodernist by definition, and if it is truly characterized in the manner in which I have indicated in the preceding paragraphs, then it has a prior claim to the name "postmodernism." But what then of the later postmodernism, the one that for the sake of clarity I will call "official postmodernism"? What of that official (primarily French) postmodernism that Rorty has woven together with strands of classical Pragmatism in order to produce his neopragmatism? I shall consider this question under two headings, even though there are others that are relevant to the current discussion.

First, Rorty's neopragmatism shares with official postmodernism what is arguably an inversion of the modernist depiction of the relation between the sciences and the arts. Modernism, with its preference for the quantitative over the qualitative, its preference for qualities that it regarded as primary over those it regarded as secondary, tended as a consequence to treat the arts as inferior or subservient to the sciences. This phenomenon was apparent as late as the middle of the twentieth century, which witnessed the last gasps of the program of logical positivism.

But now the modernist-positivist program appears to have been turned on its head by official postmodernism. This is perhaps nowhere more apparent than in the famous hoax perpetrated by physicist Alan Sokal. In 1996 Sokal submitted an essay to the influential journal of cultural studies *Social Text*, in which he argued that "physical reality" was nothing more than a social construct and that the objects of the natural sciences, including mathematics, are culturally determined. His paper, written as a parody of the texts of official postmodernism was accepted and published. When Sokal revealed his hoax, there was great indignation on the part of the journal's editors and the other targets of his spoof. Sokal responded by publishing a book in which he expanded his attempts to unmask what he took to be the faux science that he had found in the texts of some of the most influential proponents of official postmodernism.[10] Jacques Lacan, Julia Kristeva, Luce Irigaray, Gilles Deleuze, and Jean Baudrillard were among his targets. One reviewer attempted to assess the damage: "But what is the crime here? At worst these French theorists are *blufeurs*. They do not hate science; they love it too well and try to wrap themselves in its mantle."[11]

I would put matters differently. After examining the texts that Sokal presents in support of his case, I would suggest that they illustrate a mirror image or inversion of positivism, namely a romantic subsumption of technoscience to the subjective side of the arts, an attempt to involve or encase the quantitative, denotative features of the technosciences within a cocoon of self-reflexive, qualitative discourse. In these texts, the technosciences are at first deracinated and then called upon to serve the demands of high literary style.

To be fair, it should be noted that Rorty himself has not gone to the extremes that one finds in some of the texts of official postmodernism. But I believe that he has nevertheless to a considerable extent followed their lead. He interprets Dewey, for example, as having attempted to "rub out" the distinctions between the arts, technoscience, and philosophy, and to substitute for them a "vague and uncontroversial notion of intelligence."[12] But, as I have noted else-where, Rorty also seems to think that the technosciences are receding into the background and that it is the poet who is in ascendency. As for philosophy, he has suggested that it would be better to "avoid thinking of philosophy as a 'discipline' with 'core problems' or with a social function."[13] The poet is, after all, the "one who makes things new."[14]

But of course Dewey did not attempt to "rub out' the distinctions between the arts and the sciences. On that matter he was quite clear. In this sense classical Pragmatism subscribes neither to the positivist model or the standard postmodernist inversion of it. For Dewey, it is the business of the arts to express meanings, and the business of the sciences to state meanings. What this means in concrete terms is that Dewey realized that the history of human problem-solving has devel-oped at least two complementary types of approaches to the resolu-tion of situations that are unsettled. Rather than privilege either the arts or the sciences, Dewey argued that the methods that they can bring to situations that require resolution are not only different from one another, and not only cooperative, but applicable in different ra-tios depending on the nature of the required resolution. Where the overt statements of technoscience are either censored or unheeded, for example, it is often possible for the arts to motivate social change. One current example of this situation is the Iranian cinema, in which social stigmas attached to women as a group are explored in ways that are calculated to provoke the types of debate that can lead to reform. Of course the opposite situation can also obtain, that is, when the arts are censored or unheeded and the natural or social sciences are employed as vehicles for the solution of problematic situations. Ex-amples abound, and include the quantitative studies regularly pub-lished by Andrew Hacker that deal with the feminization of poverty in the United States or the research that went into the identification of the causes of AIDS. Ideally, of course, the arts and the sciences do their work as partners.

Second, with respect to the role of philosophy as tool for social engagement and change, there is also a less than ideal match between

Dewey's classical Pragmatism and Rorty's neopragmatism. Apart from Rorty's general suggestions in *Achieving Our Country* concerning ways in which liberals can and should be more patriotic, less enamored of theoretical excesses, and more imaginatively melioristic in their roles as nonspecialist private citizens, his work exhibits little that resembles Dewey's commitment to experimental work undertaken by philosophers qua philosophers.

This situation is especially evident when it comes to the respective accounts of the two philosophers regarding the role of discourse in social and political amelioration. Whereas Dewey considered discourse an important *phase* within the complex of methods he termed "denotative," Rorty's notion of discourse is more akin to that of Habermas: to the extent that discussion of the experimental dimension of Dewey's denotative method is there at all, it is buried deeply inside discussions of discourse and communicative action.[15]

This general assessment should not, however, be taken as an attempt to obscure the fact that Rorty's views concerning social and political matters seem to have changed over the course of the last couple of decades.

Responding to his work as it stood circa 1985, for example, Ralph Sleeper was particularly critical of Rorty's notion of an "ungrounded social hope."

> We are left, [Rorty] tells us, with "ungrounded social hope" and a philosophy that can provide us with nothing more than occasional illumination to dispel the gathering gloom. Philosophy, according to Rorty, is to give "edification," and there doesn't seem to be anything very edifying in Rorty's attenuation of philosophy's function to the point where it becomes indistinguishable from that of literary criticism. What rankles is Rorty's insouciant reductionism. Pragmatism—at least Dewey's sort—had seemed to offer us more than that. It had seemed to be teaching us how to transform the culture that is decaying around us, rather than just how to "cope" with its collapse."[16]

Rorty's work circa 1990 led to my own suggestion,[17] that the program of his liberal ironist resembles nothing so much as a kind of secular Calvinism. The liberal ironist, like the Calvinist, is skeptical about the efficacy of tool use; philosophy, it is said, cannot provide much in the way of help concerning how we are to orient ourselves toward our lifeworld. For both the liberal ironist and the Calvinist, the emphasis is upon individual regeneration, which might then, provided conditions are favorable, perhaps find some means of expression in the realm of the social.

Of course this analogy is far from perfect: whereas the Calvinist relies on the grace of God for redemption, the liberal ironist relies on the muse, friends, and books to stimulate his or her imagination. The liberal ironist hopes to get from friends and books the kind of literary redescriptions that will nourish the flickering flame of ungrounded hope. Moreover, it should be recalled that whereas Calvinism posited a self (read soul) that was so very palpable as to be all but substantial, Rorty's decentered self is chameleon-like by comparison. At certain times it seems to resemble nothing so much as the fractured self of official postmodernism or the centerless Humean self.[18] At other times, however, it appears in the guise of the more solid, active, integrating self that Dewey presents in *Human Nature and Conduct*. It is there, for example, that Dewey writes of a "self [that] gets solidity and form through an appropriation of things which identifies them with whatever we call myself" (MW 14.82).

More recently, and most prominently in *Achieving Our Country*, in several essays published during 1996 and 1997, and in the responses to his critics in *Rorty and Pragmatism*,[19] the social and political have taken on an expanded dimension in Rorty's work. In his essay "Globalization, the Politics of Identity and Social Hope," for example, he takes a position that seems to echo that of Habermas, namely, that nothing "can take precedence over the result of agreement freely reached by members of a democratic community."[20]

Even more to the point of my argument in this essay, Rorty attributes this view to Dewey. For both Habermas and Dewey, he suggests, "the reason this kind of philosophy is relevant to politics is simply that it encourages people to have a self-image in which their real or imagined citizenship in a democratic republic is central. . . .

This kind of philosophy, so to speak, clears philosophy out of the way in order to let the imagination play upon the possibilities of a utopian future."[21]

Rorty's preference for a social and political program that clears philosophy out of the way has also been noted by Steven Shapin, who reads him as suggesting that "philosophers should either shut up shop or take themselves off to the humbler departments of sociology, history and psychology: 'Philosophy does not make much difference to our practices, and should not be allowed to do so. . . . For most purposes, whether we have any philosophers around or not doesn't really matter.'"[22]

Rorty may describe himself as a "follower" of Dewey in these matters, but his Dewey is not one that I am able to recognize. As I read him, Dewey thought that philosophy and philosophers still have important work to do, and that most of that work can be articulated in terms of projects that are social and political. As I read him, Dewey thought that the denotative method was at the heart of philosophical inquiry. Here is Dewey in 1925, in the first chapter of *Experience and Nature*.

> The empirical method points out when and where and how things of a designated description have been arrived at. It places before others a map of the road that has been travelled; they may accordingly, if they will, re-travel the road to inspect the landscape for themselves. Thus the findings of one may be rectified and extended by the findings of others, with as much assurance as is humanly possible of confirmation, extension and rectification. The adoption of empirical, or denotative, method would thus procure for philosophic reflection something of that cooperative tendency toward consensus which marks inquiry in the natural sciences. The scientific investigator convinces others not by the plausibility of his definitions and the cogency of his dialectic, but by placing before them the specified course of experiences of searchings, doings and findings in consequence of which certain things have been found. His appeal is for others to traverse a similar course, so as to see how what they find corresponds with his report. (LW 1.389–90)

This passage reveals several aspects of Dewey's thought that are both important and at variance with Rorty's neopragmatism. For one thing, contrary to Rorty and Habermas, Dewey refuses to characterize definitions and dialectic (discourse) as primary or even central, that is, as practices within which experimentation is present but somehow remains submerged. Dewey's account turns matters the other way around. Discourse—definition and dialectic—is a phase of a larger program of experimental or inquirential activity. Since they are both postmodernist thinkers, of course, both Dewey and Rorty think that it is high time that we jettisoned the bulk of classical, medieval, and modernist metaphysics. But unlike Rorty, Dewey thinks it is part of the work of philosophers to determine how such idols of the tribe can be disposed of, and what kinds of things will take their place. And since each generation has its own metaphysical blind spots, philosophy and philosophers will still have a lot of work to do that does not fall within the scope of disciplines such as sociology, history, psychology, or even comparative literature.

In all this it is not that Rorty's goals are not admirable, for indeed they are. It is just that in this respect, at least, his neopragmatism seems somewhat timid and even nebulous when compared to the robust program of experimental reconstruction advanced as a part of Dewey's classical Pragmatism.

Dewey's commitment to, and Rorty's insouciance for, experimentalism is a matter that I have discussed elsewhere.[23] It is also a matter that James Gouinlock has taken up in his excellent essay "What is the Legacy of Instrumentalism?"[24] In my view, Gouinlock hits his mark dead center when he reads Dewey as arguing that the methods of science and the methods of democracy are not separate. Instead, he writes, "the norms of science are incorporated into those of democracy."[25] Moreover, it is the "responsibilities of schools to provide an environment in which scientific-democratic virtues will be acquired as an organic part of the learning process."[26] In short, Gouinlock argues that Dewey's scientific-democratic commitments offer much more than ungrounded social hope. In his reply to Gouinlock, Rorty admits that he finds the notion of a scientific method "pretty use-less."[27] Further, the term "method" "was not a fortunate choice. It promised more than he [Dewey] could offer—something positive, rather than the merely negative admonition not to get trapped in the past."[28] Again, "Granted that Dewey never stopped talking about 'scientific method,' I submit that he never had anything very useful to say about it."[29]

Even in the face of Gouinlock's direct challenge, then, Rorty maintains a stance toward the denotative or scientific method that is best termed vague. Unless one is dealing with Burkean conservatives or religious fundamentalists, he writes, the method is just "too noncontroversial to make a fuss about." Moreover, he doesn't see much difference between the method of a priori reasoning and the method of science except that "the former discourages, and the latter encourages, bold and imaginative speculation."[30]

Rorty's position on these matters hardly matches up with Dewey's version of Pragmatism. In our own time, just as in Dewey's, some of the most heated discussions at school board meetings take place between those who advocate teaching the methods and content of science and those who advocate teaching the methods and content of antiscientific alternatives. Whereas Dewey struggled with proponents of creationism, educators today must struggle with proponents of intelligent design.

Surely such discussions are about more than the merely negative admonition not to get trapped in the past. They are also about the successes of the denotative method in displacing disease, superstition, and bad government. They are about improvements in the methods of organizing communities of scientific research, communities of educational practice, and even communities of mutual therapeutic interests. In all this it is not simply a matter of not getting trapped in the past: it is also a matter of taking what is good from the past and building on it. Dewey's rich account of the denotative method takes into account the evolution of that very method. He correctly notes that it is the only method yet devised that is self-correcting.

And yet Rorty is correct, if only in a tangential sense, in saying that what Dewey called a method was in fact a whole complex of methods. Dewey recognized this fact, however, and that recognition is evident in his published work. In the final chapters of *Experience and Nature*, for example, Dewey discussed the ways in which the methods of the arts, sciences, technical disciplines, humanities, jurisprudence, and so on, each have unique yet overlapping bodies of method and content. He also indicated his view that one of the most important functions of philosophy was to act as a liaison officer, rendering the languages of these various disciplines intelligible to one another.

Unlike Rorty, then, Dewey thought that methods matter and that philosophy continues to be relevant. That is one of the big differences between classic Pragmatism and neopragmatism. And that may also be one of the reasons why the Rortian neopragmatist is left with ungrounded social hope.

PART TWO

TECHNOLOGY

FOUR

CLASSICAL PRAGMATISM AND COMMUNICATIVE ACTION

Jürgen Habermas

The thing set down in words is not affirmed. It must affirm itself or no form of grammar and no verisimilitude can give it evidence.

—Ralph Waldo Emerson

Nullius in verba (On no man's word)

—Motto of the Royal Society

The Federal Republic of Germany is fortunate to have in Jürgen Habermas a deeply engaged public philosopher.[1] Since the 1960s he has been a social critic of undisputed stature who has brought to numerous public debates a profound understanding of philosophy, its past and prospects, and of the human sciences in general. Some would argue that the United States has lacked a public philosopher of comparable stature since the death of John Dewey in 1952.

Even a quick scan of Habermas's recent work reveals the breadth of his interests. In numerous interviews, essays, and books, he has applied his broad and incisive intelligence to issues as diverse as the reunification of Germany, the Persian Gulf War of 1991, the neoconservative movement, the complex relations between the Federal Republic's policies on immigration, and the German sense of national identity.

Despite the broad swath that he has cut through public policy issues in Germany, however, Habermas is still best known in the

United States for his theoretical work. His early criticism of Herbert Marcuse concerning the status and prospects of technology; the paradigm shift toward an intersubjective theory of communication that his work exhibited beginning with the publication of *The Theory of Communicative Action*; his reconstruction and defense of discourse ethics; and more particularly his discussions of the origin and role of norms within human activity: these and other aspects of his thought have inspired an extensive literature of comment and criticism.

For present purposes I will restrict my attention to one area of Habermas's thought which I believe to be both crucial to his overall program and a continuing problem for it: his characterization of the role of scientific technology as a type of human activity. The persistent dualism explicit in his discussion of the forms of practice involve what he sometimes calls "technical rules" and "purposive-rational action,"[2] and other times calls "communicative action" or "symbolic interaction."[3] Since these matters turn out to be particularly problematic for his readers who approach his work from the tradition of American Pragmatism, I shall address them from that perspective.

The terms "science" and "technology" appear only rarely in the indices of Habermas's major works from *The Theory of Communicative Action* to the present. He dealt with science and technology in his early work, however, where he attempted to carve out a middle position between two competing visions of scientific technology, both of which took it as their task to avoid dogmatism. On the one hand, there was what Habermas termed the "decisionism" of the scientizing positivists. He correctly and eloquently charged them with attempting to remove from the "mainstream of rationality the pollutants, the sewage of emotionality," which are "filtered off and locked away hygienically in a storage basin—an imposing mass of subjective value qualities."[4] On the other hand there was Marcuse, who claimed all science is tinged with political considerations and there might consequently be a postrevolutionary scientific technology that was new in kind. It was Marcuse's view that if the "fatal link" within scientific technology between the domination of nature and the domination of human beings could be severed, and if human beings (and the human sciences) could be politically liberated, then "science would arrive at essentially different concepts of nature and establish essentially different facts."[5] In short Marcuse was proposing that if the human sciences were split off from the natural sciences and politically reformed, then the reform of technology would probably not be far behind.

To this suggestion Habermas replied that scientific technology is what it is for reasons that are rooted not so much in cultural or political practice as in the origins and development of the human species itself. Work and the domination of nature necessarily rely on the establishment and pursuit of inflexible goals (requiring methods known as "straight-line instrumentalism," "instrumental rationality," or, in Habermas's terms, *Zweckrationalität*). Work and the domination of nature are not merely ubiquitous expressions of human life—they are among its very conditions. Therefore, the alternatives Marcuse envisioned (but never fully developed) were and remain in Habermas's view not true alternatives after all. If scientific technology is a project at all, as Marcuse thought it, then it is a project "of the human species *as a whole*, and not . . . one that could be historically surpassed."[6] In other words Habermas didn't object to the split between scientific technology and the human sciences that Marcuse had thought necessary for the reform of both, but he did object strenuously to the suggestion that scientific technology might be reformed in ways that would substantially contribute to the advancement of the methods of the human sciences.

One of the reasons Habermas rejected the possibility of such reform was his contention that scientific technology can never be concerned with questions of practical reason, which takes as its task the interpretation and liberation of meanings. In order to do its work, scientific technology must dismiss such concerns as subjective. "The glory of the sciences," Habermas wrote, "is their unswerving application of their methods without reflecting on knowledge-constitutive interests."[7] It is not that scientific technology does not intervene in the conduct of life, but that its methods disallow the self-conscious analysis of the ways in which this occurs.[8] Since Habermas holds that scientific technology is essentially linked to straight-line instrumentalism, it is left to the hermeneutic sciences to address such matters. This is because the hermeneutic sciences operate in terms of a wholly different methodology—one which actively seeks to avoid control and domination. The methods and ideals of scientific technology are not infelicitous or wrongheaded *for* scientific technology, which is concerned with facts, but they are inappropriate at best, and destructive at worst, when applied to the human sciences, which are concerned with values.

Of course Habermas's attempt to construct a middle position between the disparate visions of scientific technology advanced by the positivist right and the Marcusean left is in some ways quite appealing. Especially given the highly positivized philosophical climate of the 1950s and 1960s, his attempt to retain what was good in Enlightenment science without yielding to scientism, and at the same time to open up more space for the human sciences, can only be applauded as farsighted. From the standpoint of a Deweyan Pragmatism, however, his project appears to suffer from several difficulties.

First, a Deweyan Pragmatist would certainly find a bit quaint Habermas's characterization of scientific technology as inherently monological, subject-object oriented, and preoccupied with control or domination. In her view, to identify the essence of scientific technology with the excesses of *Zweckrationalität* would be similar to identifying the essence of religion with the excesses of the Inquisition. She would therefore regard Habermas's treatment of scientific technology as methodologically, if not ontologically,[9] irreconcilable with the inherently dialogical project of communicative action and as tantamount to opening up an unnecessary and ultimately debilitating chasm within the domain of human inquiry. She would suggest that Habermas's unwillingness to envision scientific technology in terms of management or adjustment (which must also be operative within communicative action), rather than domination or control (which is the leitmotif of straight-line instrumentalism), or to envision scientific technology *and* communicative action as continuous with one

another and as features of a larger inquirential project, leaves Habermas with an underlying dualism from which his project continues to suffer.

Nor would her concern be merely an arcane one that involves nothing more than Habermas's "pre-paradigm shift" work of the 1970s. Even after the paradigm shift of *The Theory of Communicative Action*, this split remains very much in evidence. In his essay "Reconstruction and Interpretation in the Social Sciences," for example, published in *Moral Consciousness and Communicative Action* (in German in 1983 and in English translation in 1990), Habermas was still contrasting the attitude of the scientist (as "someone who simply says how things stand") with the attitude of the interpreter (as "the performative attitude of someone who tries to understand what is said to him.")[10]

From *The Theory of Communicative Action* to the present, then, Habermas seems just to accept the necessity of this dualism of scientific technology versus the human sciences and then go forward to develop means by which to ground and enlarge one of its sides at the expense of the other. Instead of attempting to overcome the breach by the *reformation* first of politics and then of scientific technology, as Marcuse would have had it, he seems to want to make communicative action (as the central method of the human sciences) a *bulwark* against the "colonization of the lifeworld" by the strategic action of scientific technology, and to *expand* the domain of communicative action by mounting an inquiry into the grounds of its possibility. This latter project, the expansion of the domain of communicative action (just pushing back the scientific technologies without explicitly relating them to the ever-growing domain of the human sciences) has led one of Habermas's Pragmatist critics to complain that he "has not really attempted, from the standpoint of the theory of action, to do justice to the diversity of kinds of action, and accordingly has delivered only communication as such as the jam-packed residual category of non-instrumental action."[11]

The study of communicative action has thus become for Habermas the crucial science, since it performs the two functions just mentioned, namely acting as bulwark against scientific technology, on the one hand, and expanding into its domain, on the other. Put in terms of the three areas of human interest that Habermas laid out in *Knowledge and Human Interests*, the study of communicative action that arises from practical-hermeneutic interests performs just this double function. On the one hand it limits and counteracts *technical* interests (the bulwark effect), which seek to control objectivized processes. On the other, it informs and marshals the energies of *emancipatory* interests (the expansion effect) which are concerned with the criticism of asymmetrical power relations.

But surely there must be some way to preserve the middle ground that Habermas attempts to establish between scientism and relativism without paying the price of an unresolved and debilitating dualism that writes off scientific technology as irrevocably coupled to straight-line instrumentalism and thereby committed to domination. And surely there must be a way to preserve a reasonable understanding of the objectivity of science and reject the relativism of those such as Rorty (who would reduce scientific technology to a type of literature) without insisting that there is an unbridgeable divide between scientific technology and the human sciences. If Habermas is correct in holding that no such way can be found, or that none is necessary, then the only contribution that scientific technology can make to the human sciences seems to be to supply them with facts, which then serve as raw materials for their interpretation of values or meanings.

American Pragmatism, and especially the work of Dewey, provides a potentially fruitful perspective from which to view Habermas's account of these matters. Although Habermas has appropriated some aspects of the work of Mead and Peirce, some of his readers have found it curious that he has not so far demonstrated much interest in Dewey. A few cursory remarks about Dewey appear in Habermas's early work, but most of those seem either perfunctory or wide of the mark. This situation is especially surprising given the view, widely held among Habermas's critics, that the two philosophers have so much in common. Given the fact that the work of both Dewey and Habermas is concerned with the ways in which communication functions within industrial democracies, it is probably fair to say that

Habermas's readers would like to see him engage Dewey's work at least to the extent that he has the work of Dewey's colleague Mead.

Of course I am hardly the first to suggest that there are similarities between Dewey and Habermas. Alan Ryan has gone so far as to call Habermas "the most 'Deweyan'" of contemporary social theorists,[12] and his assessment is not without its basis. Dewey would certainly have applauded Habermas's rejection of hard line scientific realism (although he would have probably have suggested that Habermas has not gone far enough in this regard). Like Habermas, Dewey held that the natural sciences are not involved in an investigation of reality "as such" but only that part of reality that needs to be engaged with respect to certain human interests. Nor would Dewey have found much fault with Habermas's characterization of the empirical sciences as disclosing "reality subject to the constitutive interest in the possible securing and expansion, through information, of feedback-monitored action,"[13] although he would have interpreted the matter more positively than has Habermas. In other words, both Dewey and Habermas reject scientific realism on the grounds that knowing is perspectival and fallible, and they both retain a limited but healthy notion of scientific objectivity on operational grounds.

But there are also important differences between their respective positions. Dewey clearly rejected Habermas's view that the human sciences proceed on the basis of a *wholly different method* than do the scientific technologies, that is, that the two methods are at bottom irreconcilable.[14] The methods of the human sciences are not observational, according to Habermas, and they are not particularly interested in the outcome of experimental operations. "Access to the facts," he writes, "is provided by the understanding of meaning, not observation."[15] The human sciences are hermeneutic in the sense that they involve the interpenetration of traditional and cultural meaning and the meanings of those who communicate with the interpreter. It is the self-reflective aspect of the human sciences, according to Habermas, that takes them beyond a concern with producing nomological knowledge to an engagement with an "emancipatory cognitive interest."[16]

A Pragmatist critic of Habermas would argue that scientific technology is far richer than Habermas's persistent characterization of it
as narrowly instrumental, that is, as occupied with intransigent goals
and oriented solely, or even principally, toward facts and domination.
Dewey developed a thick notion of scientific technology that located
it, along with other forms of productive communication, within the
context of a naturally occurring (and continually evolving) type of
human behavior he called "inquiry."

In one sense, Deweyan inquiry is an analogue of Habermasian
communicative action. Both inquiry and communicative action involve the clarification, extension, and enrichment of meanings. For
Dewey, however, inquiry is more than just hermeneutical: it is experimental, and it includes the activities of both scientific technology and
the human sciences (as well as the arts, historiography, and jurisprudence, to name but a few). Dewey's notion of inquiry is sufficiently
rich to allow him to specify ways, for example, in which natural and
human sciences can and do cooperate in the solution of pressing
human social problems. In his view these and other disciplines interact with one another as they pursue their respective goals, and they
also contribute to and borrow from a more general, overarching, and
constantly evolving pattern of inquiry that he calls "the general
method of intelligence." For Dewey, properly conducted inquiry aims
not at control or domination but at management or adjustment. And
although he did not deny the existence of straight-line instrumentalist
attempts at problem-solving, historically or in the present, he did
deny that such attempts had ever achieved much success and insisted
that they had no legitimate place among the methods of scientific
technology.

Habermas's Pragmatist critic would thus argue that Dewey's naturalistic approach to inquiry is ultimately more productive than Habermas's quasi-transcendental approach to communicative action
because it interrelates and *integrates* each of the interests that Habermas develops in *Knowledge and Human Interests*—the empirical
sciences, the historical hermeneutical sciences, and the critical sciences—within a general account of inquiry. Consequently, it bridges

the dualism exhibited by Habermas's project (or more accurately, it does not allow it in the first place). As I have already indicated, one of the ways Dewey achieved this was by emphasizing the ways in which the various disciplines interact with one another, both contributing to and borrowing from a more general notion of inquiry. Even more important, Dewey argued that each of the interests that Habermas characterizes as separate, and each of the methods to which those interests give rise, constitutes a *phase* within successful inquiry in its generic sense.

Technical Interests

From the standpoint of history, the analytical feature of subject-object distinctions displayed by what Habermas calls "*technical* interest" provided one of the keys to the successes of the revolution in seventeenth-century science. And from the standpoint of present-day scientific technology (or even of inquiry in general), technical interest is not for the Deweyan Pragmatist false or to be rejected *überhaupt*, but only if taken reductively as the ontological ground for inquiry or as a sole method of inquiry. In inquiry of all types, including the human sciences, it is often necessary to make such objectifying distinctions (arising out of what Habermas calls "third person" stances), but only as a part of the *analytical* or *solvent* phase of a particular sequence of inquiry.

Another way of putting this is that the Deweyan Pragmatist does not totally reject the objectification of essences, but tempers such objectification by functionalizing or operationalizing what is objectified. Objectification as posited *within* and as a part of inquiry is therefore for the Deweyan Pragmatist among the most important tools that inquiry has at its disposal. The difficulty comes when, as Dewey put it, the inquirer commits the "philosopher's fallacy" of "hard" reification or objectification—that is, the taking of something that is the *result* of inquiry as if it had existed in its own right *prior to* inquiry.

This is a matter of enormous importance. The failure of so-called scientific Marxism, as well as the failure of the cold war technophilia or excessive *Zweckrationalität* of the 1950s and 1960s in the United States exhibits just this type of objectification. Marcuse understood this well enough, and Habermas does too. For the Deweyan Pragmatist, however, it would be a mistake to accept these phenomena as legitimate cases of scientific technology. She would regard their failure not as a failure of scientific technology, but as a failure of intelligence to resist the kind of gratuitous reification that leads to an ossified ideology. Put another way, scientific technology is experimental, and neither scientific Marxism nor American cold war technophilia was ever sufficiently so.

Interest in Intersubjective Understanding

The same is true with respect to the interest that Habermas terms intersubjective understanding. The Deweyan Pragmatist would not view scientific-technical inquiry as excluding intersubjective understanding in principle, and she would argue that the positivists were wrong in their attempt to perform such a reduction. Seen in this light, and because of his systematic exclusion of intersubjective understanding from the "data gathering" activities of scientific technology (even if not from its metatheoretic activities), Habermas seems willing to give up a good deal more to the positivists than would a Deweyan Pragmatist.

It should also be noted that Habermas's position in this regard leaves him wide open to the criticism of feminist philosophers of science who have enumerated in rich detail the ways in which data gathering does in fact change as a result of the enlarged role of women in the scientific technologies. This new situation, they correctly contend, has altered the interpersonal dimensions of those disciplines.

To put the matter somewhat differently, since the Deweyan Pragmatist understands intersubjective interest as a *phase* in inquiry, she is obligated to reject Habermas's notion of a separate science or cluster of sciences which have a putatively proprietary claim to the methods of intersubjective understanding. Far from attempting an expansion of the intersubjective *phase* of inquiry to the point that it forms a bulwark against or exercises hegemony over other phases of inquiry, the Deweyan Pragmatist views such action as only one phase within inquiry. The intersubjective phase of inquiry is, to be sure, the phase that sets up and institutes feedback relations between ends and means and is therefore essential to the consensual objectivity that inquiry produces whenever it is successful. This is true both at the social level and at the level of (derivative) inner dialogue. But the intersubjective phase of inquiry is not *all* of inquiry, and consensus is not *all* of objectivity. Objectivity demands not merely consensus, but consensus based on experimental results. Moreover, such experimental results are often non-linguistic.

Interest in the Critical Sciences

For Habermas, the interests and methods of the critical sciences, such as the critique of ideology, also play a part in Dewey's thick notion of inquiry, since a healthy skepticism about current modes of practice is not only a feature of the scientific temperament (and therefore a part of the scientific method) but also a feature of any inquiry that can be said to be productive. The Deweyan Pragmatist would emphasize that this critical stance is an especially important feature of the social inquiry that occurs in primary and secondary education. It is for this reason that she would view both scientific technology and education as agents of the reform of social institutions. The enemies of social progress are for her not the objectification and domination that Habermas views as among the essential features of scientific technology, since she thinks that they have been only accidentally associated with scientific technology in any case. The enemies of social progress are rather the objectification and domination that are present in any species of deliberation that relies on what is reductive and intransigent and that therefore resists the application of the methods (and the appropriation of the promises) of experimental inquiry in its various manifestations.

The Deweyan Pragmatist would not deny that greed, class interest, and uncriticized tradition often work to prevent the enlargement of the meanings of human existence (a rough analogue of Habermas's "colonization of the lifeworld"). She would insist, however, that where meaning is diminished or eclipsed, scientific technology is not the culprit. In her view, if men and women are not free then it is not the fault of too much, but too little scientific technology (understanding scientific technology as the intelligent use of tools to solve perceived problems). And if there are problems in the public sphere, it is not the fault of too much, but too little democracy (understanding democracy as "belief in the ability of human experience to generate the aims and methods by which further experience will grow in ordered richness") (LW 14.229).

One of the crucial differences between Habermas and Dewey on these issues, then, seems to be that Dewey's notion of inquiry is much more complex and at the same time much more flexible than Habermas's notion of communicative action. This is because Dewey's account of inquiry does not rest on an untenable dualism. Further, because Dewey did not ground communicative action on quasi-transcendental norms, but instead on the historical-cultural-existential situatedness of a human organism that adjusts by means of the experimental use of tools of many different sorts, his theory of inquiry was much more open-ended and evolutionary in terms of its prospects. To put this another way, because Dewey emphasizes the situatedness and the prospects of inquiry, he does not need to make the covert foundational move that Habermas does when he, Habermas, writes that "the use of language with an orientation to reaching understanding is the *original mode* of language use, upon which indirect understanding, giving something to understand or letting something be understood, and the instrumental use of language in general, are parasitic."[17]

Like the dualism of which it is a feature, then, Habermas's quasi-transcendentalism continues to worry his larger project. In *The Past as Future*,[18] he seeks to distance himself from what he regards as the apriorism of John Rawls and Robert Nozick, whom he thinks "design the basic norms of a 'well-ordered' society on the drafting table."[19] For Habermas, norms are not given by theorists or technocrats: they are instead *"encountered* in practice."[20] Dewey, too, thought that norms emerge from the practical phase of inquiry. But when one gets down to the details of how such norms emerge, the two thinkers reach very different conclusions. (This may be a result of Habermas's close association with Karl Otto Apel, who reads American Pragmatism in terms of what some have described as an overly "transcendentalized" Peirce.)

Habermas thinks that norms "have to proceed from particular pragmatic presuppositions, in which something like communicative reason emerges."[21] In brief, norms seem to emerge out of communicative action in two ways. They emerge when parties to unhindered communication come to consensus, to be sure. Most often, however, they seem to emerge as such communication reveals the grounds and conditions of its own possibility.

For Dewey, by way of contrast, norms emerge as the *by-products* of experimental inquiry, in which unhindered communication that ends in consensus plays a part in, but does not constitute the whole of, inquiry. Because of his rich notions of technology and science, Dewey thought that experimental *tests* are essential to the construction of norms, that the ability to perform such tests is gained through education in techniques of inquiry, and that there is a continuity between inquiry of a quotidian variety and inquiry in the sciences.[22] This is precisely Dewey's argument in the first chapter of his 1903 *Studies in Logical Theory* (MW 2.298–315). After a discussion of the ways in which an "undefined range of possible materials becomes specific through reference to an end," Dewey continues with the claim that "in all this, there is no difference of kind between the methods of science and those of the plain man [Dewey's analogue of Habermas's lifeworld]. The difference is the greater control by science of the statement of the problem, and of the selection and use of relevant material, *both sensible and conceptual*" (MW 2.305, emphasis added).

In this essay I have suggested that Habermas's project rests on an unstable dualism of strategic action versus communicative action that was developed in his early work and continues to the present. Habermas's Pragmatist critics have suggested that his project places too much weight on the noninstrumental side of the breach, where communicative action occurs,[23] that it consequently fails to give experimentation its proper weight,[24] and that it sells short the historicist (adjustive) aspect of the human situation. I have attempted to flesh out some of these criticisms and to suggest some of the ways in which Dewey's project, because it is both richer and more flexible than Habermas's, avoids the pitfalls of the latter by avoiding its explicit dualism, as well as the quasi transcendentalism that is nested within that dualism. I have also offered the modest proposal that, given the great similarities between the work of the two philosophers and the positive contributions already made to Habermas's work by the two American Pragmatists Peirce and Mead, Habermas's readers would be greatly rewarded if he were to engage Dewey's work more systematically.

FIVE

FROM CRITICAL THEORY TO PRAGMATISM

Andrew Feenberg

Over the course of more than two decades, during which he has published an impressive number of books and essays, Andrew Feenberg has established himself as an important representative of a new generation of Critical Theorists.[1] Consistently insightful and articulate, he has developed a trenchant critique of technological culture that has taken as its point of departure the humanistic Marxism of his mentor, Herbert Marcuse. In his recent book *Questioning Technology*, he presents what is arguably his most successful attempt to construct a major revision of the critique of technology advanced by Marcuse and other first-generation Critical Theorists and the succeeding generation, including Habermas. At one level his work can be read as fulfilling a promise that Marcuse offered but left vague. At a deeper level, however, *Questioning Technology* can be viewed as a move away from some of the core ideas of Marcuse and the earlier Critical Theorists.

As a student of Marcuse, Feenberg might be thought to belong to the second generation of Critical Theory. Following Joel Anderson's excellent essay on the history of the Frankfurt School, however, our best option is to place Feenberg's work squarely within Critical Theory's third generation. The first generation was interested in emancipation from instrumental rationality as ideology by means of reflective social science. The second generation focused on the development of communicational tools to promote moral development and respect for constitutionality, as well as to overcome social pathologies such as extreme nationalism, xenophobia, and the colonization of the lifeworld by technoscientific rationality. The third generation, whose experiences were formed by the events of 1968, has abandoned the essentialist and substantialist views of its forebears in favor of positions that are more thoroughly functionalist and constructivist. This generation has turned its attention to problems of pluralism, multiculturalism, and globalization, and has tended to view problems of technoscience not as separate from, but as a part of social life.[2]

To those familiar with the central ideas of American Pragmatism, some of the planks in Feenberg's platform will therefore appear remarkably familiar. More specifically, Feenberg's revisions of Marcuse have the interesting effect of moving his critique noticeably in the direction of the instrumental version of Pragmatism that was developed in the first half of the twentieth century by Dewey. It is perhaps not surprising that this should have occurred, given attempts by Habermas and Apel, second-generation Critical Theorists, to appropriate the insights of Peirce, and the influential studies of Mead by Hans Joas, who has influenced third-generation Critical Theorists.

But this similarity between the Feenberg of *Questioning Technology* and Dewey's Pragmatic critique of technology, I suggest, is all the more significant given the fact that Feenberg has not given his readers much evidence that he is aware of this situation. In *Questioning Technology*, for example, he devotes a total of about a half page to Dewey, in which he discusses Dewey's treatment of democratic deliberation and then dismisses him as having exhibited an "uncritical confidence in science and technology."[3] Ten pages later, however, he reminds us that Dewey foresaw how "the dispersion of the technological citizenry" and other factors, including a "media-dominated public process," would account "for the passivity of a society which has not yet grasped how profoundly affected it is by technology" (QT, 146).

The apparent conflict between these two assessments may in fact not be so great as it at first appears. Although Dewey did have a measure of confidence in science and technology, or what is now frequently termed "technoscience," his attempts to present a democratized critique of technology are remarkably similar to those that Feenberg himself is now advancing. For those who are sympathetic to the programs of the American Pragmatists, as I am, what I have termed "Feenberg's Progress" is therefore a matter to be applauded.

It is probably best to begin by looking at Feenberg's history of the philosophical critique of technology. Presenting "before and after" snapshots in the preface to *Questioning Technology,* he describes what he views as "a fateful change in our understanding of technology" (QT, vii). What is this change? Put simply, before philosophical critiques of technology began to exhibit functionalist accounts of the current democratization of the technical sphere, they were almost universally essentialist. On the cultural and political right, there were the romantics: the John Ruskins and the Heideggers who viewed technology as the root cause of all that was dehumanizing. On the cultural and political left there were socialists and progressives who tended to an uncritical acceptance of everything that came off the engineers' drawing boards. But it should not be thought that these opposing and frequently conflicting camps had nothing in common. As Feenberg views matters, they "all agreed that technology was an autonomous force separate from society, a kind of second nature impinging on social life from the alien realm of reason in which science too finds its source" (QT, vii).

It is worth noting that although first-generation Critical Theorists Horkheimer and Adorno were constructivists with respect to "the social world," they were essentialists with respect to technology (which they placed over against the social). Marcuse shared their view in a slightly weaker form: although he never worked out the details, his view was apparently that political reform was a necessary, but not sufficient, condition for the reform of technology.[4] Moreover, it will hardly be news even to casual readers of Habermas that his early work advanced a version of technological essentialism. He reduced technoscience to "instrumental rationality" and fact-gathering, a view he has since neither rejected nor revised.

The situation has since changed. Conditions of emerging and expanding democratization have led critics to question essentialism, let alone the more extreme view, advanced by Jacques Ellul and others, that the essence of technology is nefarious through and through. For Ellul, technology is a thing: a debilitating, all-consuming, autonomous force. As a response to these new conditions, Feenberg thinks, it now seems important to move technology from the "autonomous/ other" column into a column that might be labeled "our social matrix." Put another way, the idea of the essentialists that technology occupies a location separate from the places where meaning and value are constructed has given way to the notion that meaning and value are also constructed in the context of technoscientific decision-making.

Feenberg's response to this changed situation has been to issue a manifesto. "The time has therefore come," he writes, "for an antiessentialist philosophy of technology" (QT, viii). His book is dedicated to working through what he thinks will be the characteristics of this new anti-essentialist philosophy.

The new anti-essentialism will in his view be an invigorated constructivism that allows for the possibility of difference where there was only the monolithic "technology as thing," and that therefore takes into account, as he puts it, the "social and historical specificity of technological systems, the relativity of technical design and use to the culture and strategies of a variety of technical actors" (QT, x). As I have already indicated, Horkheimer and Adorno were also constructivists. But their constructivism was limited to what they regarded as the social world—a world they perceived as existing over against the world of technoscience, in which instrumental rationality held sway, and also over against nature, which was treated as just "given."[5]

What does this mean in practice? For one thing, it means that
Feenberg has adopted a more comprehensive and explicit construc-
tivist position, which holds that technology is neither determining
nor neutral.[6] Feenberg indicates that he is following the suggestion of
Don Ihde that "technology is only what it is in some use-context"
(QT, 213).[7]

But of course this notion is Instrumentalist as well as constructivist, and it has a fairly long pedigree. It recalls McLuhan's insight that
media are the extensions of "man," and also what Melvin Kranzberg
was fond of calling "Kranzberg's First Law,"[8] namely that technology
is neither positive, nor negative, nor neutral. Does this mean that the
methods and devices of technology are vectorless, that they do not
possess momentum? Of course not. The point asserted by these Instrumentalists is just that even though technological artifacts often
possess a high degree of momentum, even to the degree that it is
sometimes almost impossible to overcome their motion, there is nevertheless a relation of feedback between the selection of tools and
methods and the influence that those tools and methods have over
our lives. As McLuhan put it, we shape our tools; thereafter they
shape us.

It is also worth noting that this type of Instrumentalism-construc-
tivism had already been well articulated long before it resurfaced during the 1960s in the work of media theorist McLuhan and historian
Kranzberg. One version, for example, was developed at the end of the
nineteenth century and the beginning of the twentieth by Dewey. The
very name he gave to his version of Pragmatism might well have
served as a clue to sharp-eared philosophers of technology that they
might find something of interest in his work: he called his view Instrumentalism. Given the long history of Instrumentalism-construc-
tivism as an approach to the philosophy of technology, therefore,
Feenberg's manifesto—that "the time has therefore come for an anti-
essentialist philosophy of technology"—has an odd (but welcome)
ring to the ears of this Pragmatist.

From the negative side, as part of his rejection of the technological
determinism evident in Horkheimer and Adorno and lurking in

Marcuse, as well as from the positive side, as a part of his emerging commitment to an invigorated constructivism that includes techno-science, Feenberg has argued that technology is not just a matter of the rational control of nature. Both the development and the impact of technologies are intrinsically social: "Technologies are not physical devices that can be extricated from contingent social values. The technical always already incorporates the social into its structure" (QT, 210).

He has further insisted, "This view undermines the customary reliance on efficiency as a criterion of technological development . . . [which] opens broad possibilities of change foreclosed by the usual understanding of technology."[9] If one reads this statement in the light of Horkheimer, Adorno, and Marcuse, then "efficiency" should probably be understood as "instrumental reason" or what Langdon Winner has called "straight-line instrumentalism," and "the usual understanding of technology" should probably be read as the views espoused by the first and second generations of Critical Theorists.

In short, Feenberg is attempting to replace the monolithic models of technology with a flexible one, which puts the decisions about its tools, methods, and techniques within the sphere of the normative-evaluative, or what some have called "the lifeworld." In his view technology is not something foreign to human life. It is not, as his predecessors thought, ideology by another name. It is not an unrestrained quest for efficiency nor the domination of nature.

What then *is* technology? It is a natural activity of human beings, a part of their attempt to secure transitory goods and improve the conditions of their lives, both as individuals and as groups. It is a method of decision-making in which means and ends are weighed against one another in a process of continual readjustment. It is complex, multifaceted, and, with the requisite amount of effort, even reversible. It is possible to speak of technological progress and regress as well. Given the factors that I have listed in this paragraph, it should be clear that Feenberg's break with the first-generation Critical Theorists is massive and dramatic. More important for present purposes, however, this paragraph also contains a pretty good representation of Dewey's Pragmatic technology.

As I have already indicated, anyone who finds Dewey's Pragmatist critique of technology attractive can only applaud Feenberg's Progress. The fact is that his position now resembles that of Dewey much more than that of his teacher, Marcuse. Already in the 1890s Dewey was articulating a critique of technology that comprehends most of the elements I just listed. He continued to refine that critique right up until his death in 1952.

First, like Feenberg, he viewed technology as a multifaceted enterprise. For Dewey, this meant that technology was more or less interdefinable with inquiry in the broad sense of the term. Dewey rejected essentialism early on, calling for a functionalized understanding of what philosophers from the Greeks to the moderns had called essences. According to his functionalist view, the essence of an event, object, or institution amounts to those aspects which we ("we" in this instance meaning members of various publics or communities of inquiry) find of sufficient relevance to our own needs and interests that we select them to characterize that event, object, or institution.

Dewey claimed that essentialists tend to commit what he called "the philosophical fallacy," namely the taking of something that is the result of inquiry as if it had existed prior to that sequence of inquiry in precisely the form that the inquiry determined it to be. Dewey's philosophical fallacy is, of course, more or less what Alfred North Whitehead would later call "the fallacy of misplaced concreteness," which is in turn the very fallacy that Feenberg condemns in the closing pages of *Questioning Technology*. When technology is stripped of its values and social context, Feenberg writes, as sometimes occurs in engineering and management contexts, "technology emerges from this striptease as a pure instance of contrived causal interaction. To reduce technology to a device and the device to the laws of its operation is somehow obvious, but it is a typical fallacy of misplaced concreteness" (QT, 213).

Like Feenberg, but unlike Marcuse, Dewey refused to accept the explicit separation between facts and values the early Critical Theorists made to drive a wedge between technoscience as the rational gathering and deployment of facts and technoscience as a realm of meanings and values developed in the context of a lifeworld. For Dewey, as for Feenberg, technological decision-making is at each fork in the road precisely about which of many possible values will be secured.

For Dewey, moreover, decision-making in the spheres of technoscience is never a matter of starting from scratch. It operates against the backdrop of two sorts of assumptions: those things that are valued in fact and those things that are valued by experimental deliberation. For Dewey there are no pure, contextless facts ready to be gathered by activities of putatively value-free technosciences. Instead, it was Dewey's view that the technosciences operate in much the same way as do other areas of human inquiry: facts are always facts of a case, selected by individual human agents or groups of them, embodied at a particular time and place and carrying forward a particular history against a particular cultural backdrop. For Dewey and Feenberg, but not for the early Critical Theorists, there is no contextless technoscience.

Perhaps even more important, however, both Dewey and Feenberg honor the idea that means and ends are not isolated from one another, that in productive forms of technology neither means nor ends should be viewed as dominating the other. Feenberg's position is clear enough in his discussion of the ways in which various theories of technology have tended to treat this issue.

> Deterministic theories, such as traditional Marxism, minimize our power to control technical development, but consider technical means to be neutral insofar as they merely fulfill natural needs. Substantivism shares determinist skepticism regarding human agency but denies the neutrality thesis. Ellul, for example, considers ends to be so implicated in the technical means employed to realize them that it makes no sense to distinguish means from ends. Critical theories, such as Marcuse and Foucault's left dystopianism, affirm human agency while rejecting the neutrality of technology. Means and ends are linked in systems subject to our ultimate control. This is the position defended here, although I work it out differently from Marcuse and Foucault. (QT, 9)

Feenberg's difference with Foucault and Marcuse on this issue, as well as with what he calls the "common sense" view, seems to be as follows. For the common sense view, technology is neutral and thus available to serve values and ends that are formulated independently. In the views of Foucault and Marcuse, however, "choices are not at the level of a particular means but at the level of a whole means-ends systems" (QT, 7).

Feenberg's own view is similar to that of Dewey. He posits two dimensions of what he terms "technical objects." The first is their social meaning and the second is their cultural horizon. The point of the first dimension is that engineering goals hardly ever have the last word, even when successfully articulated. Although it may turn out to the disappointment of the engineers in question, social meanings, some of which are quite different from original engineering goals, also enter into the life of technical and technological objects. On this functionalist approach, straight-line instrumentalism gives way to the ramification of multiple possibilities. As Feenberg puts the matter, "Differences in the way social groups interpret and use technical objects are not merely extrinsic but make a difference in the nature of the objects themselves."[10] Dewey would, of course, have applauded this conclusion.

The second hermeneutic dimension, the cultural horizon, refers to cultural background assumptions. In the medieval period of the Latin West this involved a preoccupation with religious signs and symbols, and in our own milieu it involves rationalization. Apparently unaware that he is echoing remarks that Dewey made more than six decades ago, Feenberg has concluded that "technology is thus not merely a means to an end; technical design standards define major portions of the social environment" (QT, 97).

For Feenberg technological choices are made by "social alliances." Such alliances appear to be more or less what Dewey termed "publics" in his 1927 book, *The Public and Its Problems*. Here is Feenberg: "A wide variety of social groups count as actors in technical development. Businessmen, technicians, customers, politicians, bureaucrats are all involved to one degree or another. They meet in the design process where they wield their influence by proffering or withholding resources, assigning purposes to new devices, fitting them into prevailing technical arrangements to their own benefit, imposing new uses on existing technical means, and so on. The interests and worldview of the actors are expressed in the technologies they participate in designing" (QT, 10–11). Feenberg's invigorated constructivism holds that "technology is social in much the same way as are institutions" (QT, 11). In Feenberg's vision of a "deep" democratization of technology, his alternative to technocracy, the activities of such social alliances will be wedded to "electoral controls" on technical institutions.

As I have already indicated, this vision, and the detailed analysis that supports it, of increasing electoral control by overlapping networks of educated and informed publics over the various "social alliances" that contribute to technoscientific decision-making, is precisely what Dewey was arguing for in 1927 in *The Public and Its Problems*.

In that work Dewey was highly critical of technological determinism. "There are those who lay the blame for all the evils of our lives on steam, electricity and machinery. It is always convenient to have a devil as well as a savior to bear the responsibilities of humanity. In reality, the trouble springs rather from the ideas and absence of ideas in connection with which technological factors operate" (LW 2.323). Furthermore, he argued, "The instrumentality becomes a master and works fatally as if possessed of a will of its own—not because it has a will but because man has not" (LW 2.344).

Nor is this Feenberg's common sense view of technoscientific neutrality. For Dewey technoscientific artifacts teem with meanings, and this because such artifacts are the subjects of intent and desire, and intent and desire are inevitably social in nature. "Primarily," writes Dewey in 1925, "meaning is intent and intent is not personal in a private and exclusive sense. . . . Secondarily, meaning is the acquisition of significance by things in their status in making possible and fulfilling shared cooperation" (LW 1.142).

In 1939 Dewey specifically rejects the idea, still held by the Critical Theorists who were now working a stone's throw from his office at Columbia University, that "science is completely neutral and indifferent as to the ends and values which move men to act: that at most it only provides more efficient means for realization of ends that are and must be due to wants and desires completely independent of science" (LW 13.160). In other words, he rejects the split between a world of technoscientific facts and a lifeworld of meanings and values.

In 1946, in a revised introduction to *The Public and Its Problems,* Dewey puts this even more clearly.

> Science, being a human construction, is as much subject to human use as any other technological development. But, unfortunately, "use" includes misuse and abuse. Holding science to be an entity by itself, as is done in most of the current distinctions between science as "pure" and "applied," and then blaming it for social evils, like those of economic maladjustment and destruction in war, with a view to subordinating it to moral ideals, is of no positive benefit. On the contrary, it distracts us from using our knowledge and our most competent methods of observation in the performance of the work they are able to do. This work is the promotion of effective foresight of the consequences of social policies and institutional arrangements. (LW 2.381)

How is this "promotion of effective foresight of the consequences of social policies and institutional arrangements" to be effected? Dewey cannot tell us directly, for his Instrumentalism incorporates perspectivism, contextualism, and fallibilism. But if he cannot do this, he can at least discuss the conditions under which such a "great community" will be possible. Such conditions include the free flow of information that is secured by means of experimental inquiry, among various overlapping publics which refine and express their interests in ways that make them amenable to discussion and compromise, and an educational system that is committed to the development among children of an intelligence of the type that prepares them for participation in a great community. Experts will be relied on not to

make policy but to clarify for the various publics the various consequences of alternative scenarios. It will require that the tools and
methods of technology be employed to assure a level of material and
emotional security that is the precondition for such a community.

> If the technological age can provide mankind with a firm and gen-
> eral basis of material security, it will be absorbed in a humane age.
> It will take its place as an instrumentality of shared and communi-
> cated experience. But without passage through a machine age,
> mankind's hold upon what is needful as the precondition of a
> free, flexible and many-colored life is so precarious and inequita-
> ble that competitive scramble for acquisition and frenzied use of
> the results of acquisition for purposes of excitation and display
> will be perpetuated. (LW 2.370–71)

These remarks anticipate Feenberg's claim that technology will be
democratized not solely, or even primarily, through the legal system,
but through greater "initiative and participation" that would result
in the "creation of a new public sphere embracing the technical background of social life, and a new style of rationalization that internal-
izes unaccounted costs borne by 'nature.' "[11]

In sum, Feenberg follows Dewey on the following points: He has
a) moved from an essentialist to a functionalist understanding of
technology, b) developed a vigorous form of social constructivism, c)
rejected a Heideggerian romanticism in favor of a naturalized technology, d) rejected the Critical Theorists' notion of technology as ideology, e) accepted the idea that the project of Enlightenment
rationality is not as much of a threat as the Critical Theorists had
imagined, f) proposed the idea that technical decisions are made
within a network of competing factors in which one weighs various
desired ends against one another, g) warned against the reification of
the results of inquiry as if they had existed prior to inquiry (Dewey's
"philosophic fallacy"), and h) recast technology in a way that crosses
the line between artifacts and social relations. Did Dewey go beyond
Feenberg? The short answer is yes. Dewey developed a philosophy of
education and a deep analysis of "actor networks," which he termed
"publics." He also developed a detailed philosophy of democracy,

which is the centerpiece of his philosophy of technology. Taken with his theory of inquiry, and taken seriously, these aspects of Dewey's work provide the context for changing the way we talk about technology. My point in this chapter, however, has been to suggest that Feenberg's progress toward a Pragmatic reading of the philosophy of technology is the right move at the right time.

A NEO-HEIDEGGERIAN CRITIQUE OF TECHNOLOGY

Albert Borgmann

There is a great deal to admire in Albert Borgmann's neo-Heideggerian critique of the ways in which contemporary men and
women interact with technology.[1] His suggestions about how such
interactions can be improved are both serious in tone and richly suggestive. He encourages us to go beyond what he calls "the device paradigm" in order to consider "focal things and practices," about which
we are able to communicate by means of what he calls "deictic"
discourse.

As I understand it, his device paradigm is more or less what has
come to be known as the program of the domination and commodification of nature advanced by Enlightenment rationality, and the
crass version of means-ends relationships that Langdon Winner[2] has
called "straight-line instrumentalism." Focal things and practices, on
the other hand, are matters of transcendent importance, or what Borgmann calls "ultimate concern." What is focal, he tells us; "gathers
the relations of its context and radiates into its surroundings and informs them."[3] Deictic discourse, is our way of talking about focal

things and practices; its purpose is to express and reveal. Deictic, in Borgmann's vocabulary, means "to show, to point out, to bring to light, to set before one, and then also to explain and to teach."[4]

What is deictic is contrasted to what is "apodeictic" or explanatory. Although deictic and apodeictic forms of communication share the trait of being fallible, apodeictic communication is more limited in its scope. It "cannot disclose to us how it gets underway, i.e., how its laws are discovered and how something emerges as worthy or in need of explanation."[5] It is in this sense that neither science nor technology can furnish the ends-in-themselves that Borgmann thinks lie outside those fields and provide human life with its ultimate meanings.

It is not hard to see what is salutary about this account. Only a few true-believer free-marketeers would want to disagree with his claim that most of us in Western industrialized countries have a tendency to get too tightly locked into patterns of consumption, and this without reflecting on the place of our behavior within the broader picture. This pattern of behavior includes activities such as buying things that we do not really need, that we only briefly desire and soon tire of, and with money that we do not yet have. Such behavior is frequently exhibited at the personal level and at the social and political levels as well.

At the personal level this pattern of commodification is sometimes found even in religious practice. The attitudes advanced by fundamentalist televangelists, for example, seem based not so much on the teachings of the financially insouciant Jesus, who urged a spiritual revolution, as on the agenda of the well-heeled Euthyphro, who was sure he could find the best way of doing business with the gods. In their straight-line instrumentalist worldview, for example, even the heaven of the fundamentalist Christian becomes commodified as the equivalent of a kind of eternal Caribbean cruise: a heavily advertised and expensive commodity that must be purchased well in advance, on the testimony of celebrities, and with the stipulation that all sales are final.

At the social and political level, patterns of consumption distract attention from established ecological problems such as global warming, as well as from the types of engagement that an informed citizenry would otherwise have with pressing local, regional, national, and international issues, such as the growing gap between rich and poor. Once there were citizens who initiated informed debates concerning issues of public importance. Now they seem to have been replaced by consumers who buy and use prepackaged ideas. In all this, something has been lost. Some may want to call it "the larger picture," others "the aesthetic dimension of life," and still others "the ground of our Being." Borgmann calls it "focal things and practices."

So Borgmann thinks that our view of focal things and practices, or ends-in-themselves, has come to be obscured by the smog generated by the device paradigm. How can we dispel the smog? We don't need to tinker with the sciences, since even though they cannot tell us anything about ends or values they are at least able to provide information about the "lawful fine structures of reality." We don't need to reassess the "deictic" discourses either, since they are our best hope of diminishing the effects of the device paradigm by allowing focal things to shine.

Borgmann's solution to the problem of obscured focal things and practices is to enter technology under two columns. One is the bad part of technology (the device paradigm), which involves manipulation and transformation and therefore disburdens us from intimate contact with focal things and practices. The other is the good part of technology, which operates in the background supporting focal things and practices. At the personal and familial level, television, stereos, central air conditioners, and dining out are bad, while piano music, wood-burning fires, and eating in are good. At the public level, cathedrals are good and the space shuttle is bad.

This is a matter of crucial importance to understanding what Borgmann wants to tell us, so it deserves to be stated in his own words. In matters personal and social, private and public, the thing to remember is that technology will never be reformed from *within* the device paradigm. Reform is only possible from the outside, as he puts it, by means of "*the recognition and the restraint* of the [device] paradigm."[6] Borgmann's proposed reform of technology, then, intends "to restrict the entire [device] paradigm, both the machinery and the commodities, to the status of a means and let focal things and practices be our ends."[7] This plan of action would lead, in his view, to a "simplification and perfection of technology in the background of one's focal concern and to a discerning use of technological products at the center of one's practice."[8] In other words, small is beautiful and big is bad. Hands-on crafts and directly legible texts (such as printed words and musical scores) are good, and machine manufacture and electronic communication (such that machines are required to read the text) are bad.

Borgmann's program has some interesting similarities with other critiques of technology, past and present. Like Lewis Mumford, Borgmann is concerned that the machine tends to mangle the organic. Like Jürgen Habermas, he is concerned that technology has begun to colonize the lifeworld of communicative action. Like Langdon Winner, he is sharply critical of the idea that ends of production and consumption tend to determine and justify their means. Like E. F. Schumacher and Hazel Henderson, he thinks that small is usually beautiful and that big is usually ugly. And like Amory Lovins, he favors a technology that is decentralized and self-sufficient. As important as these connections are, however, it is in the work of Martin Heidegger that we find Borgmann's spiritual taproot. He follows Heidegger in complaining that contemporary technological practice (the device paradigm) distracts us from the "great embodiments of meaning."[9] He also follows Heidegger in claiming that technology (the device paradigm) has been responsible for a kind of diaspora of focal things and practices. For both Heidegger and Borgmann technology provides the ground for a kind of negative hope. The vacuity of technology (again, the device paradigm) serves as an opening or clearing in which focal things can once more be engaged with clarity and purpose.

To Borgmann's credit, however, there are also crucial points on which he seems to part company with Heidegger. First, whereas Heidegger seems to want to return to pretechnological enclaves as part of his romanticized search for poetic meaning, Borgmann recognizes the futility of such thinly veiled Luddism. He tells us that he wants instead to go forward toward a reformation of the device paradigm from the outside in a way that will result in leaner, more appropriate forms of technology. He recognizes that we can't live entirely without devices, such as pianos and wood-burning stoves; he just wants us to live without the big, complex, distracting ones, such as televisions, computers, and space shuttles. In other words, whereas Heidegger apparently wanted to go all the way back to stone bridges, Borgmann says that he wants to go forward by going only part of the way back, to acoustical instruments and home cooking.

Second, whereas the social dimension of focal things seems to drop out of Heidegger's work, especially after his disastrous affiliation with the Nazis, Borgmann wants to emphasize the political and social contexts of such focal things and have them play their part in helping us develop more sympathy and tolerance for one another. If we can just strip our devices down to the bare minimum so that we can focus more intently on matters of ultimate concern, this way of thinking can begin to permeate our social and political lives.

In all this, then, Borgmann is clearly advancing one of the best neo-Heideggerian critiques of technology now available. He supplants the romantic Luddism of Heidegger's later period with a kinder, gentler form of romanticism that attempts to give technology—at least in some of its more limited forms—its due. What's more, he attempts to introduce an agenda of social and political reform into his analysis of technology in a way that almost makes us forget the disastrous consequences of Heidegger's own maladroit program.

In sum, Borgmann thinks that we need about the same amount of explanation but much less transformation and manipulation. We need to be less occupied with the malleability of things, and we need to downsize our dependence on devices. We need more expression, more revealing, and more articulation. We need much less big technology, about the same amount of science, much more small technology, and, which he thinks comes down to pretty much the same thing, much more art.

Even those who are sympathetic with some of Borgmann's goals, as I myself am, might nevertheless find themselves tempted to tweak some of the details of his program. First, I believe, that he has cast the net of his condemnation of the device paradigm too broadly. He does this by reducing the many and varied functions of certain devices to one essential property. Television, for example, is unequivocally bad because it displaces social relations.[10] But surely television does more than that. Granted, there is much that is stupid on television. Nevertheless, the medium sometimes informs and educates, sometimes serves as soporific or aphrodisiac, and during times of crisis it can even bring people together. It functions in lots of other ways, too. In other words, whether we want to dismiss a particular tool or artifact as contributing to what we think is bad about our technological culture really has more to do with the function of that particular tool or artifact within a specific context than with some property that is claimed to be its essence. My first objection to Borgmann's program, then, is that it rests on a rigid essentialism. I believe that a flexible functionalism can take us further down the road to understanding the complexities of our technological milieu.

Second, there is the matter of his focal things and practices. The issue here is not so much whether we often discourse about matters that are "transcendent" in some sense, and of "ultimate concern" to us, but whether someone might want to give a different account of what such things are, how they arise, and how they function. Simply put, I believe that Borgmann has given too much weight to the integrity of focal things and practices. He does not seem to be interested in their origins and he does not think that they are amenable to testing. Taken together, these two objections amount to a criticism of his account of means-ends relationships.

Before I get into these matters in more detail, however, I want to take a step back in order to examine the ways that Borgmann characterizes some of the accounts of technology that compete with his own. Several years ago I wrote a review of *Technology and the Character of Contemporary Life* for the journal *Research in Philosophy and Technology*.[11] In his generous reply to my review, Borgmann indicated that his discussion of rival theories was only a "disciplinary aspect" of his work, and subordinate to its "substantive concerns."[12] I think he may have been too modest in this regard, however, and that his discussions of theories that rival his own do in fact shed considerable light on some of the more substantive parts of his account.

He thinks that all theories of technology can apparently be fit into one of three boxes—or four, if you count his own. The first three of these boxes are labeled substantivist, instrumentalist, and pluralist. The substantivist view holds that "technology appears as a force in its own right, one that shapes today's societies and values from the ground up and has no serious rivals."[13] Jacques Ellul is cited as a proponent of this position. Borgmann thinks this view unduly pessimistic, and for the most part opaque, too, since it tends to stop the quest for explanation in the face of a menacing, vague, and unalterable force. Anyone who has spent much time reading Ellul probably won't be moved to quarrel with Borgmann on this particular point.

The instrumentalist view, on the other hand, holds that "there is a continuous historical thread that leads from our ensemble of machines back to simple tools and instruments. We may think of both machines and tools as affording possibilities of which we can avail ourselves for better or worse."[14] Borgmann thinks that the several varieties of this position, including those he calls "anthropological instrumentalism" and "epistemological instrumentalism," have some important elements in common. First, they treat tools as value neutral. Second, they tend to treat matters of ultimate concern as something to be established by efforts that are essentially private.

The worst of the worst in Borgmann's account are these instrumentalists. In order to go about their everyday business, he suggests, they have to assume and make use of the reality delivered to us by the scientists. But this is the very reality that they fail to treat with sufficient respect. They seem only to be interested in how things can be used. They are not really interested in fundamental reality beyond what is concrete and quotidian, and they think that abstract science is full of "convenient and useful formalisms."[15] The instrumentalists are bad because they keep telling us that "whatever works is good."

Borgmann characterizes this view as shortsighted because it ignores the fact that tools are never mere means, but are instead "always and inextricably woven into a context of ends."[16] If substantivist views collapse from the weight of their own totalizing ambition, then instrumentalist views suffer from their inability to see the big picture and from their lack of common sense.

The third theory of technology is advanced by those whom Borgmann calls "pluralists." This view attempts to take the complexity of technology seriously as a "web of numerous countervailing forces," but it "fails reality," as he puts it,[17] because it ignores overall patterns, pervasive social agreements, and coordinated efforts. If the substantive view is a kind of black hole that collapses in on itself on account of its own gravity, and if the instrumentalist view is little more than froth, with no discernable direction of movement apart from what works at the moment, then the pluralistic view tends to go flying into a thousand pieces because there is no force at its center capable of holding it together. As we shall see, Borgmann wants his own view to have the gravity of a good solid center, but he doesn't want that center to suck in everything around it.

As a working Pragmatist of an eclectic sort, I am obliged to suggest that Borgmann's taxonomy of theories of technology is at least one short. Several years ago I published a Pragmatic account of technology that has its own taproot in the work of John Dewey.[18] This view, which I will call Pragmatechnics for short, doesn't quite fit into any of Borgmann's three categories. It does overlap with some of them, however, as well as with some of the features of his own view, which I will call Focaltechnics. Pragmatechnics is not substantivist, for example, since it holds no brief for reifications or foundations of any sort, whether they be scientific or metaphysical. It doesn't treat technology as a "thing" or "force" as does Ellul. In fact, it is even less substantivist than Focaltechnics, which appeals to the "lawful fine structures of reality."

Pragmatechnics does not fit into the box that Borgmann labels "pluralist." Not content with merely describing experienced complexities, it is instead a thoroughgoing program of problem-solving that involves analysis, testing, and production: production of new tools, new habits, new values, new ends-in-view, and, to use Borgmann's phrase, even new "focal things and practices." Pragmatechnics thus takes up a matter that appears to be absent in Focaltechnics, that is, how we come by focal things and practices in the first place. Like Focaltechnics, Pragmatechnics argues that if technology is to be responsible then it must be socially and politically engaged. But unlike Focaltechnics, Pragmatechnics argues that if technology is to be responsible then it must also be able to test our focal things and practices.

Pragmatechnics is not an instrumentalist view in the sense in which Borgmann employs the term. It holds that a genetic or historical understanding of tools and artifacts is important, and therefore that scientific discourse can in fact disclose how it gets underway. But it also holds that human beings are much more than simply tool makers and users. It holds that there are vast and important areas of human experience that do not involve conscious tool-use since they do not call for deliberation. Like Focaltechnics, Pragmatechnics holds that focal things and practices generally have to do with aesthetic experience, sympathy, and enthusiasm. Unlike Focaltechnics, however, Pragmatechnics holds that we sometimes need to examine our enthusiasms, aesthetic experiences, and sympathies, to subject them to tests of relevance and fruitfulness, and then to honor the ones that serve common goals and reject the ones that are unproductive because they are based on what is merely personal or sectarian.

Although some of the features of Pragmatechnics overlap those of Focaltechnics, then, there are important differences as well. One of the most important differences is that Pragmatechnics holds that value-determination, including assessment of our most cherished "focal things" is an activity of intelligence, and that intelligence is not located outside of human technological activity. For Pragmatechnics, the tools and artifacts of our culture require ongoing evaluation, and such evaluation must be done in context. We cannot say a priori, or even on the authority of some end-in-itself, that small-scale devices are more appropriate than large-scale ones. We cannot say up front that learning to play the piano is more appropriate or meaningful than learning to play an electric guitar or learning to appreciate recorded music. Pragmatechnics just doesn't admit this type of reduction: it holds that intelligence demands that what is *techne* be subjected to a *logos*, whether the *techne* in question involves basic activities such as using wood-burning stoves or more complex ones such as building a space station. For Pragmatechnics, the *logos* of *techne* is technology.

So Focaltechnics seems to want to characterize device-technology reductively as an addiction to the disburdenment from attending to focal things and practices, and then to work for its reform from the outside, using science and deictic discourse to achieve a small-is-beautiful "appropriate technology" alternative in which such disburdenments are reversed. Pragmatechnics, on the other hand, characterizes technology more broadly as the invention, development, and deliberate use of tools and other artifacts to solve human problems. It does not distinguish between large- and small-scale devices a priori, or even on the authority of some end-in-itself, but only in the context of problems and issues as they are critically articulated. It holds that technical failures are usually due to a failure of intelligence, and that most devices, especially complex ones, exhibit a whole range of values and functions from which it is the job of intelligence to select the best and most meaningful. Appropriate technology is thus for Pragmatechnics not a question of essence or scale but of function and context. Pragmatechnics argues that when we encounter a problem we can only start where we are, and not where we are not. And where we are is on the "inside" of technology in the sense that our culture uses a wide range of devices, both large and small, both complex and incomplex, some of which are used in ways that enrich human life and some of which are used in ways that are not. This is a distinction of enormous importance. I hope that it will become clear during the course of the next few pages that it is a distinction that makes a real difference.

Borgmann has written that he thinks there are two big differences between our two views.[19] The first difference involves the question of whether a strong reform of technology is needed. The second and related difference concerns whether matters of ultimate concern are testable.

As regards the strong reform of technology, Borgmann is mistaken when he identifies the type of liberalism that Dewey advocated, and that I advocate, with the type of weak or feckless reform program that ignores excellence, as he puts it, because it is content to settle for progress in the areas of justice and prosperity. Dewey also argued against that type of liberalism. In his book *Liberalism and Social Action* (LW 11), for example, he identified that particular type of liberalism as outdated and called for its replacement by a more robust type that would treat individual excellence as a social goal, and not as something that occurs haphazardly or as the effect of an "invisible hand." But the point of that book cannot be properly understood without remembering a point that philosophers often tend to forget, namely that Dewey was deeply involved in educational experimentation.

In *Democracy and Education* (MW 9), as well as in *The School and Society* (MW 1) and *The Child and the Curriculum* (MW 2), excellence was precisely what Dewey was after. It is true that he thought that the pursuit of such excellence is facilitated when certain conditions are satisfied, and that these include social justice and a decent level of material well-being. Even though some of our current political leaders seem to want us to ignore the fact, it is difficult to start a school day on an empty stomach. But social justice and a decent level of material well-being do not suffice to produce excellence. The sufficient causes of excellence are many and varied, so we cannot say in advance what they are. But education, both in the schools and in a lifelong curriculum, remains one of the best means of determining such causes on a case-by-case basis.

Borgmann thinks that the type of liberalism that Dewey and I propose is faulty because it leaves the pursuit of excellence to the private sphere. This may be true of some varieties of neopragmatism, but it is not true of the view I am defending here. Pragmatechnics treats learning as a public activity that engages its wider context. Dewey, for example, did not write about the school *or* society, but the school *and* society. And whereas much of current educational theory focuses extraordinary attention on either the child *or* the curriculum, Dewey emphasized the interrelatedness of the child *and* the curriculum.

Borgmann also criticizes the type of Pragmatism that Dewey and I propose on the grounds that its program for reform is weak because it is piecemeal. Although he sees some merit in such an approach, because it is sometimes the only type of reform available to us, he is nevertheless afraid that it will lead to a "featureless landscape wherein piecemeal meliorism is the only kind of reform that remains."[20] Borgmann contrasts this view with his own, which he says aims at "knowing and revealing, as distinct from making and transforming."[21] It is difficult to know precisely what to make of this claim, since even the small technology that Borgmann places on the good side of the ledger requires some degree of making and transforming. As near as I can determine, it seems to involve a covert dualism in which ends are separated from means. For Pragmatechnics, knowing and revealing are not separable from making and transforming, since making and transforming are the means by which knowing and revealing are brought to fruition, and it is by treating knowing and revealing as ends-in-view that making and transforming are made meaningful. In other words, the two types of activities are related as means and ends.

This leads directly into the second big difference that Borgmann sees between his own view and mine. It involves the question of whether and to what extent matters of ultimate concern are testable. He thinks that they are not testable, but that they are contestable and attestable. I think that in many or most of the cases in which ultimate concerns come into conflict, which is to say when they become problematic, they are also testable.

Far from being mysterious or ineffable, then, matters of ultimate concern manifest themselves in terms of whether they contribute to the enrichment of the individual and the community. The problem is that what some call matters of ultimate concern are sometimes little more than idols of the tribe or the marketplace. Were matters of ultimate concern not testable, then there could be no systematic reform of any sort, and therefore no progress.

Even though Borgmann denies that matters of ultimate concern, or final commitments, are testable, he does allow that they are "contestable, attestable, and, alas, fallible." "If my ultimate concern is impoverished or oppressive," he suggests, "you are to contest it by attesting in your speaking and acting to one that is richer or more generous."[22] Focaltechnics thus privileges speaking and acting over experimental testing, and this places it at odds with Pragmatechnics, which treats ends as ends-in-view, or artifactual and provisional, and thus as subject to experimental tests. But whereas Focaltechnics places speaking and acting over against experimentation, Pragmatechnics holds that experimentation includes speaking and acting and much more as well.

There is more than a verbal difference in describing something as testable, on the one side, and contestable and attestable, on the other. It is true that there are times and circumstances when adequate tests are not available, and when all we can therefore do is attest or contest. It is also true that there are circumstances in which there is a subtle gradation in which testing, on the one side, and attesting and contesting, on the other, shade into one another. But it seems to me that if a strong reformer of technology has any obligation at all, it is to seek to develop such tests wherever there are differences of opinion about ultimate concerns. The strong reformer of technology cannot be satisfied with merely attesting and contesting. To fail to take the next step beyond attesting and contesting runs the risk of endless discussion, endless claims and counterclaims, with little hope of reform, either weak or strong. Attesting and contesting, as I understand the terms, have to do with *doing*, which may or may not be productive, whereas testing has to do with *making*, or the production of new consequences.

At one point Borgmann mounts a parody of the idea of testing final commitments: "For me to test [a profound mutual commitment] the way the Consumer Union tests cars would be to jeopardize and perhaps to destroy it."[23] In raising this issue, he has alluded to a matter that is of high importance to the Pragmatist: tests are only appropriate, and indeed only possible, when there is a perceived problem. Deliberation is only required, and is only possible in any meaningful sense, when there is an experienced difficulty. Further, means and methods will vary according to the nature and context of a doubtful situation. We do not test scientific hypotheses in the same way that we test works of art, and we do not test cars in the same way we test ultimate concerns.

I must confess, then, that I have some serious questions about the way that Borgmann treats the matter of ultimate concerns. As I have indicated, he tells us that they are not antiscientific. "Focal practices," he writes, "are at ease with the natural sciences. Since focal things are concrete and tangible, they are at home in the possibility space that the sciences circumscribe." Moreover, "the reform of technology would rest on a treacherous foundation if focal things and practices violated or resented the bounds of science."[24]

But he also tells us that focal things and practices are "unprocurable and finally beyond our control."[25] A focal practice is "the resolute and regular dedication to a focal thing. It sponsors discipline and skill which are exercised in a unity of achievement and enjoyment, of mind, body, and the world, of myself and others, and in a social union."[26]

Technology, on the other hand, at least in the sense of what I regard as his overly inclusive "device paradigm," does seem to Borgmann to be hostile to focal things and practices. His device paradigm is overly inclusive because it is concerned with things in their malleability, and especially as they become increasingly malleable as a result of our increased scientific understanding of them. I am afraid that I find more than just a hint of a kinder, gentler version of Platonism lurking in the background of this vision: what is transformable and malleable is put on one side, as inferior, and what is an end-in-itself, "unprocurable and finally beyond our control," is put on the other, as superior. The problem, then, lies not so much in his criticism of his device paradigm (since Pragmatechnics also criticizes reliance on faulty means-ends relationships) but in the fact that he has made his device paradigm include too much. Consequently, Focaltechnics seems to be anchored in what is unprocurable and finally beyond our control, rather than in what is amenable to tests and evaluation.

It might be objected that by arguing that ultimate concerns are testable the Pragmatist is left with nothing to ground her focal things, that is, her most cherished values. Such an objection would be both correct and incorrect. If asked to ground one of her ultimate values such as her faith in democracy as a method of association in "the lawful fine structures of reality," the Pragmatist would simply deny that such grounding is possible. She is, after all, a robust antifoundationalist. What she holds most dear is not grounded in this way.

But even if what she thinks valuable is not grounded in this way, that does not mean it is arbitrary or without substance. With Dewey, she would say that what is valuable is constructed, but that it is not constructed out of nothing. It is constructed out of the raw materials and intermediate stock parts that we get from our histories, from our cultural interchanges, and from our personal interactions. It is constructed by common political or social action to solve common problems. And it has been subjected to the tests of long series of experiments that have culled out a good many forms of social and political organization that did not work. In fact, it is subject to ongoing tests.

What is of ultimate concern to the Pragmatist may change over time as new ideas and ideals are generated, and as new methods are found to bring about what is most cherished. Moreover, what one generation counts as ultimate concern may be of little account to the next. There are abundant examples of this phenomenon, from the Crusades to the Inquisition to the institutions that attempted to justify slavery. This is why a Deweyan Pragmatist would argue that democracy is equivalent neither to a set of institutions nor to a set of desired outcomes, but is instead a set of provisional methods (self-correcting as long as they are actually applied and as long as they continue to be tested) for finding solutions to common problems. As Dewey put it in an address in 1939, "Democracy is belief in the ability of human experience to generate the aims and methods by which further experience will grow in ordered richness. Every other form of moral and social faith rests upon the idea that experience must be subjected at some point or other to some form of external control; to some 'authority' alleged to exist outside the processes of experience" (LW 14.229).

Now there is a way of reading Borgmann's program that saves it, at least from the perspective of the Pragmatist. On this reading, the device paradigm would be identified as only those aspects of technology that most informed critics, upon ongoing reflection and experimentation, find to be counterproductive or undesirable. Other aspects of technology—including big-ticket items such as most medical research and most of the space program and small-ticket items such as research into sustainable agriculture in developing countries—that have led to and supported what progress we have been able to make would then be absorbed into or counted as a part of what is outside of the device paradigm. Such items would thus take their place with goals, or ends-in-view, and science on the good side of the ledger, and only the crass straight-line instrumentalism of the device paradigm would be left on the bad side of the ledger.

But I think that Borgmann would object to being read in this way, since what seems to be his preferred dividing line between device-technology, including most of electronic technology, on the one side, and small direct-access technology, science, and focal concerns, on the other, would have been substantially redefined. I think that he would object to this model because it would have the effect of placing what he takes to be questionable, namely manipulation and transformation, on the good side of the ledger where he thinks they do not belong. What appears to be his deep distrust of instrumentalism and his profound devotion to ends-in-themselves seems to militate against this way of looking at matters.

I conclude with a brief example. One of the ultimate concerns that Borgmann turns to again and again involves the family. This type of discussion is, and should be, a part of any discussion of the reform of technology for several reasons. For one thing, the family is or should be a primary place of education. For another, our social and political institutions, including our ideas and practices regarding what families are and how they should be supported, are themselves constructed artifacts. Discussions of the nature and function of the family are heard today in almost every quarter, and almost all of the parties to these discussions claim to hold the integrity of the family as a matter of ultimate concern. How, then, can there be so much disagreement about what a family is and should be? And more important, how can these profound disagreements be resolved?

Borgmann tells us that we need to demonstrate, to show, to reveal, what a family can be by our practice. If we do so, in his view, we will go beyond any type of technological treatment of the subject and attest to our ultimate values in ways that will move others to action. I believe that there is a great deal of truth in this suggestion. But we must go further. This is only one strategy among many for restoring the family to its proper place as a locus of social intelligence. Other strategies involve demographic studies, longitudinal psychological studies, and other types of experimental tests that can help us determine whether our intuitions about what is worthy of ultimate concern in these matters are warranted.

It is hardly a secret, for example, that many gays and lesbians want to be accorded the benefits that accrue to legitimized family relationships. They want to be able to adopt children, to make decisions about an ill or deceased partner, and to be eligible for the survivor's benefits normally provided by life insurance policies and retirement programs. In short, they want to be recognized and respected as families in the same way that heterosexual families are. For individuals who are a part of such relationships, these are focal things. They are matters of ultimate concern.

But there are some people whose ultimate concerns run directly counter to such aspirations. Such people tell us that their ultimate concerns demand that they fight such recognition, legitimization, and respect. They see in the ultimate concerns of gays and lesbians the seeds of moral decay, transgression against what they take to be the will of God, and the corruption of the young. In states such as Colorado and Oregon they have mounted ballot initiatives designed to roll back even the civil rights that gays and lesbians currently enjoy.

How are such fundamental conflicts over ultimate concerns to be addressed?

I believe that Borgmann is correct when he says that attesting and contesting constitute a part of the solution to this crucial and urgent social problem. Many gay and lesbian political activists would agree. They attest to their ultimate concern by refusing to conceal their sexual orientation and by bearing the scorn of their neighbors in a public fashion. Since they do not have access to public legitimization for their domestic unions, they attest to their love and commitment to one another in private religious ceremonies. In debates, in discussions, and in the courts they contest the customs, institutions, and statutes that are arrayed against them. They contest what they take to be unfair practices by challenging existing laws, retirement programs, and adoption policies. Sometimes they even engage in civil disobedience and go to jail. It is right that they should do these things, and it is certainly the case that their attesting and contesting constitute a step toward the reform of the social pressures that often serve to stress their family relationships and render them more fragile than they would otherwise be.

Attesting and contesting in these ways is an important step toward the solution of this pressing social problem. By itself, however, it is not enough. The fact is that ultimate concerns such as those associated with family life are testable. Some of the tests involve quantifiable data. It is possible, for example, to quantify the benefits to health and psychological well-being that accrue to individuals living in stable, committed, monogamous relationships. It is also possible to test the effects on children of growing up in a same-sex household. Such studies have been undertaken, and they continue to be undertaken. To any fair and open-minded person, their results are unambiguous. Such tests reveal that in this case, where two widely diverse sets of ultimate concerns are in conflict, one is well founded, promotes health and harmony, and is salvific. The other is uninformed and moved by fear of what is not known or understood.

Such experimental results may fail to convince those whose ultimate concerns render them incapable of accepting objective evidence.

This was certainly the case during the civil rights struggles in the South during the 1960s, and it is still the case during the civil rights struggles of the current decade. But such results do matter to fair-minded people. They do matter in terms of the official positions of professional health organizations. And they do matter when conflicts enter the legal system.

This is only one example of what the Pragmatist means by testing ultimate concerns. I could have discussed any number of equally important matters, such as disputes concerning the direction that our form of democracy should take, or whether wilderness areas should be preserved from development. These matters also involve ultimate concerns, and they are also hotly contested.

I believe that the type of appeals I have just discussed, though they may appear too "instrumental" to some purists, will turn out to have greater positive long-term effects than any appeal to ultimate concerns as ends-in-themselves. This claim, too, is at least potentially testable.

My intuition is that Borgmann recognizes that there is this danger in talking about "final structures," "ultimate concerns," and "things in their own right," and that he tries to temper his treatment of these matters by appeals to science, or "the lawful fine structures of reality." He does so because he is also a democrat, a pluralist, and a person who believes deeply in the possibility of reform. I suspect that he also knows that public policy decisions are best made on the basis of experimentally informed discussion and open-minded debate, rather than on the basis of appeals to ultimate concerns. This is because what is accepted as ultimate is hardly ever also universal.

As I have tried to indicate, I am in general sympathetic with some of Borgmann's goals for the reform of technology. We need to move beyond narrow consumption and use-models for living, and we need a new commitment to social intelligence. Further, I think that his emphasis on ultimate concerns will be especially attractive to those whose lives are influenced by the claims and interests of liberal theology and those who already feel strongly about environmental issues.

Nevertheless, I wonder if Borgmann's suggestions will enjoy wide appeal. Some of his readers, especially those who live in urban areas, will probably be uncomfortable with his suggestion that when we get beyond the simplest of devices such as acoustical musical instruments and wood-burning stoves then we have allowed our ultimate concerns to become clouded. Some of his readers, especially those who are struggling with inherited religious and other cultural values that don't seem to be applicable to their everyday lives, will probably be uncomfortable with his view that ultimate concerns are unprocurable and finally beyond our control. And some of his readers, especially those who view electronic communication as one of the antidotes to provincialism, may reject his argument that our culture has too much technology and that technology is the source of our current political and social ills. I myself am uncomfortable with these ideas because my conception of technology is pluralist and functionalist. My Pragmatism leads me to think that where technology fails us, it is not technology that is the problem. It is ourselves. It is our lack of interest, our lack of insight, and our lack of devotion to the solution of pressing problems. And above all, it is our lack of ability to invent new tools and to criticize our own highly cherished values.

SEVEN

DOING AND MAKING IN A DEMOCRACY

John Dewey

Understanding has to be in terms of how things work and how to do things. Understanding, by its very nature, is related to action; just as information, by its very nature, is isolated from action . . . only . . . by accident.

—John Dewey

Advancing a claim once regarded as radical and still widely misunderstood, John Dewey argued that most of his philosophical predecessors, even those who had claimed the methods of science as their own, had been guilty of a failure to recognize the importance of technology.[1] He suggested this was due in part to their prejudice against the impermanent materials used by artisans and craftspeople, in part to their tendency to deprecate the social classes whose members have traditionally dealt with doing and making in the practical sphere, and in part to their rejection of what he took to be the democratizing tendencies of technological methods.

Analysis of the web of technical artifacts and methods that humankind weaves, lives in, and works in was for Dewey a lifelong task.[2] His early work, between 1892 and 1898, exhibits a preoccupation with the relations between the sciences and the industrial arts and between what were then known as "normal" and "technical" schools. His middle work, from 1899 to 1924, contains discussions of the ways in which intelligence is related to the use of technological artifacts, and of the ways in which concrete tools such as agricultural implements are related to less tangible tools, such as logical connectors.

Dewey's later work, from 1925 until his death in 1952, including *Experience and Nature* (1925) and *Art as Experience* (1934), developed these themes in detail. He articulated an account of the philosophical implications of technology during its classical, modern, and contemporary periods, and he anticipated many of the issues and debates which now occupy those working in the philosophy of technology. In this connection, chapters four and five of *Experience and Nature*, central chapters in what is regarded by many as Dewey's most important work, are devoted almost entirely to a critique of technology. Moreover, those of his later works that focus on science, education, religion, and democracy are richly furnished with examples and metaphors from the technical sphere.

It was Dewey's contention that his philosophical predecessors had for the most part misplaced technology with respect to science, metaphysics, and social thought. Plato and Aristotle, each in his own distinctive way, had attempted to relocate technology outside the work of the artisan and outside the interactions between humans and changeable matter. Plato, especially in the *Timaeus*, did this by establishing a kind of grand artisan outside the realm of nature. Aristotle did so by making nature itself the grand artisan whose task it is to establish fixed ends fit to be contemplated as ends-in-themselves, not as instruments for further ends.

What resulted was not just a perversion of technology, but a stunting of the growth of science and social inquiry as well. *The Republic* richly documents the consequences for social thought in general, and for democracy in particular, of this turn against experience in its full-bodied sense. It is there that Plato relegates *techne*, the activities of the technical artisan, to the lowest rung of his socio-political hierarchy, and at the same time characterizes an attenuated and immaterial form of *techne*, that of the totalitarian social engineer, as the purest and most important of social activities.

It was Dewey's contention that Plato had placed the artisan at the bottom of the social hierarchy for the same reason that he had so adamantly demanded censorship of the plastic and dramatic artists: the methods of *techne* are too powerful to be left in the hands of artists and craftsmen. Unhindered by the repressive legislation of the perfect guardians, the practitioners of *techne* in its concrete sense would have proved a threat to the "thinkers" of the Republic.

As for Aristotle, it was Dewey's view that the *Politics* fosters a view of the city-state so constructed that its justification rests on ends "given" by nature. The activities of the practitioner of *techne* are, as they were in Plato, refined and sublimated. For Aristotle, however, the beneficiary of his transference is not a system of supernature contemplated by the philosopher-king but nature itself, which becomes the grand artisan. Just as Plato had, but less perniciously so, Aristotle plundered the creative and social significance of the artisan's work and relocated its content elsewhere.[3]

Dewey read the Greek attitudes toward science as part and parcel of their unfortunate attitude toward *techne*. He argued that the Greeks' abhorrence of the mutability inherent in the tasks and materials of technology had led to a science of "demonstration," a science of contemplation, an attempt to possess something already finished, "out there" and complete. In fact, they had invented not so much science as the idea of science. He issued the warning that when inquiry is focused in the sphere of objects esteemed for their own intrinsic qualities—whether that sphere be supernatural or extranatural, as it was for Plato, or natural and immanent but complete, as it was for Aristotle—then such inquiry will fail to increase our knowledge of things as they are, whether that inquiry concerns itself with materials and artifacts, conceptual models of nature, or the ways in which social organization takes place.

As for modern science, the science of Copernicus, Galileo, Kepler, and Newton, it was Dewey's view that its advances were attributable more to what its practitioners were *doing* than to what they *thought* they were doing. While the novelty of their theories certainly advanced the practice of their science, their metatheory—their metaphysics and epistemology—often failed to grasp the novelty in those theories. Dewey had high praise for the new mathematical techniques of substitution, and suggested that they constituted a "system of exchange and mutual conversion carried to its limit." The objects of science thus became "amenable to transformation in virtue of reciprocal substitutions" (LW 1.115). But the metaphysics and epistemology of the new science were still wedded to the old ideas of a finished universe.

Dewey's claims in this regard are by no means uncontroversial. Desmond Lee, for example, in the introduction to his translation of the *Timaeus*, rejects the view that the contempt held by the Greeks for the work of the artisan discouraged experimentation and hindered the development of technology. He argues that the aristocracy of seventeenth-century England, a time and place of enormous technological development, had at least as much disdain for the artisan as had the Greeks. He further suggests that inhibitions of technological development in the classical world were not always aristocratic. The Roman contractor, whom he identified as a "fairly rough type, often a freedman,"[4] would certainly have been glad to have profited from technological development if it had been possible for him to do so. Instead, Lee argues, the weakness of ancient metallurgy and a lack of precise instrumentation were among the inhibiting factors. But why should these technological materials and instruments not have developed? Lee suggests that there was a conceptual reason: the Greeks had tied science to philosophy, and "philosophy is concerned to understand rather than to change."[5] For Lee, the contribution of Galileo to the advancement of experimental science was that he took the technical tools and artifacts available to him, tools and artifacts that had gradually become much more sophisticated than those developed by the Greeks, and used them to "untie" science from philosophy.

Dewey repeatedly rejected any view of philosophy that had as its goal understanding without change, for he thought that understanding of any legitimate sort entails change. He also argued that hope of financial gain, even by the most "rough and ready" of contractors, is in itself insufficient to promote technological development. It may in fact thwart or divert such development. On one point at least, his position is consonant with that of Lee. They agree that experimental science requires active transaction with environing conditions.

Dewey thought that his predecessors and contemporaries who failed to see that this is also true of philosophy had not fully appreciated the scientific revolution of the seventeenth century. Put in the socio-political terms by means of which he had analyzed the fate of *techne* among the Greeks of the fourth century BCE, it was Dewey's contention that the new science of the seventeenth century exhibited a surge of democratic methods and an assertion of adaptive practice. But there was a broad gulf between what the new science said it was doing and what it was actually about.

The official view of what modern science was about was still conservative and authoritarian. Its apologists continued to traffic in antecedent truths, demonstrations, and certitudes. They held fast to what we today call foundationalism and the correspondence theory of truth. Moreover, its metatheory continued in this vein long after the new science had enjoyed the prodigious successes that resulted from its practical commitment to the treatment of natural ends as instruments for further inquiry and transaction with nature, rather than as fixed objects of contemplation. Thus did the practice and first-order theories of seventeenth-century science relocate technology de facto in terms of its new spirit of practical experimentalism, even if its metatheory did not do so. Dewey thought that the genius of the new science was its discovery that "knowledge is an affair of *making* sure, not of grasping antecedently given sureties" (LW 1.123, Dewey's emphasis).

Nevertheless, many of the metatheorists of seventeenth-century science, among whom were some of the most respected metaphysicians of the time, did not understand that the taproot of the new science was in practice. It was the growing body of tools and artifacts that made systematic science possible.

Contemporary historians of science and technology continue to commit this error. The following description by Daniel Boorstin of the work of Galileo the telescope-maker is illustrative of this mistake: "With no special insight into the science of optics," Boorstin writes,

"Galileo, a deft instrument-maker, had made his device by trial and error. But if Galileo had been merely a practical man, the telescope would not have been such a troublemaker."[6]

Dewey would have found in this characterization a vestige of the very mistake made by most of the early philosophers of modern science. His view was that Galileo was not so much proceeding by means of trial and error as he was "thinking" with his materials, inquiring into their possibilities in a way that had much more in common with the activities of the artists and craftsmen of Plato's Greece than the philosophers of the modern period realized. Dewey's view of what Galileo was doing is closer to the description of his activities provided us by Paolo Rossi: "Kepler was to lay the foundation of the new optics in the *Paralipomena* of 1604, but it was to be a scientist-technician like Galileo who was to muster up the courage 'to look' by using the telescope. He skillfully transformed a use-object which had progressed only 'through practice,' partly accepted in military circles but ignored by the official scientific establishment, into a powerful instrument of scientific exploration."[7]

Dewey argued that inquiry into materials such as was practiced by Galileo precedes and conditions inquiry of a more conceptual variety. It also informs its methodology and terminates its activity in further concrete application. This was perhaps Dewey's most important contribution to the debates concerning the relations between science and technology. Even though the craftsman who thinks in and with materials may not translate that thought into the conceptual sphere, and conversely even though those who think by means of conceptual tools are frequently unable to bring their work to fruition in practical terms, there is nevertheless no reason to posit a methodological gap between the two enterprises.

It is only the infelicitous social prejudice regarding the media in which inquiry is undertaken, the misunderstanding of the talents and dispositions of those who direct the inquiry, and the unfortunate social and cultural boundaries assumed to exist between those modes of inquiry that perpetuate the appearance of a gap that is not in fact justified from the standpoint of methodology. In short, intelligence with respect to materials is fully the equal of intelligence with respect to those enterprises we normally consider "conceptual" (for example, science and social thought). Not only are their methods basically the same, but it is only by the cooperation of each with the other that human knowledge is advanced.

Dewey made this point forcefully in *Art as Experience*. "Any idea," he wrote, "that ignores the necessary role of intelligence in production of works of art is based upon identification of thinking with use of one special kind of material, verbal signs and words. To think effectively in terms of relations of qualities is as severe a demand upon thought as to think in terms of symbols, verbal and mathematical. Indeed, since words are easily manipulated in mechanical ways, the production of a work of genuine art probably demands more intelligence than does most of the so-called thinking that goes on among those who pride themselves on being 'intellectuals'" (LW 10.52). He was careful to include the "practical" or "technological" arts in this characterization. "Art," he suggested, "denotes a process of doing or making. This is as true of fine as of technological art" (LW 10.53).

It was Dewey's claim, then, that philosophy during its modern period, from the seventeenth to the nineteenth centuries, failed to locate technology properly because its allegiance was still tied to the metaphysics of contemplation, of antecedent truths, demonstration, and certitude. But his analysis did not simply take the part of the Empiricists against the Rationalists. Some modern philosophers, he pointedly reminded us, surrendered the antecedent truths of reason only to accept antecedent truths of sensation. Modern Empiricism, according to his view, committed itself to an equally egregious form of foundationalism.

For the bulk of philosophy in its modern period, nature was thought to be a vast machine. Living in the shadow of Darwin as he did, Dewey rejected the metaphor of the machine and replaced it with the organism. But even to those who have transcended the metaphor of world-as-machine there is still the fact of machines and the problem of how to relate to them. A machine can be contemplated as something finished and its workings discovered and admired. Further, it can be examined as something complete but in need of occasional repair. Or it can be treated as something ongoing, unstable, and provisional—as a tool to be used for enlarging transactions of self and society with environing conditions. It was Dewey's contention that the discussions of the nature of the world-as-machine in the seventeenth and eighteenth centuries were primarily focused on the first two of these attitudes. Of course each of these three possibilities involves some level of interaction with nature. But it is only with the third that there comes to be genuine transaction with nature, awareness of such transaction, and inclusion of that awareness in the meta-theories of science.

In the political sphere, of course, it was a great advance over the old supernaturalist and extranaturalist views to think of the world as repairable, even if it was not yet fully open to transaction. In *Liberalism and Social Action*, Dewey praised the advances made by Bentham on just these grounds. But he also warned of treating the world-machine as something to be *merely* examined and repaired. He cautioned against Bentham's acceptance of humankind as "a reckoning machine" (LW 11.24). The old machine metaphors of Bentham and others neglected the fact that relations between human beings and their political environments are always "relations of ongoing affairs characterized by beginnings and endings which mark them [the ongoing affairs] off into unstable individuals" (LW 1.127). These individual relations are in need of continual and intelligent reevaluation and reconfiguration by means of practical inquiry.

Failure to make this conceptual shift from machine-as-finished-though-imperfect-and-repairable to machine-as-incomplete-and-unstable-instrument has precipitated in our time a situation well described by Stuart Hampshire in a polemic against Utilitarianism, a cluster of positions against which Dewey also argued. In its emphasis on repair as opposed to transaction, Hampshire suggested, much recent thought has led to "new abstract cruelty in politics, a dull, destructive political righteousness: mechanical, quantitative thinking, leaden academic minds setting out their moral calculation in leaden abstract prose, and more civilized and more superstitious people destroyed because of enlightened calculations that have proved wrong."[8]

It might be objected that it was during this modern period of science that the United States of America, the most influential democracy of the contemporary world, was founded. It might further be argued that among the framers of that democracy were deists, practitioners of a form of religious faith that explicitly regards God as artisan and a virtually finished universe as His handiwork. But among these social experimenters were also gadget-makers, mechanics, and tinkerers. Thomas Jefferson, whom Dewey greatly admired, consistently spoke of political and social experimentation in a manner that echoed his transaction with clocks, agricultural methods, and gadgets of many sorts. Jefferson repeatedly referred to the government that he helped establish as an *experiment*, moreover, one whose institutions and laws would be in need of recurring modification by each succeeding generation. For government, as for nature, contemplation had been replaced by examination, and that in turn by experimentation, whose goal was constant attention to possibilities of adjustment and amelioration.

Jefferson's transactionist orientation to technology, to social thought, and to the broader world of his experience stands in stark contrast to the examinationist program of Descartes a little over a century earlier. L. J. Beck gives the following account of Descartes' attitude toward Galileo's telescope as exhibited in his *Dioptrique* of 1637 and his correspondence with Jean Ferrier:

> Already at La Flèche, Descartes had probably heard of the discoveries made by Galileo through the use of the telescope. Descartes wishes to draw up a plan for the construction of an even better one, and above all of a more powerful lens. This cannot be done until, he tells us, it is known, what happens when light traverses several lenses, until the law of refraction has been established and the problem of the *linea anaclastica* solved. Then only can the plan of the various curves of the lenses be worked out. Descartes works these out but, as one can see, the unfortunate Ferrier is unable to carry out in practice the difficult requirements set by Descartes. Galileo cannot solve the problem of the *linea anaclastica*;

he does not know the law of refraction, but he manages to construct an instrument which gives a substantial magnification. Kepler, slightly more theoretical, knew only of approximations to the law of refraction but his description of the telescope provided a working model for future astronomers. Descartes required the exact measurements for his lenses, and failing this, he lost interest in the whole topic.[9]

It was precisely this debate between the transactionist craftsmen-practitioners of modern science and technology and those seeking to examine its hypothetical and metaphysical foundations that was a matter of intense interest to Dewey. It provided evidence for his thesis that metaphysicians of the period had mislocated the place of technological practice. Writing of the controversy between the Cartesian school and that of Galileo and Newton, he lauded the triumph of the latter because of its emphasis on "experience." And his characterization of experience made extensive use of examples of inquiry in the technological sphere (LW 1.14–15). In a rather sad aside he suggested, "We may, if sufficiently hopeful, anticipate a similar outcome in philosophy. But the date does not appear to be close at hand; we are nearer in philosophic theory to the time of Roger Bacon than to that of Newton" (LW 1.15).

Dewey wanted to locate technology in a realm that is neither supernatural nor extranatural, an organic realm in which the only telic elements are those of the natural ends of objects, individuals, and events, all of which in turn may be used as means to further ends. It was his view that the legitimate place of technology is alongside science and social thought as one of several branches of inquiry. On his reading, technology is not inferior to its brother and sister branches, and may in some respects even be more important than they in that its unique qualities serve to inform, enhance, and promote those siblings in ways that they are incapable of reciprocating.

What are these unique qualities? I have already alluded to his commitments to what Don Ihde would later call "the historical-ontological priority of technology over science."[10] In 1925 Dewey argued the historical component of this claim when he suggested that in spite of the obvious fact that "the sciences were born of the arts—the physical sciences of the crafts and technologies of healing, navigation, war and the working of wood, metals, leather, flax and wool; the mental sciences of the arts of political management, . . . it is still commonly [and erroneously] argued that technology is merely 'applied science'" (LW 1.105).

He further argued that modern science "represents a generalized recognition and adoption of the point of view of the useful arts, for it proceeds by employment of a similar operative technique of manipulation and reduction. Physical science would be impossible without the appliances and procedures of separation and combinations of the industrial arts" (LW 1.108).

In addressing the "ontological" (read "functional") component of his claim, Dewey reminded us that what is peculiar to human interaction with the world is not its enjoyment, but the necessity of grappling with it at the technological level and the knowledge, or science, which follows upon that interaction. In Dewey's words, "It was not enjoyment of the apple but the enforced penalty of labor that made man as the gods, *knowing* good and evil instead of just having and enjoying them" (LW 1.100).

To contrast knowing and having, as Dewey did in this remark, is to allude to his treatment of knowledge as hypothesis, pointing to an unfinished future in which inquiring human beings accommodate themselves to environing conditions, environing conditions are adapted to human needs, and the two processes are jointly known as "adjustment."

This is a view that would re-emerge in Heidegger's essay, "The Question Concerning Technology." Technology is there differentiated into a tool of science, the activities of the craftsman (*techne*), and, its ultimate sense, *aletheia* or revealing. It is this last sense of technology that is most basic to Heidegger's account: "Instrumentality is considered to be the fundamental characteristic of technology. If we inquire, step by step, into what technology, represented as means, actually is, then we shall arrive at revealing. The possibility of all productive manufacturing lies in revealing."[11] Again, "Technology is a mode of revealing. Technology comes to presence . . . in the realm where revealing and unconcealment take place, where *aletheia*, truth, happens."[12]

I have recalled Heidegger's account of the ontological priority of technology over science because of the light it sheds on Dewey's own account. For Dewey, it is technological instrumentality (what Heidegger calls "revealing") that characterizes the most primitive relation between the activities of men and women and the world of their experience. Such instrumentality ties together the myths that tell of the manner in which labor entered the world and the myths that constitute our most up-to-date theories of political economy.

But if technology is prior to science both historically and ontologically, it also is responsible for the prestige enjoyed by science. Dewey argued that the successes of science have been due not so much to what he called "scientific temper" as to "scientific technique." In his essay "Human Nature and Scholarship," Dewey argued that "scientific technique, as distinguished from the scientific temper, is concerned with the methods by which matter is manipulated. It is the source of special technologies, as in the application of electricity to daily life; it is concerned with immediate fruits of a practical kind in a sense in which *practical* has a special and technical meaning—power stations, broadcasting, lighting, the telephone, the ignition system of automobiles" (LW 11.457). Further, "The inherent idealism of the scientific temper is submerged, for the mass of human beings, in the use and enjoyment of the material power and material comforts that have resulted from its technical applications" (LW 11.458).

What was Dewey's view of the location of technology with respect to epistemology? "Knowledge ceases to be a mental mirror of the universe and becomes a practical tool in the manipulation of matter" (LW 11.457).[13] Dewey reiterated his radical position in *Experience and Nature*: "In the practice of science, knowledge is an affair of *making* sure, not of grasping antecedently given sureties" (LW 1.123).

Dewey not only viewed technology as the primary means of inquiry open to those individuals cut off from what normally goes on in laboratories, observatories, and places of special research; he suggested that technology was a special avenue of inquiry open to those individuals living in closed societies where social inquiry is suppressed. But he was neither idealist nor utopian. He knew that even in open societies there would be those who prefer appeals to tenacity, authority, or the a priori to free and open inquiry as methods of fixing their beliefs. It was with this in mind that he suggested that technology may also operate as a buffer between the forces of antiscience and science.

I do not think that he would have been surprised that those who now attempt to promote the teaching of a literal reading of the Genesis myth of creation do so while claiming to march under the banner of science. The advances of science propagated in the technological sphere have made moot many of the old antiscientific arguments, or at least required that they be masked in scientific jargon. Dewey repeatedly demonstrated his conviction that the work of those who take the pluralistic values of free and open inquiry seriously will never be finished. This is a central aspect of his philosophy of education.

But if technology for Dewey forms a buffer between the forces of antiscience and science, it also functions as a means by which science may be appropriated by the scientifically uninformed. There are two ways in which this takes place: not only have the fruits of technology become ubiquitous, but the methods of science, historically and ontologically dependent on technology, may be reintroduced into the field of technological practice and used with new authority. But with these two outcomes of technology—one immediate, the other mediate—come two dangers. The first is the one indicated by José Ortega y Gasset, that technological men and women may become like the aboriginal forest or jungle dweller, just picking the technological fruits as if they had been supplied by a natural system beyond their understanding or control. The second is that technology will once again become mislocated with respect to science, that is, that it will once again suffer the deprecation it suffered during the period of classical, modern, and much of contemporary philosophy. These are dangers to social organization in general, and to democracy in particular, because they signal the truncation of the full spectrum of inquiry necessary to the transaction of human beings with their environment and the consequent knowing of things as they are and can be.

In his 1944 essay, "Democratic Faith in Education," Dewey made even more explicit his concern regarding the dangers to technology and to social inquiry. He could have been writing of our current situation when he characterized the first of these dangers as "laissez-faire naturalism." To those who would appeal to the forces of the "invisible hand" or "the [undefined] laws of the marketplace," Dewey had this to say: "Technically speaking the policy known as *Laissez-faire* is one of limited application. But its limited and technical significance is one instance of a manifestation of widespread trust in the ability of impersonal forces, popularly called Nature, to do a work that has to be done by human insight, foresight, and purposeful planning" (LW 15.253). He applied this assessment to planning in national and international affairs, suggesting that the refusal to apply the methods of the technological sciences in those areas had led to a state of imbalance and "profoundly disturbed equilibrium" (LW 15.254).

A second danger to technological and social inquiry lies in the attitudes and activities of the "humanist" who attacks technology as "inherently materialistic and as usurping the place properly held by abstract moral precepts" (LW 15.255). He suggested that such moral precepts had remained abstract precisely because those defining them had divorced ends from the means by which they are to be realized.

Dewey specifically criticized the Hutchins program, which set out to separate technical training from liberal education—a situation which has both become a fact of our universities and is seen by many as tending to create a permanent social wound as it becomes more widely practiced in our secondary schools. When the putrefaction of the wound is eventually discovered, the blame will likely be located at the door of "technology," and not in its proper place, namely, the failure to apply the inquiry which is characteristic of experimental science and technology at its best to all areas of human endeavor.

In that same essay Dewey mentioned a third threat to technological and social inquiry. It is consequent on the activities of contemporary Luddites, especially of the theocratic variety. They resist the application of scientific and technical methods to the field of human concerns and human affairs because they tend to think of themselves as outside of and above nature and because they prefer a return to the medieval prescientific doctrine of a supernatural foundation and outlook in all social and moral matters. He further suggested that this group erroneously believes that the methods of science and technology have been applied to every area of human concern—and found wanting.

A special variety of this third faction has become even more militant than it was at the time Dewey issued his warning. Both antiscientific and antidemocratic, Christian fundamentalists of the extreme Right have nevertheless adopted the tools of electronic technology to advance their aims. Dewey was aware that technological advances could be appropriated by authoritarian forces, and discussed this phenomenon in detail in his 1936 essay, "Religion, Science and Philosophy."

The two forces that particularly concerned him in that dangerous year, a year which saw the growing power of Fascism throughout the world, were what he called "political nationalism" and "finance-capital," both important allies of the religious Right in our own time. He called these movements "new religions." They, like religious fundamentalism, depend on the a priori and the putatively revealed as substitutes for intelligent inquiry. They, like religious fundamentalism, have their "established dogmatic creeds, their fixed rites and ceremonies, their central institutional authority, their distinction between the faithful and the unbelievers, with persecution of heretics who do not accept the true faith" (LW 11.460).

They share a further important characteristic of religions: they dote on the *terminus a quo* rather than on the *terminus ad quem*, a doctrine of "original intent" rather than a careful attention to consequences. Dewey's *Experience and Nature* warns of the capture of applied science by these elements: they work to channel it toward "private and economic class purposes and privileges. When inquiry is narrowed by such motivation or interest, the consequence is in so far disastrous both to science and to human life" (LW 1.130–31). Dewey reminded us that these potential disasters are not due to the practical nature of technology, but to the defects and perversions of morality as it is embodied in institutions and the effects of such institutions upon personal disposition.

This chapter would remain incomplete were I not to quote an extended passage from an address prepared by Dewey and delivered at a celebration of his eightieth birthday. There is perhaps no more eloquent characterization of the interaction between inquiry at its various technological, scientific, and political levels in all of Dewey's writings. Belief in democracy is there characterized as a

> belief in the ability of human experience to generate the aims and methods by which further experience will grow in ordered richness. Every other form of moral and social faith rests upon the idea that experience must be subjected at some point or other to some form of external control; to some "authority" alleged to exist outside the process of experience. Democracy is the faith that the process of experience is more important than any special result attained, so that special results achieved are of ultimate value only as they are used to enrich and order the ongoing process. Since the process of experience is capable of being educative, faith in democracy is all one with faith in experience and education. All ends and values that are cut off from the ongoing process become arrests, fixations. They strive to fixate what has been gained instead of using it to open the road and point the way to new and better experiences.
>
> If one asks what is meant by experience in this connection my reply is that it is that free interaction of individual human beings with surrounding conditions, especially the human surroundings, which develops and satisfies need and desire by increasing knowledge of things as they are. Knowledge of conditions as they are is the only solid ground for communication and sharing; all other communication means the subjection of some persons to the personal opinion of other persons. Need and desire—out of which grow purpose and direction of energy—go beyond what exists, and hence beyond knowledge, beyond science. They continually open the way into the unexplored and unattained future. (LW 14.229)

PART THREE

THE ENVIRONMENT

EIGHT

NATURE AS CULTURE: JOHN DEWEY AND ALDO LEOPOLD

Genuine experimental action effects an adjustment *of* conditions, not *to* them: a remaking of existing conditions, not a mere remaking of self and mind to fit into them. Intelligent adaptation is always a *re*adjustment, a reconstruction of what exists.

—John Dewey

Nature is made better by no mean but nature makes that mean.

—William Shakespeare

The Guiding Stars of Dewey's Pragmatic Naturalism

It is as unfortunate as it is unfair that John Dewey has been read as an unabashed apologist for industrial expediency and business boosterism.[1] One consequence of this has been the assumption that his work has little relevance to current debates regarding the status of nonhuman nature.[2]

It is true that Dewey was at one time the leader of a school of Pragmatism known as "Instrumentalism," but his Pragmatism was never the vulgar sort that valorizes bald expediency. Nor was his Instrumentalism the "straight-line" variety that works toward fixed goals, heedless of the collateral problems and opportunities that arise during the thick of deliberation.

It is also true that Dewey consistently argued that experimental science is necessary to ameliorate the deplorable conditions under which much of humanity subsisted during his lifetime (many of which conditions have since deteriorated). But his notion of experimental science was more comprehensive and revolutionary than his contemporaries ever grasped. He conceived its place in human experience as a partner with, not as overseer of, other forms of inquiry, including the arts, law, and politics. He consistently held that to view science as a tool for the domination of nature is to honor a conception of science, as well as a conception of nature, that has become outdated.

What, specifically, does Dewey have to contribute to the current debates regarding the relations of human beings to nonhuman nature? To a casual observer, Dewey may lack the authenticity that other writers on nature have. Unlike Henry David Thoreau, he did not go to the woods to articulate an alternative to the stuffy life and genteel transcendentalism of Concord; unlike John Muir he did not develop an evolutionary pantheism in the course of a thousand-mile walk from Indiana to the Gulf of Mexico; and unlike Aldo Leopold he constructed neither land ethic nor land aesthetic based on experiences in the arid American Southwest and the lush farmland of Wisconsin. In short, Dewey was not a field naturalist. Although his boyhood was spent in the small towns and countryside of Vermont, his adulthood was in the city. Apart from his recreational retreats to mountains, seashores, and his farm on Long Island, from 1894 until his death in 1952 he lived first in Chicago, then in New York City.

But if Dewey was no field naturalist, he was a naturalist nevertheless. As a committed evolutionary naturalist, Dewey argued for the view that human beings are in and a part of nature, and not over against it. It was his contention that human life constitutes the cutting edge of evolutionary development (but not its telos), because, as he put it, humans make self-reflection a part of evolutionary history when they come to consciousness by means of social intercourse.

For Dewey, the principal difference between human beings and nature is not human communities' unique powers of communication, but human beings' unique ability to control their own habit-formation and consequently alter their own evolution and the evolution of their environing conditions. In other words, it is only with the advent of human beings that systematic choice, and consequently systematic morality, become a part of life on earth (EW 5.53), and it is only as human beings come to consciousness that nature comes to have "a mind of its own" (MW 4.29).

One of the clearest statements of Dewey's naturalism is found in his reply to George Santayana, who had charged him with advancing a "half-hearted" and "short-winded" naturalism. Santayana had argued that Dewey was only interested in "foreground," and that consequently the "rest of nature [in his philosophy] is reputed to be intrinsically remote or dubious or merely ideal."[3] To put a fine point on it, Santayana was accusing Dewey of ignoring, or worse, idealizing nonhuman nature.

Dewey had thought his own naturalism such an obvious and fundamental part of his philosophy that he was astounded by Santayana's criticism. His reply was that "if the things of experience are produced, as they are according to my theory, by interaction of organism and environing conditions, then as Nature's own foreground they are not a barrier mysteriously set up between us and nature. Moreover, the organism—the self, the 'subject' of action,—is a factor *within* experience and not something outside of it to which experiences are attached as the self's private property" (LW 14.17).[4]

As further evidence of his naturalism, Dewey cited his appropriation of the radical empiricism of William James: "My theory of the relation of cognitive experiences to other modes of experience is based upon the fact that *connections* exist in the most immediate noncognitive experience, and when the experienced situation becomes problematic, the connections are developed into distinctive objects of knowledge, whether of common sense or of science" (LW 14.18).[5]

Finally, he responded that "the proof of the fact that *knowledge* of nature, but not nature itself, 'emanates' from immediate experience is simply that this is what has actually happened in the history or development of experience, animal or human on this earth—the only alternative to this conclusion being that in addition to experience as a source and test of beliefs, we possess some miraculous power of intuitive insight into remote stellar galaxies and remote geological eons" (LW 14.19).[6]

In his response to Santayana, then, Dewey reveals the reference points by which the course of his naturalism has been charted. The first is his Instrumentalism, which is his way of avoiding the traditional problems of both realistic and idealistic views of nonhuman nature. On the side of ontological realism, for example, seventeenth-century science and philosophy tended to view nonhuman nature as a clock-like machine, complete in itself. On the side of ontological idealism, some contemporary environmental philosophers have argued for a panentheistic version of the Gaia hypothesis, which in its extreme form holds that the Earth is not only a self-regulating superorganism, but is also capable of deliberation in terms of its own ideals.[7] Looked at from a different angle, epistemological realists, including most neopositivists, have argued that knowledge of nature is secured as its features are "mirrored" in separate human minds; and epistemological idealists, such as Berkeley, have contended that nature is a correlation among ideas.

For Dewey's Instrumentalism, however, nature, as a *complex* of objects of knowledge, is neither complete in itself apart from human interaction, nor the locus of extrahuman deliberation. It is neither directly given nor a mental correlation. Nature is instead a multifaceted construct that has been slowly and laboriously built up over thousands of years of human history by means of various tools of inquiry, including the arts, religion, magic, hunting, manufacture, and experimental science, to recall just a few. Nature is a construct, or cultural artifact, but it has not been constructed out of nothing. The raw materials of previous experiences and experiments, unanticipated events, chance insights, moments of aesthetic ecstasy, habits, traditions, and institutions have all been continuously reshaped and refined by tools that have included religious rituals, philosophical treatises, novels, poems, scientific hypotheses, television documentaries, and many more.

The Instrumentalism that supports Dewey's concept of nature-as-culture bears scant resemblance to the "straight-line" variety of instrumentalism advanced by seventeenth-century philosophers and scientists. His post-Enlightenment Instrumentalism calls for careful attention to ends-means relationships at every step of deliberation. This is no less true when the domain of inquiry is nonhuman nature than when a musician chooses a subject for her song. Tools must be continually revised if they are to be appropriate for new tasks. Tasks must likewise be continually reevaluated in light of the tools available for their execution.

Nature, conceived as cultural artifact, is never finished. Because the rush of time and the jolt of novelty are observable features of experience, nature too, as a complex of objects of knowledge, becomes subject to ongoing reevaluation and reconstruction in order to effect adjustment to changed and changing conditions. We may be able to get it better and better, truer and truer, but we never get it completely right. This is Dewey's fallibilism.

One of the most important features of Dewey's naturalism, so important that it almost becomes synonymous with his larger program, is his distaste of claims to transcendent knowledge. His antitranscendentalism would have led Dewey to reject attempts by some environmental ethicists to "sacralize" nature as a thing-in-itself with values, interests, or rights that are purely intrinsic to it, and independent of human interests. What would he have made of the view of Carolyn Merchant, for example, that "all living things, as integral parts of a viable ecosystem, . . . have rights"?[8] Should the remaining samples of smallpox virus be set free from captivity, for example, because of its inherent rights as an integral part of a viable ecosystem? And what would he have thought of the biocentrism of Paul Taylor, with its claim that nature has "intrinsic" value, or value apart from its being valued "either intrinsically or instrumentally, by some human valuer"[9] Dewey would, I think, have characterized Merchant's "rights" talk and Taylor's suggestion—that an ecological ethic can only be grounded in values never experienced, and perhaps not capable of being experienced, by human beings[10]—as having abandoned naturalism altogether for an excursion into an ideal realm.

Dewey thought it the function of intelligence to expand and enrich experience, with a view to adjusting experienced situations to new demands. Such adjustment is neither the alteration of environment for the sake of the experiencing subject, nor the accommodation by the experiencing subject to its environment. Because environments include experiencing subjects as parts, it is both accommodation and alteration.

If Dewey's naturalism eschews the transcendent, it is holistic nonetheless. Since human beings are a part of nature, their enriched experience of nature enriches nature's experience of itself. This is what Dewey means when he says that the production of the objects of knowledge involves the interaction of one part of the environment with other parts of the environment. At the same time, however, as he argued in his now famous essay "The Reflex Arc Concept in Psychology," (EW 5.96–109) there is no knowledge without prior interest because it is interest that serves to initiate and focus inquiry. Our knowledge does not come to us fully formed from any region in which we have no interests. Some may wish to call this view anthropocentric, but it is neither more nor less than a recognition of the fact that human beings transact business within environing conditions beginning where they are, and not where they are not. If "biocentrism" means taking a perspective that is other than human, then Dewey was no biocentrist. If it means, on the other hand, that it is characteristic of human intelligence that it continually broadens its purview, and that its best and most productive perspective is holistic, then Dewey's work from the 1890s onward was biocentric.

Another component of Dewey's naturalism was his antifoundationalism. This is the view, now recognized as one of the central theses of postmodern thought, that the search for epistemic foundations is both futile and unnecessary. One consequence of this is that the individual thinking self is not privileged, as it was for the architects of modern philosophy, Descartes, Locke, and Kant. The self is itself a construct, and as such it is experienced neither foundationally, immediately, nor privately, but just as are other parts of the built-up environment of human knowledge. It further follows that there is no objective nature to provide a foundation for knowledge. Nature is not a "thing" but instead a complex and fecund matrix of objects and events, experienced in part as an expanding source of novel facilities and constraints, but nevertheless constructed within the history of human inquiry.

Dewey's radical empiricism[11] includes the claim that noncognitive experience is capable of grasping relations. This is very important for an understanding of nature-as-culture because it means that we can grasp what hangs together in all of nature—human and nonhuman alike and together—as features of our most immediate and basic aesthetic experiences. In a moment I will suggest that this grasping-of-things-together was also an important stage in the development of the thought of Aldo Leopold.

Dewey recognized that it is notoriously difficult to retain moments of aesthetic insight. Even the most intense delights have a way of turning to dust in our hands. It is at this point that the cognitive portion of experience enters the picture. Cognition develops experienced relations by relating them to one another and making something new and more secure out of them.

But radical empiricism doesn't just say that we experience relations; it also says that at the edges of the focal points of noncognitive experience there are unfocused areas, or fringes. This amounts to a powerful antidote to the tendency to go transcendent, to posit a nonhuman world filled with independent values of its own.

It turns out that radical empiricism provides the benefits of transcendent views without their disadvantages. It allows us to acknowledge that there is a "beyond" to experience, just as transcendent views do. But it doesn't commit the fallacy of transcendent views, which is their attempt to say something *definitive* about what is experienced only as horizon. Regardless of where the focus of experience moves, according to radical empiricism, it is always fringed by vague areas of which we are only dimly aware but which may provide the opportunity for refocusing. Such refocusing is itself often the occasion for the production of new objects of knowledge.

What all this means is that we can get more and more intimately involved in terms of our experience of nonhuman nature without having to posit a realm in which animals and plants which are not conscious of themselves or in control of their own behavior have independently inherent "rights," or into which we may only enter provided that we have abandoned the perspective of human beings. The function of cognition is to extend human interest, and therefore human knowing, into areas of experience that had theretofore been no more than fringes or horizons of working knowledge. Properly nurtured, aesthetic delight gives rise to interests, which in turn motivate the kind of inquiry that eventuates in a robust interaction with ever wider dimensions of the human environment.

Radical empiricism does the work of transcendent views of nature, and it does it better. It describes and prescribes ways in which nonhuman nature can enter into the domain of human concerns, and thus into the widening circle of the moral, without appealing to a priori or ad hoc devices. Radical empiricism embraces a genuinely evolving naturalism that is rooted in the histories of natural events and that seeks to play a part in their further evolution; it is not, as are some versions of the Gaia hypothesis or most theories of "inherent rights of nature," a short-cut or ersatz naturalism based on the discontinuities of mysticism or logical leaps.

Taken together, radical empiricism and Instrumentalism argue that what is cognitive arises out of what is noncognitive by the intervention of intelligence. But the reverse is not true. Unlike Bertrand Russell, for example, Dewey is no reductionist: he does not claim that the cognitive can be reduced to something primitive and noncognitive.

Phylogenetically, historically, then, the cognitive emerges from the noncognitive. This is Dewey's genetic argument. Whenever we think seriously about anything, ontogeny recapitulates phylogeny. Cognition is advanced and enhanced whenever it takes its own history into account. The roots of the normative aspects of any discipline grow in the fertile soil of the history of that discipline. By implication, if we are to advance normative claims with respect to nonhuman nature, then the history of inquiry in that area, including the history of religious, aesthetic, scientific, and technological inquiries, must be taken into account.

Dewey's constructivism is a thread that runs through each of the other components of his naturalism, and thus deserves emphasis. Nature may be conceptualized in retrospect as nature-as-nature, or what is in fact experienced as immediately and unreflectively valued. In its richer sense, however, nature is also nature-as-culture, an artifact or complex of ideas that has proven valuable and continues to provide grounds for successful action. Nature-as-nature may be, and often is, the source of romantic or mystical responses that are deeply satisfying in their consummatory moments. But nature-as-nature is nature experienced haphazardly; experienced values have not been secured because their meanings have not been worked out and linked to one another. Nature-as-culture, on the other hand, is the product of conscious attempts to extend and link the meanings of nature in ways that secure experienced values by testing them one against the other in order to determine what can continue to prove valuable.

It is Dewey's constructivism that links these two conceptions of nature. In other words, the functional separation of nature-as-nature, or nature-as-valued, from nature-as-culture, or nature-as-valuable, does not render Dewey vulnerable to the charge of having regressed to a dualism of fact and value, or even a dualism of nature and culture, since what is valuable is a development that grows in ordered richness out of what is valued, and culture is thus continuous with and a part of nature. Nature-as-nature and nature-as-culture are not ontologically separate, but only functionally so. They are phases, earlier and later, of the expansion and extension of the meanings of situated human experience.

Dewey's position avoids the traditional split between facts and values by means of his contention that: a) values and relations are experienced (his radical empiricism); b) facts are not just given but always selected from a busy and complex environment as facts-of-a-case, that is, always and only in the context of a particular inquiry (his Instrumentalism and his anti-transcendentalism); and c) what is valuable is so only as a result of tests that have proven it to be a reliable basis for further action (his constructivism and his fallibilism).

Dewey's Pragmatic Naturalism and Leopold's Land Ethic

If these are the guiding stars of Dewey's naturalism, what course do they indicate for an environmental philosophy? One way of answering this question is to set Dewey's naturalism alongside that of Aldo Leopold, allowing each to take the measure of the other.

Chapter seven of Max Oelschlaeger's *The Idea of Wilderness*[12] provides an excellent guide to Leopold's work. Leopold's land ethic, writes Oelschlaeger, "which states that humans ought to act to preserve the integrity, stability, and beauty of natural systems, gives Leopoldian ecology an explicitly normative dimension. . . . In Leopold's normative ecology the human species is viewed as a part of rather than apart from nature. Subsequently, the membership of sentient beings in the community of life entails obligations to preserve the land."[13]

This statement sums up in an admirable way the diverse and sometimes conflicting elements within Leopold's work. As a professional scientist, a forester, he had been trained to accept the demands of a *modernist* or imperial ecology—an ecology based on a search for epistemological foundations—a faith in quantification, a vision of linear and inevitable progress, an acceptance of the physical sciences as paradigmatic of all rationality, and a conception of nature as machine to be dominated and exploited.

On the other side, however, because of his own profound aesthetic sensibility, Leopold also felt the claim of a *postmodernist* or arcadian ecology that had been adumbrated by Thoreau and Muir, an ecology that rejected each of these modernist claims and sought to establish others in their stead. This would be an ecology that emphasizes human situatedness within nature, that holds that science is only one of many productive areas of human experience, that views progress as fragile and attainable only in piecemeal fashion, that treats knowledge as relative because perspectival and fallible, and that denies any absolute or final split between fact and value or between culture and nature.

By now it should be obvious that each of these components of postmodernist ecology was also a component within Dewey's naturalism.

In Oelschlaeger's story, Leopold's thinking moves through several developmental stages. From an initial acceptance of the modernist views, learned at Yale University and in the employ of the USDA Forest Service, he moved first to an intuitive, aesthetic appreciation of the connectedness of natural events (bordering on a mystic organicism), and thence to an attempt to construct a land ethic of amelioration that takes into account "the interconnections between the cultural and natural worlds."[14]

Within this later phase, however, Leopold's vocabulary is complex and sometimes conflicted. He variously employed, according to Oelschlaeger's account: 1) an organic model of nature whose key idea is management, 2) a social model of nature whose central idea is community, and 3) an enriched organicism that held that "*natural species possessed intrinsic rights* to existence and that these sometimes took precedence over human rights."[15]

Leopold's field naturalism and Dewey's Pragmatic naturalism turn out to have a great deal in common. Dewey's radical empiricism, for example, provides a key to understanding the incipient phase of Leopold's shift from modernist to postmodernist ecology. (Conversely, Leopold's shift provides an excellent example of Dewey's radical empiricism.)

Leopold's initial break with Forest Service doctrine was patently noncognitive. He was profoundly influenced by the relations that he discovered within his aesthetic experience. Tempted to remain within the confines of that experience, he flirted with a transcendent, organic vitalism. "Possibly, in our intuitive perceptions," he wrote, "which may be truer than our science and less impeded by words than our philosophies, we realize the indivisibility of the earth—its soil, mountains, rivers, forests, climate, plants, and animals, and respect it collectively not only as a useful servant but as a living being."[16]

But Leopold soon realized that it would be impossible to continue indefinitely this celebration of his noncognitive experience. Mysticism qua mysticism does little work in the public sphere.[17] Beyond the continued celebration of it, the consummatory moment in aesthetic experience can be prolonged only by developing its connections to other experiences. He came to realize that his noncognitive vision must be reconstructed into an instrument that can function in the sphere of public science and public opinion. His subsequent vocabularies of management, community, and the rights of species represent various stages of his attempt to reconstruct his initial experience in ways that would prove sufficiently valuable to have broad appeal and therefore to effect what he took to be ameliorative change.

Leopold never lost sight of the aesthetic dimension of his experience, however. He appealed to both elements within his experience, the noncognitive and the cognitive alike, in his 1932 remark that a successful ecology must take into account a "residual love of nature, inherent even in 'Rotarians,' [that] may be made to recreate at least a fraction of those values which their love of 'progress' is destroying."[18] On the cognitive side, the term "management" appears as a key word in the title and the chapter headings of Game Management, one of his major works during this period.[19]

Leopold's "Rotarian" remark also contains a genetic argument. Evolutionary history equips human beings (even the most ardent land speculator) with a noncognitive sensibility toward nature that may, if properly managed, stimluate an enriched cognitive response to nonhuman nature that can take into account more than the narrowly economic and utilitarian.

His remark is also constructivist and antifoundational. He has recognized that any concept of nature that does real work in the domain of public affairs is a cultural artifact. "Although Leopold never escaped entirely from thinking of ecological facts as 'out there,'" writes Oelschlaeger, "he knew that the objective order of nature was a useful fiction. His research had repeatedly confirmed that Homo sapiens and nature were internally related."[20]

There are numerous parallels to Leopold's conceptual shift in the contemporary literature of environmentalism. Biologist Nathaniel T. Wheelwright, for example, has argued for respect for nature on the grounds of its "resplendence." Contending that it is "poor conservation strategy to bank on the arguments of ecologists or economists alone," Wheelright has pointed out that the deterioration of natural environments and the loss of species diminishes what is "intricate," and "irreplaceable," and that aesthetic experience is thereby diminished.[21] This is an excellent example of an appeal to what most human beings feel about nature, which is something that can be reconstructed in such a way that it performs work in the public sphere.

To what extent is Dewey's Pragmatic naturalism consistent with Leopold's environmentalism? Two out of the three metaphors that Oelschlaeger has identified as central to Leopold's thought are also found in Dewey's work. Dewey's Pragmatic Instrumentalism is an encouragement to "management," in just the Leopoldian sense, that is, as an intelligent reworking of what is unsatisfactory in order to render it more satisfactory. It is true that Dewey used the word "control," in connection with his Instrumentalism, and that this has been the occasion for some of his critics, especially those of neo-Heideggerian temperament, to dismiss his views as unrepentantly modernist. But Leopold also wrote of control. What both men meant by control is intelligent interaction within a situation in order to effect its improvement.

The second of Leopold's central metaphors, community, also occupies an important place in Dewey's work. There are two important senses in which nature can be understood as community. In the first, nonhuman nature would be said to constitute a community in the sense of interacting populations, food chains, and so on. "Communication" within nature's community would, on this model, be a way of talking about equilibrating forces within an ecological system that maintain its stability as a whole and with respect to which human beings are either not involved or involved only marginally. This view of communication has the disadvantage of tending toward an idealization of nature that renders it transcendent of human interests.

In the second sense of community, however, there is no break between human and nonhuman nature, and human beings themselves
are regarded as one of many forces within the larger domain of nature. Communication would then be transaction among all relevant
parts of nature, including the human part, that is, the part in which
self-conscious intelligence emerges.

The term "management" takes on radically different meanings
when applied to these two views of nature's community. The first
view presents two scenarios. In the first scenario, that of the ontological idealist, the idea of management is replaced by the idea of respect,
since nature is something that possesses ideals apart from those of
human beings. In the second, the scenario of the ontological realist,
management is imposed on a nature no less apart than that of the
idealists, but which is, in this case, a machine to be maintained and
repaired. Both of these positions have their roots in modernist
thought. In the second view of nature's community, human manage-
rial skills become an active part of the ongoing evolution of a system
of which human beings are also a part.

Both Leopold and Dewey understood "community" in the second
of these senses, that is, in the postmodernist sense. Civilization is not,
Leopold wrote, "the enslavement of a stable and constant earth. It
is a state of *mutual and interdependent coöperation* between human
animals, other animals, plants, and soils, which may be disrupted at
any moment by the failure of any of them."[22] In short, evolution
evolves. Continuing communication (ongoing adjustment of the various parts of the entire system to one another) is the condition for
the continuing success of the whole.

This is also Dewey's sense of community, and it is his sense of
management. In his 1898 essay "Evolution and Ethics," Dewey argued
against the position taken five years earlier by Thomas Huxley in his
Romanes Lecture. Huxley had taken the view that there has been a
radical break in evolutionary history. The rule of the earlier "cosmic"
processes had been struggle and strife. This was nature "red in tooth
and claw." The rule of the emergent but now radically distinct "ethical" process would be sympathy and cooperation. And whereas the

goal of the cosmic process was survival of the fittest, the goal of the ethical process would be that of fitting as many as possible for survival. Huxley had argued that "the ethical progress of society depends, not on imitating the cosmic process, still less in running away from it, but in combating it."[23]

Dewey thought that Huxley had capitulated to an unwarranted and dangerous form of dualism. In his reply he uses Huxley's own analogy of a garden in order to undercut his separation of nature from culture. "The ethical process," he writes, "like the activity of the gardener, is one of constant struggle. We can never allow things simply to go on of themselves. If we do, the result is retrogression. Oversight, vigilance, constant interference with conditions as they are, are necessary to maintain the ethical order, as they are to keep up the garden" (EW 5.37).

But what is the relation of the ethical (the cultural) to the process of evolution as a whole (the natural)? Dewey answers that "we do not have here in reality a conflict of man as man with his entire natural environment. We have rather the modification by man of one part of the environment with reference to another part. Man does not set himself against the state of nature. He utilizes one part of this state in order to control another part. . . . He introduces and maintains by art conditions of sunlight and moisture to which this particular plot of ground is unaccustomed; but these conditions fall within the wont and use of nature as a whole" (EW 5.37–38).

In other words, human activity, and therefore culture, is one part of nature. It is one of the ways that nature transacts business with itself. In intelligent gardening, just as in any other intelligent activity, one part of the environment is modified with respect to another part of the environment. Deliberation and intelligent management enter into the history of evolution.

It might be objected that Dewey has already gone too far, that he has allowed just anything that human beings happen to do to amount, by definition, to progress with respect to the whole. But Dewey meets this objection head-on by means of his Pragmatic Instrumentalism. Since the part of human beings within the evolutionary process is intelligent choice, it is not action *simpliciter*, but

intelligent action that produces improved results and therefore advances the process of evolution. Doing nothing and doing just anything are equally unintelligent, since they do not enhance the
adjustment of one part of the environment to another.

Dewey's argument in this essay hinges on his notion of temporal-
ity. "Every one must have his fitness judged by the whole, including
the anticipated change; not merely by reference to the conditions of
today, because these may be gone tomorrow. If one is fitted simply to
the present, he is not fitted to survive. He is sure to go under" (EW
5.41). "The past environment," Dewey writes, "is related to the present as a part to a whole" (EW 5.46). Further, "Evolution is a continued development of new conditions which are better suited to the
needs of organisms than the old. The unwritten chapter in natural
selection is that of the evolution of environments" (EW 5.52).[24]

If Dewey has undercut the grounds for a dualism of evolution and
ethics, nature and culture, we are still left with the question of just
how it is possible for communication among the features of the natural environment to occur. This is a matter that Dewey takes up in
1925 in the fifth chapter of *Experience and Nature*, where he presents
his theory of communication as an essential ingredient of his naturalism. "Where communication exists," he writes, "things in acquiring
meaning, thereby acquire representatives, surrogates, signs and impli-
cates which are indefinitely more amenable to management, more
permanent and more accommodating, than events in their first state.
By this fashion, qualitative immediacies cease to be dumbly raptur-
ous" (LW 1.132).

In other words, communication involves taking naturally occurring experiences and making them more meaningful by relating them
to other naturally occurring experiences. This is an art that involves,
in its turn, careful attention to the qualitative moments of experience
in order that their traits may be made manifest, or expressed, by
working out their implications.

Communication is a multiplier. More than the expression of already existent material, it is the "cooperation in an activity in which
there are partners, and in which the activity of each is modified and

regulated by the partnership" (LW 1.141). Communication opens up the doors of perception. We become "capable of perceiving things instead of merely feeling and having them. To *perceive* is to acknowledge unattained possibilities; it is to refer the present to consequences, apparition to issue, and thereby to behave in deference to the *connections* of events" (LW 1.143).

Late in his career, apparently as a reaction to the neopositivism that was beginning to dominate academic ecology,[25] Leopold seems to have retreated to an organicism that holds that "*natural species possessed intrinsic rights* to existence and that these sometimes took precedence over human rights."[26] This is Leopold's third model of nature, and what he seems to have regarded as the basis for his now famous "Land Ethic." But Dewey's naturalism leads him to reject this, as well as other varieties of free-standing or transcendent treatments of nature. He rejects foundations in earth as well as sky.

Like many other ethicists, Dewey held that moral rights exist only in the context of a community of moral agents. This is so because of the linkage between rights and obligations. Because there cannot be obligation in the absence of choice, and because it is only with the advent of human life that choice becomes fully a part of evolutionary history, it is a mistake to attribute intrinsic rights either to nonhuman species or to nonhuman individuals.[27] To speak of nonhuman species or nonhuman individuals as the possessors of intrinsic rights would in Dewey's view amount either to anthropomorphizing nonhuman nature or to opening up a chasm between human and nonhuman nature by positing a domain of moral rights that does not involve moral agency and is therefore entirely separate from what human beings understand by the term.[28]

Does this mean that Dewey's naturalism regresses to a modernist anthropocentrism? Does his naturalism open the door to treating nonhuman species in any way we choose? It does neither. In order to understand why this is so it is necessary to return to his radical empiricism and his idea that human beings experience nature noncognitively as well as cognitively.

At the noncognitive level, nature, both domesticated and wild nonhuman nature, is a source of intense and immediate aesthetic delight. Because of its immediacy, this type of aesthetic experience requires no warrant. It just is. Hunting, fishing, hiking, boating, bird-watching, celebration of the seasons, and many other forms of interaction with nonhuman nature, such as the enjoyment of pets, offer the occasion for such delight. The delights of breathing clean air, drinking pure water, and the enjoyment of forests untouched by acid rain—all this is valued in its immediacy.

Dewey's radical empiricism also allows for the immediate experience of a "beyond" in the sense that immediately experienced delight possesses sensible fringes. Hints, gaps, leads, and clues are experienced on the fringes of focused experiences. In its noncognitive phase, then, nature is the source of both felt delight and wider expectation. Because of its commitment to radical empiricism, Dewey's naturalism is capable of promoting a piety with respect to nonhuman nature that is not encumbered by the epistemological problems of transcendent views of nature. A fringe is a vague indication of what may be to come, under the proper circumstances; of what is open to possible development, given sufficient interest.

It is at the cognitive level, however, that appreciation of nature is enlarged. Nature is understood by means of the arts, as aesthetic experiences are secured and enriched, and by means of the sciences, as experiences are enlarged and related to one another through experimentation, abstraction, and quantification. Both the arts and the sciences function in Dewey's work to expand the meanings of experience, and to secure what would otherwise have been immediate and transitory; but they do so in different ways. The arts "express" meanings, as he puts it, and the sciences "state" meanings.

Another way of putting this is to point out that Dewey undercuts the distinction that plagued Leopold throughout his career, namely the distinction between facts and values.[29] In order to do this, Dewey distinguished between what is or has been valued and what has proven or might prove to be valuable. Values in nonhuman nature, and in human nature as well, are most often just experienced. As such they have not been secured as valuable, that is, they have not been reconstructed as platforms for further action. Dewey thought that values are secured as valuable just as their meanings are developed, enlarged, and interrelated. This may be accomplished in the arts, as certain traits and qualities of materials are expressed in ways that single them out from others that are less interesting, less fecund, or less evocative of further experience. It may also be accomplished in the sciences by means of experimentation, or the instrumental interaction with natural processes in which mere endings are replaced with consequences and consummations that are worthy of celebration and suggestive of further paths of deliberation.

Dewey's naturalism thus treats noncognitive nature both as immediately *valued*, and as raw material for the construction of nature as culture, that is, nature as human artifact or nature as *valuable*. Given the complexity of human culture, with its many overlapping and competing interests, including the economic, the artistic, the political, and the religious, to name just a few, it is nature-as-human-artifact that enters into public debates regarding the adjudication of conflicting interests. This is because one noncognitive experience, since it is immediate, has no way of holding its own against the claims of other, potentially competing noncognitive experiences. Its implications have not been worked out. But in nature-as-culture, implications have been drawn, connections made, and tentative conclusions reached.

Environmental Pragmatism and Environmental Preservation

The upshot of this is that Dewey's naturalism is capable of supporting Leopold's land ethic, that is, the view that humans ought to act to preserve the integrity, stability, and beauty of natural systems, but without Leopold's occasional lapses into an appeal to a realm of transcendent rights. This can be done by demonstrating that the integrity, stability, and beauty of nonhuman nature is immediately experienced as valued, and further that these factors have proven valuable as a

source of continually emerging values, including those that are aesthetic, economic, scientific, technological, and religious. Each of Leopold's terms, "integrity," "stability," and "beauty," however, because
it is a tool of inquiry and not an absolute whose meanings have been
determined for all time, must undergo continual reevaluation and reconstruction with respect to changing conditions.

Dewey's naturalism is consistent with and anticipatory of at least
one current version of the Gaia hypothesis. As Frederic L. Bender
characterizes it, Gaia presents four major challenges to traditional
thinking about nature. First, traditional notions of individuality are
challenged; second, traditional notions of fitness are challenged;
third, Gaia intentionally blurs the traditional boundary between life
and nonlife; and fourth, Gaia's holism rejects the traditional focus on
individual ecosystems in favor of attention to global relationships.[30]

Each of these points is also Dewey's. He argued that individuals
are only so in the context of environing factors; that the notions of
"fitness" must be greatly expanded (see his reply to Huxley); that the
difference between life and nonlife is primarily a matter of level of
organization (LW 1.195); and that intelligent deliberation takes as
broad a view as possible. As I have noted, however, Dewey rejected
extreme views of Gaia, which hold that the global ecosystem has intelligence apart from that of human beings.

If my analysis of his work is correct, then Dewey would also have
rejected the view advanced by Eric Katz and others who have argued
that the only real nature is nature that is "permitted to be free, to
pursue its own independent course of development."[31] Katz thus valorizes an extreme version of what I have called nature-as-nature, or
nature as undisturbed, and he deprecates nature-as-culture, which he
treats as a kind of forgery. The problem with this view, from Dewey's
perspective, is that nature-as-undisturbed is also nature-as-unknown,
since knowledge involves experimental interaction and therefore
some measure of "disturbance." I have already addressed the epistemic fallacy that is committed by such views of nature-as-transcen-
dent. The problem is this: what can human beings know of the values
of nonhuman nature with which they, by definition, have had no

contact? Katz's critique of the Enlightenment notion of "domination" of nature is of course well founded, but it does not address
Dewey's position. As I have argued, Dewey's naturalism was also critical of Enlightenment "domination" or straight-line instrumentalism.

Dewey's naturalism is consistent with, and anticipatory of, some
forms of "restoration" ecology, such as that advanced by William R.
Jordan.[32] Like Dewey, Jordan's leading metaphor is the garden, with
its ancillary metaphors of "maintenance" and "reconstitution."
Among the objects of his restoration interest are various portions of
the Wisconsin prairie.

Like Dewey, Jordan recognizes that human life is not a "perni-
cious" factor outside environmental change, but one part of it. His
goal is thus not to "protect" nature from human beings, but to "provide the basis for a healthy relationship between nature and culture."[33] He recognizes that restricting human participation in natural
events (idealizing nature) is merely another way of fighting nature
(the obverse of treating nature as machine), and that the real challenge of restoration ecology is to find ways in which human beings
can come to view themselves as participating members of their
environments.

Traditional nature activities such as boating, hunting, and fishing
are consequently parts of his program. "All of these are integrated
into an event that is constructive rather than consumptive—as each
of these particular activities is in its traditional form."[34] It is by means
of these reconstructed activities that Jordan intends to "bring to our
attention aspects of our relationship with nature that otherwise we
might not recognize."[35]

In short, Jordan thinks that the older versions of environmentalism (which I have argued rest on modernist versions of realism or
idealism) have failed because of their fruitless attempts to isolate nature from culture. He thus sees his own restoration model as Pragmatic. His intent is to increase the relevance and enlarge the
application of Leopold's land ethic.

A key element in Jordan's restoration ecology is ritual celebration.
By beginning with the immediate delight afforded by communal and

festive (noncognitive) interaction with natural events, such as pro-
grammed prairie burns, he believes that the basis can be laid for an
enriched cognitive appreciation of the place of human life within its
natural setting, and consequently that restoration will come to be
seen as "both an effective [scientific] process and an expressive [artis-
tic] act." "The idea," he continues, "is not merely to *decorate* restoration, but to develop it to enhance its expressive power."[36]

Because of his interest in scientific inquiry, Dewey would have ap-
proved of setting aside wilderness areas so that they can serve as laboratories for environmental scientists. But this is not to treat wild
nature as apart, ideal, or "untouched." It is instead to preserve it as
source of experimental data which would otherwise be lost. As Leopold notes, "A science of land health needs, first of all, a base datum
of normality, a picture of how healthy land maintains itself as an organism . . . . Wilderness, then, assumes unexpected importance as a
laboratory for the study of land-health."[37]

As a synthesis of the aims of preservationist and restorationists,
the work of The Nature Conservancy is also consistent with Deweyan
naturalism. As it continues its task of purchasing and protecting wild-
life habitats checkered within developed areas, both the scientific and
the aesthetic dimensions of human experience are served and expanded. Each of these models of naturalism—restoration, preservation, and The Nature Conservancy synthesis—can play a part in the
wider project of adjusting one part of our environment to other parts
in order to effect amelioration of the whole.

If my reading of Dewey is correct, then, his naturalism allows him
to accept and defend the central tenets of Leopold's land ethic without the appeal to an idealized nonhuman nature that sometimes surfaces within Leopold's work. I have argued that Leopold's attempt to
provide a foundation for his ethic by this means is the least workable
and the least defensible feature of his otherwise excellent project. If I
have made my case, then Dewey's work locates itself in the thick of
current debates regarding the relations between human beings and
nonhuman nature, and it offers the promise of continuing insights
within this arena of experience.

NINE

GREEN PRAGMATISM

Reals without Realism, Ideals without Idealism

This essay builds on the material presented in the preceding chapter, in which I argued that the field naturalism of Aldo Leopold and the environmental naturalism of John Dewey have a great deal in common and that Dewey's Pragmatism can broaden our understanding of Leopold's life and legacy.[1] In this chapter I shall discuss the relevance of Dewey's ideas to more recent philosophical debates among environmental philosophers such as Bryan Norton, Holmes Rolston III, J. Baird Callicott, and Michael Zimmerman.

As I have already indicated, Dewey was one of the first philosophers to advance a rigorous and broad philosophical critique of technological culture. He was also an evolutionary naturalist who rejected what he regarded as the extremes of scientific realism and romantic idealizations of nature.

Dewey advanced his critique of technology on two fronts. On the first front he addressed readers of diverse types in his role as a public

intellectual. He closely followed developments within the technosciences and interpreted their social, political, educational, and religious consequences. He was one of the first major philosophers to do
this in a systematic way, and his efforts met with considerable success.
On the occasion of his ninetieth birthday, the *New York Times* hailed
him as "America's Philosopher."[2]

On the second front he addressed his professional colleagues in his
role as a technical philosopher. He reworked the tools he had acquired from his study of the history of philosophy—especially its
Greek and Enlightenment phases—to develop a highly sophisticated
critique of technology. (For an extended account of this aspect of his
work see chapter 7.)

Dewey thought that technology needed to be investigated on several levels. On the first level are the tools, machines, software, and
other artifacts that are invented and used by ordinary people, especially by craftsmen and engineers. On a more general level is the technological milieu that furnishes the leading metaphors that help us as
a culture define our place and time with respect to other milieux. On
this level the character of our particular historical context is influenced not only by the crafts and engineering, but also by the theoretical sciences, historiography, jurisprudence, and the arts, among
others. On a still more general level is what Dewey called "the general
method of intelligence." This is a general method of inquiry or problem-solving that draws on the methods of the various disciplines just
mentioned and feeds back into them. At this most general level, technology may be characterized as the invention, development, and cognitive deployment of tools and other artifacts, brought to bear on raw
materials and intermediate stock parts, with a view to the solution of
perceived problems. At this level, more than any other, it becomes
apparent that technology involves tools and artifacts that are intangi-
ble as well as those that are tangible.

Since this last point has been the source of some confusion, I offer
two comments by way of clarification. First, Dewey thought that
technology at its most general level is pervasive, but not ubiquitous.
Since technology has to do only with deliberation, and since most of

human life involves behavior that is habitual or otherwise unreflective, the domain of the nontechnological is much larger than the domain of the technological. Second, the most general level of technology is intimately related to philosophy. There are two reasons for this. First, Dewey thought that philosophy, as a generalized criticism of criticisms, functions as a kind of "liaison officer" with respect to the various non-philosophical disciplines. It functions as a kind of go-between and translator. It supports their interaction with one another. Second, the *theory* of this most general level of technology—inquiry into inquiry—Dewey identified as *logic* (for more on this subject, see chapter 12).

Put somewhat differently, we might say that Dewey saw, and attempted to make clear to his readers in the philosophical community, the continuities between the kind of thinking that invents the telephone and builds bridges and the kind of thinking that solves problems in ethics and attempts to think about the generic traits of being. Even more important, he recognized that in order to solve the problems generated by our technologies in particular, and by our attitudes toward our technological milieu in general, then we must develop a specialized set of techniques—which he called technology in its most generalized sense. He thus championed a new way of thinking about traditional philosophical problems designed to take account of the pushes and pulls of life in industrial democracies. This would be a new set of tools and techniques designed especially to deal with the problems of technology-as-culture. And it would be self-consciously analytical and self-corrective.

Why did Dewey risk the confusion that would be the inevitable result of referring to each of these different levels of concern as "technology"? I believe he did so for two reasons. First, he was keen to demonstrate his plans for healing the splits and discontinuities within experience that he thought Greek philosophy bequeathed us and early modern philosophy exacerbated. He thought these problems resulted from a failure to treat knowing as an affair of construction and reconstruction. Second, he thought that technology—as the invention, development, and cognitive deployment of problem-solving tools and other artifacts—goes all the way back in the history of human self-consciousness; all the way forward in terms of its prospects; all the way down within quotidian or everyday life; and all the way up in terms of the abstractions we construct and utilize in our attempts to understand culture in a comprehensive fashion. This, in fact, is a fair statement of his evolutionary naturalism as it pertains to the arena of human life.

As a public intellectual, Dewey saw his task as the invention and development of some of the tools we will need to tune up the workings of quotidian life in technological cultures. As a technical philosopher, he saw his task as the invention of new tools for thinking about technology in a more general sense, that is, for subjecting our critiques of everyday affairs to a metacritique. In the end, as I have already indicated, he regarded philosophy as the discipline that does just this kind of work, and he referred to it as "a criticism of criticisms" (LW 1.298).

I have argued elsewhere[3] that Dewey was the first major philosopher to write extensively about technology on these various levels. In this matter he anticipated the work of Heidegger by several decades, even though Heidegger is still widely (and erroneously) thought to have been the first to introduce the subject into mainstream philosophical discourse.

Dewey sometimes referred to his most general criticism of technology—his criticism of criticism—as "Instrumentalism." Since this has been the occasion for some misunderstanding, it would probably be better if we referred to it as "Pragmatic Instrumentalism" in order to differentiate it from the kind of vulgar opportunism that Langdon Winner has appropriately labeled "straight-line instrumentalism" and that the Frankfurt School has famously treated under the heading of *Zweckrationalität*. Although his Pragmatic Instrumentalism rests on several interconnected theses, I want to emphasize his rejection during the 1900s of both representative and sensationalist varieties of realism, at one extreme, and both subjective and objective varieties of idealism, at the other.

Robert Westbrook has described this aspect of Dewey's work with his usual precision: "The source of difficulty for idealists, sensationalists, and those . . . who tried vainly to synthesize transcendentalism and empiricism lay in their requirement for 'a total contrast of thought as such to something else as such' (SLT, 330). This, Dewey argued, was to commit a mistake by now familiar to readers of his work: the erection of functional distinctions within experience into distinct entities."[4] Dewey thought that this mistake had been a major feature of the history of philosophy. That is why he called it "the philosophic fallacy."

The commission of the philosophic fallacy was in Dewey's view much more than simply a matter of concern for technical philosophers. He thought it an important move in a high-stakes game because it involved practical consequences: the error, as he put it, had led philosophers to state "the terms upon which thought and being transact business in a way so totally alien to concrete experience that it creates a problem which can be discussed only in terms of itself— not in terms of the conduct of life" (MW 2.308). What Dewey wanted to substitute for these traditional epistemologies—realistic as well as idealistic—was a new kind of inquiry or logic that would be a "natural history of thinking as a life-process having its own generating antecedents and stimuli, its own states and career, and its own specific objective or limit" (MW 2.309).

The consequences of Dewey's insights for understanding technology were, and remain, considerable. He was keen to reject what he regarded as two extreme positions, both of which involve an element of truth, but both of which are incomplete in the form in which they are usually advanced. The first was scientific realism, with its emphasis on representationally given facts, its reliance on a correspondence theory of truth, and its assumption of a split between facts and values that favors facts. The second was idealism, which included the so-called "humanistic" or "spiritual" critique of scientific technology, with its emphasis on values grounded elsewhere than an experienced world, its reliance on a coherence theory of truth, and its assumption of a split between facts and values that favors values.

Dewey thought that there was a reasonable way out of this un-happy stand-off. He invited us to notice that the general method of intelligence (or the set of techniques that involves a critique of cri-tiques) is reducible neither to attempts to "dominate" an objective world that exists independently of our experience, effected by means of a series of "adaptations" of it, nor to attempts to "accommodate" the subject to a set of values which also exist in some region beyond what we are able to locate and secure through processes of inquiry.

The failure of both of these programs—realist and idealist alike—was in his view a result of their lack of attention to the ways in which facts and values, ends and means, and intrinsic and instrumental goods are related in cases of actual deliberation. In his view, the ex-treme positions made one-sided attempts either to elevate means over ends, as scientific realist acounts of nonhuman nature often do, or to elevate ends over means, as idealist accounts often do.

Dewey simply bypassed the chasm this debate had opened. He pro-posed we recognize that the two sides—the one that emphasizes facts and the one that emphasizes values—are at bottom connected as *phases* or *moments* within inquiry. Whereas both facts (as facts-of-a-case) and values (as ideals, or ends-in-view) are essential components of problem-solving activities, realism errs when it attempts to make a fact into something independent that exists prior to its being experi-enced as a fact-of-a-case in the context of discriminative inquiry. And idealism commits a similar error when it attempts to make a value into something independent that exists outside of and apart from the ideals (ends-in-view) that arise from active discrimination of the fea-tures of our lived experience.

Dewey called our attention to the following readily observable situ-ation: since we human beings are reflectively conscious organisms who live forward into the future, we continually engage in activities that involve various techniques—we plan, resolve, construct, and re-construct. These activities are central features of human affairs, and each of them involves the formulation and testing of both reals (as either felt preferences or selected data to be organized into facts-of-a-case) and values or ideals (as ends-in-view to be tested with refer-ence to the facts-of-a-particular-case).

In essence, Dewey was arguing that even the modernist epistemologies which attempt to provide ontological descriptions or taxonom-
ies that divide portions of our experience into what is "external" and
"internal" are themselves artifacts: the product of certain techniques.
They are the consequences of inquiry, not its antecedents. Inquiry is
thus a technological enterprise because it involves techniques: the invention, development, and cognitive deployment of tools and other
artifacts (such as rules of inference), brought to bear on raw materials
(such as data) and intermediate stock parts (such as the results of
previous inquiries), to resolve and reconstruct situations which are
perceived as problematic. Inquiry is a technique for producing new
outcomes, including new habits of action.

This view of technology as critique of critiques—as a method of
experimentation, resolution, and reconstruction—turns out to have
some interesting consequences for environmental philosophy, and especially for our understanding of nature. Dewey argued that once unreflectively perceived events and relations begin to be ordered and
reconstructed into facts-of-a-case, and once those facts-of-a-case are
checked against ends-in-view and consequently transformed in ways
that result in new knowledge, then new artifacts have ipso facto been
produced. And since inquiry always involves broadened significance,
it has dimensions that are social as well as individual. Its artifacts have
meaning and authority within our cultural milieu.

When the delights of unreflectively experienced nonhuman nature,
for example, or what in the previous chapter I called nature-as-nature, enter into deliberation as facts-of-a-case, then they take on the
quality of cultural artifacts. Such artifacts are constructed by myriad
culturally based deliberative enterprises including religion, science,
industry, cinema, literature, and philosophy, to name but a few. Nature-as-nature relinquishes its status as immediately and evanescently
enjoyed and becomes more secure and sharply defined. It becomes a
construction, an artifact, we do well to recognize as nature-as-culture.

One important consequence of this view is that value is no longer
understood as either what is immediately experienced as valued or

what is posited as an ideal end-in-view, but as what has been experimentally ascertained and secured as valuable. What is experimentally determined to be *valuable* is constructed from the *inside* of what Dewey called deliberative situations, or what some have described in more general terms as deliberation within a "lifeworld." What is valuable thus does not intrude into a situation ready-made from some source external to the deliberative situation, whether that source be a neutral and determinate body of empirically given facts as posited by scientific realists, or freestanding and self-certifying values located in some uncognized or uncognizable domain as posited by idealists.

Another important consequence of this view is that "intrinsic value" and "instrumental value" come to be understood as relative terms, just as "means" and "ends" are relative terms. Something valued as "intrinsic" is just, Dewey reminds us, what "occupies a particular place in life; it serves its own end, which cannot be supplied by a substitute. There is no question of comparative value, and hence none of valuation" (MW 9.247–48).

But of course things that are valued as intrinsic in one situation may, in a new situation, be seen as incompatible with other intrinsic things. And things that are intrinsic for one person or group may be instrumental for another. Such conflicted situations call for choices, and choices call for deliberation. What was accepted as an intrinsic good in one situation may become the subject of analysis in another. We are then faced with the necessity of examining the object or event in question in order to determine its instrumental value for bringing about the good of that new situation.

In sum, Dewey was reminding us that some things are unreflectively valued, either because they are just *immediately enjoyed* in the absence of any inquiry at all (for example, an evening of food and wine with friends), or because they have been *deemed to have* intrinsic value—that they are irreplaceable or invaluable—on the basis of some prior sequence of inquiry (as is the case with human infants and certain nonhuman species) and their value is therefore no longer questioned. But when there is a clash of values, inquiry is called for. Arguments about action to be taken with respect to stands of trees, nonhuman animal species, and sometimes even human infants involve real conflicts for which there is usually no facile solution. In each situation, deliberation must proceed with care. Facts-of-the-case must be determined, ends-in-view must be considered, and intelligent reconstruction must be undertaken.

Something that is regarded as intrinsically good in one situation or to one inquirer may be instrumentally good—"good for"—in another situation or to another inquirer. We then use the techniques of intelligent criticism of our concepts and other tools, or what Dewey also called *technology*, to make such determinations: we use various types of tools in the resolution and reconstruction of situations which present value conflicts. The aim of such situations is to produce new artifacts, that is, new situations that are balanced and harmonious. In all of this it is essential to recall that for Dewey the meanings of the terms "instrumental" and "intrinsic" are always context-sensitive.

Bryan G. Norton and J. Baird Callicott

Dewey's treatment of these matters has some interesting applications to current debates within environmental philosophy. His views turn out to be quite similar to the views of several contemporary environmental philosophers and constitute a criticism of the views of several others. In this section I will discuss the work of two philosophers whose views are similar Dewey's. In the next section I will discuss the work of two whose views differ from his.

In his essay, "On the Intrinsic Value of Nonhuman Species," J. Baird Callicott distinguishes between the source of value and the locus of value. "I concede," Callicott writes, "that, from the point of view of Scientific Naturalism the *source* of all value is human consciousness, but it by no means follows that the *locus* of all value is consciousness itself or a mode of consciousness like reason, pleasure, or knowledge." From this he concludes that "something may be valuable only because someone values it, but it may also be valued for itself, not the sake of any subjective experience . . . it may afford the valuer."[5]

In order to make his view more perspicuous, Callicott strips the notion of "intrinsic value" of one common meaning, thus, we might say, distinguishing *intrinsic* value, or value in the sense of "for its own sake as meaningful to some reflectively conscious being," from *inherent* value, or value in the sense of "in itself apart from its being meaningful to some reflectively conscious being." "An intrinsically valuable thing," he writes, "is valuable *for* its own sake, *for* itself, but it is not valuable *in* itself, i.e., completely independently of any consciousness."[6]

Callicott's position in this essay is similar to Dewey's. Both are eager to reject the subjective idealist's claim that what we experience is only our own experience, or as Callicott puts it, the idea that "the *locus* of all value is consciousness itself or a mode of consciousness like reason, pleasure, or knowledge."[7] And both are also careful to reject the claim of the "objective" or absolute idealist, that there are things that are valuable in themselves, without qualification, apart from anyone's reflective experience of them. Moreover, Callicott and Dewey emphasize valuing in its honorific sense as *valuation*, that is, as something that comes at the end of a sequence of productive activity, and that is therefore the result of deliberate choice. Callicott does this—although somewhat less robustly than Dewey—in the context of his remarks on intentionality. For his part, Dewey identifies valuation as the outcome of experimental deliberation with respect to choices among alternatives. "There is no value [in the sense of what is valuable]," Dewey writes, "save in situations where desires and the need of deliberation in order to choose are found, and yet this fact gives no excuse for regarding desire and deliberation and decision as subjective phenomena" (MW 8.35).

Callicott provides two examples of the locus of intrinsic value, as he uses the term: human infants and nonhuman species. Dewey also employs the language of location: in his view, we might say, both human infants and nonhuman species occupy "a particular place in life." Both serve their own ends, and those ends cannot be supplied by a substitute. Moreover, "there is [normally] no question of comparative value, and hence none of valuation" (MW 9.247–48). Under most circumstances, we neither need to ask what they are good for, nor would it be appropriate to do so: they are invaluable.[8]

As Callicott reminds us, however, the notion of inherent value, as the value of something which is such as it is whether or not anyone ever experiences it as valuable (or meaningful), seems to be muddled from the very outset. The very idea of inherent value assumes that we can engage some putative something, located outside or beyond the range of experimental deliberation, and then say something meaningful about it.

Why should this distinction make a difference in our decisions about environmental issues? Our accounts of valuation—of what is valued versus valuable as well as what is intrinsic versus instrumental—cannot be articulated otherwise than from the perspective of our own experience as members of a human community. That is the only perspective from which we can experience things as immediately enjoyed or valued. It is also the only perspective from which we can begin to deliberate when we must test what is merely valued, or what is tentatively posited as an end-in-view, in order to ascertain whether it is also valuable. Like Dewey, but unlike some of the idealists whom I shall discuss in a moment, in this essay Callicott is chary of "detached and impersonal axiological reference point[s]," and he views his account as an antidote to the accounts of those who would "submerge the value of the present ecosystem in a temporally and spatially infinite cosmos."[9]

Callicott does not say in this essay, but his account implies it, that when we work outward from the human standpoint then we work from shared, constructed histories and institutions that provide platforms from which we can extend and enrich common experiences. But when we work inward from the outside, from what putatively transcends experience or is absolutely ideal with respect to common, practical interests, we often fail because of the subjectivism, the sectarianism, or the a priori considerations that taint such attempts to ground our experience.

One of the chief difficulties with working from the outside inward, of course, is that such claims as they are usually articulated are not falsifiable. As William James reminded us, however, the "cash value" of such beliefs—the consequences they have for our beahvior—*are* testable, provided they are based on options that are live, forced, and momentous. This in fact turns out to be what redeems certain strains of environmentalism that are grounded on religious doctrines. It is not their theology but the behavioral consequences of their theology that sustains their position.

Two problems limit the successes of such approaches. First, theological claims, because they are non-empirical, often distract attention from, even undercut, acceptable or even honorific behavioral consequences. And second, such non-empirical arguments are only effective when addressed to an audience already predisposed to accept the theological premise advanced. Arguments of this sort consequently suffer from a limited appeal that is to a great extent self-imposed.

In a more recent paper, Callicott has argued that "we base environmental ethics on our human capacity to value nonhuman natural entities for what they are—irrespective both of what they may do for us and of whether or not they can value themselves. And this we can do regardless of the nature of the object of our intentional act of intrinsic valuation as long as we think we have *good reasons* to value it intrinsically. We can value species (such as the Devil's Hole pupfish), ecosystems (such as Cedar Bog Lake), the oceans, the atmosphere, the biosphere—all for what they are in themselves as well as for their utility."[10] It is of course *intrinsic* value (the value of something that is meaningful *in* itself to someone), as opposed to *inherent* value (the value of something *for* itself, apart from its meaningfulness to someone), that Callicott employs in the last sentence.

In a still more recent paper, however, published in 2002, Callicott seems to back off his earlier position. He appears to move nearer to the position of environmental philosophers such as Holmes Rolston III who argue from *inherent* value. He is particularly displeased by Pragmatic environmental philosophers such as Andrew Light and Bryan G. Norton, who, he complains, have wanted to bracket discussions of intrinsic value and get down to the nuts and bolts of environmental policy. "Pragmatist philosophers," he writes, "now carp and cavil against the concept of intrinsic value in nature as more nonsense on stilts."[11] He wants to accommodate the view that it is humans who do valuing, whether instrumental or intrinsic, but adds that "lots of other forms of life can also 'do' a bit of valuing."[12] Given his defense of the various positions laid out by Rolston, however, as well as his self-description as a "pro-intrinsic-value-in-nature theorist,"[13] and his claim that it is he and Rolston and not the Pragmatists who are doing a better job of raising the public's consciousness of environmental conditions, it is difficult to know precisely how far he wants to push this argument. For the present purposes, however, it is enough to recall that Callicott's earlier work honors a distinction—between the source of value and the locus of value—that is a slightly less robust form of a position that was also Dewey's.

In his essay "Anthropocentrism and Nonanthropocentrism," Bryan G. Norton also advances a distinction that Dewey had anticipated many years earlier. He distinguishes between "felt" preferences and "considered" preferences. "A felt preference," Norton writes, "is any desire or need of a human individual that can at least temporarily be sated by some specifiable experience of that individual. A considered preference is any desire or need that a human individual would express after careful deliberation, including a judgment that the desire or need is consistent with a rationally adopted world view—a world view which includes fully supported scientific theories and a metaphysical framework interpreting those theories, as well as a set of rationally supported aesthetic and moral ideals."[14] He then adds that "when interests are assumed to be constructed merely from felt preferences, they are thereby insulated from any criticism or objection. . . . A considered preference, on the other hand, is an idealization in the sense that it can only be adopted after a person has rationally accepted an entire world view and, further, has succeeded in altering his felt preferences so that they are consonant with that world view."[15]

If we combine Callicott's distinction between source and locus of value and Norton's distinction between felt and considered preferences, it is easy enough to see that Dewey not only laid out a similar theory of valuation almost a century ago, but he also elaborated on these very distinctions. He thought that what is experienced merely as *valued* (which is more or less what Norton calls "felt preferences") usually involves a quality of an experience that is just unreflectively enjoyed, or else just posited as an end-in-view to be tested. Such felt preferences might involve an immediate aesthetic response to an animal in the wild, to a wilderness area, or to a waterfall or sunset. Such felt preferences might also involve the conclusions or consummations of previous inquiries that we continue to enjoy, that is, that do not present an occasion for renewed deliberation.

But what is determined to be *valuable* (which is more or less what Norton calls a "considered preference") is a deliberately (technologically) mediated and enriched relation between an inquirer and the subject matter of his or her inquiry. The locus (to use Callicott's term) of what is experienced as considered preference may be anywhere within the experienced field or situation. It is in fact one of the functions of inquiry to fix more precisely the locus of something that is just haphazardly experienced as valued, so that it can be more securely placed within the historical-cultural context of a person's life-world and thereby be made more secure qua valuable. It is in this sense that inquiry involves technological mediation.

Questions about the locus of the unreflectively valued could well be unanswerable. Felt preferences, since they are unreflective and therefore lack inquiry, do not inquire into locus. The objects and events of felt preferences are enjoyed just as they are, no questions asked. But the locus of the valuable lies within a deliberately *reconstructed* field of experience where it has been related to other parts of that field. This is because, as Dewey reminds us, the determination of something as valuable always involves some sort of choice, that is, some sort of reconstruction of what had been unreflectively enjoyed but has ceased to be so because of some conflict or other. Competing feelings are adjudicated with respect to one another, conflicts are resolved, and the situation is remodeled or reconstructed. In the process, what is valuable is located and secured with respect to a newly organized whole.

To put this somewhat differently, it makes little sense to ask about the locus of what is unreflectively valued, since to pinpoint locus involves reflection. But the locus of something that is experimentally determined to be valuable is ascertained by means of inquiry. This applies equally to other humans, to institutions, and to things such as stands of trees, spotted owls, and the Devil's Hole pupfish.

There is no recourse to a distinction between subject and object in Dewey's account of the locus of the valuable. He simply rejected the modernist epistemology that proposes a distinction. He argued that the distinction between subject and object is itself a result of isolating and then locating with respect to one another various elements within an experienced field: subject and object are artifacts of inquiry. To establish the locus of what is valuable is to produce new artifacts. Dewey thought that one of the primary uses of deliberation is to extend and enrich the meanings of human experience. This would of course involve the extension and enrichment of the meanings of the environments by means of which we live, including the enrichment of our appreciation of wild nature and nonhuman species.

Developing this line of thought somewhat further, we can see that Dewey held something similar to what Norton has called a "weak" form of anthropocentrism. In Norton's terms, "A value theory is *strongly anthropocentric* if all value countenanced by it is explained by reference to satisfactions of felt preferences of human individuals. A value theory is *weakly anthropocentric* if all value countenanced by it is explained by reference to satisfaction of some felt preference of a human individual or by reference to its bearing upon the ideals which exist as elements in a world view essential to determinations of considered preferences."[16]

Dewey frequently contrasted his version of naturalism, which is similar to Norton's weak anthropocentrism, with a myopic strong anthropocentrism founded on an unremitting subject/object dualism that pits human life against an "external" environment and sanctions the domination of nature. The assumption of strong anthropocentrists, whom he identified as realists, was that since nature and its transcript science are value-neutral, just any means at all may be used to satisfy human desires, or felt preferences.

But if Dewey was no strong anthropocentrist, he was an anthropocentrist nonetheless. He thought that both human life and its wider context, nonhuman nature, are unintelligible absent the recognition that it is only with the advent of reflective consciousness that nature comes to have *deliberate* preferences. It is only with the advent of reflective consciousness that nature comes to have "a mind of its own."

Dewey's Environmental Conversation

Dewey had already turned his attention to what we today call environmental philosophy in an essay he wrote in 1909 to help celebrate the fiftieth anniversary of the publication of Darwin's *Origin of Species*. The essay, originally published as "Is Nature Good? A Conversation," takes the form of an interchange among several discussants, among whom are Eaton, a Pragmatist, Moore, an ironically[17] named absolute idealist, and Stair, a mystic.

Moore, the idealist, argues that nature exhibits evil as stubbornly as it does good, and that consciousness is merely a "temporary bird of passage . . . doomed to ultimate extinction" (MW 4.25). Therefore, only the real value behind the apparent value—the permanent value beyond the temporary value, and the inherent value beyond the instrumental value, so to speak—is ultimately real (MW 4.26).

We can see in this argument an adumbration of an idealist answer to the thought experiment known among environmental philosophers as the "last person" problem. In one of its versions, we are invited to determine whether there would be moral considerations involved in the decision by the last person on earth who had the power to push a button that would destroy the planet, whether or not to do so at the moment of their death.

Were Moore the last person on earth and about to die, he would certainly view his life as an individual, conscious human as a "temporary bird of passage" against the backdrop of the absolute or inherent *rational* value of Nature (with a capital N). He would therefore, *on those grounds*, take no action that would harm his environment. The idealist does not reject *überhaupt* the claim that "considered preference," or, in Dewey's terms, what has been determined to be valuable, is of high importance; he simply considers human rationality merely a small part of the larger rationality of the Absolute. In terms of contemporary debates, Moore might well be a proponent of the strong version of Gaia, which holds that the entire planetary system is capable of some sort of rational deliberation, or at least capable of some sort of super self-consciousness.

To this Stair, the mystic, says that Moore has mistaken reason or intellect as the final umpire. Reason or intellect is only a source of discord; the ultimate organ of unity and truth resides elsewhere. Words like "feeling, sensation, immediate appreciation, self-communication of Being," he says, can't quite do the job he wishes them to do, but they can be offered as an invitation "to woo you to put yourselves into the one attitude that reveals truth—an attitude of direct vision" (MW 4.26). In our own time Stair would perhaps be a proponent of some more mystic version of Gaia, or some version of panentheism, or a blend of the two.

One supposes that Stair's response to the "last person" problem would be similar to Moore's, but justified on different grounds. For Stair, the value that grounds what is cognitively experienced as valuable is romantically or aesthetically felt, rather than rationally discerned, but it is real nonetheless. He thus inverts Dewey's Pragmatist position, which treats what is romantically or aesthetically felt-as-valued as something to be reconstructed (in the event that it becomes problematic). Stair's position calls to mind the post–World War II work of Heidegger, and the work of Charles Hartshorne as well.

Zimmerman and Rolston

The idealistic positions assumed by Moore and Stair, positions that are criticized in Dewey's essay, have their counterparts in contemporary environmental philosophy. Michael Zimmerman, for example, writing in 1988, thought he had found the basis for environmental ethics in a form of mystic idealism known as "panentheism." He thought that the primary virtue of panentheism for environmental philosophy is that it avoids the dualism of Western metaphysics. In his nutshell characterization, "Panentheism . . . claims that the Creator is both transcendent of and immanent in creation. This state of affairs is paradoxical for cognitive rationality, but not for nondualistic awareness."[18] Not surprisingly, Zimmerman found support for his view in the work of the later Heidegger, although he did not—at least in this essay—mention his debt to the most famous twentieth-century proponent of panentheism, Charles Hartshorne.

Zimmerman's position in this essay seems to combine elements of positions taken by Dewey's characters Moore and Stair. His view is idealistic because it posits a ground or source of value beyond what is, or even what could be, a part of cognitive experience. And his view is mystical because of its suggestion that a spiritual-perceptual gestalt shift is necessary in order for that source of value (which is located beyond what is cognitively determined to be valuable) even to be glimpsed. Zimmerman urges his readers to take up a "nondualistic awareness" that seems to be supported more by direct perception than by cognition. The ideal object of "nondualistic" awareness thus becomes, in his view, a tool by means of which we are to evaluate what is cognitively constructed.

Like other forms of idealism, however, panentheism attempts to import what is of value into experience from what is external to it, in this case from a Creator who is both transcendent and immanent in creation. Such a creator is a thinker who thinks himself, or as a "process" theologian might put it, a God who experiences growth and knowledge of Himself through the growth and increased self-understanding of His creations.

This is of course a weaker form of idealism than some of its cousins, such as the several varieties of absolute idealism that were popular at the time that Dewey wrote "Is Nature Good?" But it is idealism nonetheless. It rehearses the usual claim of idealisms, namely that it is an antidote to dualism. And like other forms of idealism, it turns out to replace an overt form of dualism with one that is covert. In

Zimmerman's terms, what is absolutely noncognitive but available through an apparently mystical or intuitive "nondualistic awareness" is split off from the cognitive in a way that the former appears paradoxical to the latter.

In an essay published in 2004, Zimmerman develops these ideas even further, arguing that there are themes within Continental philosophy that are appropriate to environmental philosophy but that have not yet been tapped. He calls for a re-enchantment of the world, and more particularly for environmental philosophers to take "religion seriously not merely as an interesting cultural practice, but also as giving institutional expression to profound and to some extent verifiable insights."[19] Although Zimmerman pitches a very broad tent, it is clear that at least some of its occupants answer to the description that Dewey gives of Moore and Stair, his idealist and his mystic.

The work of Holmes Rolston III, I believe, exhibits yet another idealistic strategy for bringing what is valuable, in the sense in which I have used the term, into our lifeworlds from the outside, unmediated, or so it appears, by human deliberation. In his examples (which are articulated in terms that call to mind the work of the later Heidegger), the value of wild nature as well as certain other things, such as communion wine, is said to be not so much *resource* as *source*. "Before . . . the sacred [communion wine]," he writes, "one is not so much looking to resources as to sources, seeking relationships in an elemental stream of being with *transcending integrities*."[20]

Rolston thinks that we need "to get ourselves defined in relation to nature, not just to define nature in relation to us."[21] He writes of the type of experience that "moves value outside ourselves" and he tells us that "value is not just a human product."[22] He tells us that value is what "makes a favorable difference," whether in the life of an organism or an ecosystem.[23] Wilderness is said to be "the most *valuable* realm of all, the struggling womb *able* to generate all these adventures in *value*."[24]

In fact Rolston seems to have just inverted the Pragmatist's analysis of valuation. For the Pragmatist, what is *valued* is unstable, fragile, and fleeting, but what is *valuable* has been secured by means of experimental deliberation. For Rolston, however, what is *valuable* is primary and originary: it generates and grounds what is *valued*. As he puts it, "We have too much fallen into the opinion that the only values that there are, moral or artistic or whatever, are human values, values which we have selected or constructed, over which we have labored. Modern philosophical ethics has left us insensitive to the reception of nonhuman values."[25] Moreover, "it is the autonomous otherness of the natural expressions of value that we learn to love, and that integrity becomes vain when this value secretly requires our composing."[26]

The radical empiricism of Dewey and James presents a very different picture of these matters. Since they do not recognize a subject/object split in nonreflective experience, they hold that immediate value is "located" neither in subject nor in object. It is in fact not located at all: it just is. On reflection, of course, what was immediately valued prior to deliberation can be located within an experienced field, a field from which subject and object can then also be isolated as parts or moments. Dewey and James observe, and they invite us to do so as well, that unreflective enjoyment, because it is unreflective, is *prior* to subject/object distinctions, which are the byproducts of processes of inquiry. The subject/object distinction comes only in the context of an analysis of an experience (and even then only in the event that conditions call for such an analysis). For Rolston, however, immediate value seems to come forth already well formed: even prior to our experience of it, he tells us, it already has a "transcending integrity."

For Dewey and James, wild nature is a cultural/historical artifact. For Rolston, wild nature is just given. Rolston's attempts to ground value in a nature which has never been subject to the reconstructive and transformative activity of human deliberation would, I think, have appeared to Dewey as commission of the philosophers' fallacy—a reification and an anthropomorphizing of a great "Source." This move was arguably also made in the work of the later Heidegger.

Because of the Pragmatist's rejection of the realistic hypothesis, of course, she would also reject the notion that wilderness areas must be developed in an economic sense to be deemed valuable. "Transformation" or "development" or "management" of a wilderness area in this context would mean, for example, that it is located with respect to other features of our cultural landscape and that it is treated in ways that involve as much intelligence as possible, given our current tools and techniques. Such management might well mean setting it aside for scientific research or for non-intrusive human visitors, or even reserving it exclusively for its nonhuman natural inhabitants, thus placing it out of bounds for use by the current generation of humans. This is very similar to the way in which Aldo Leopold spoke of the "management" of natural settings.

I must admit that I find Rolston's split between "source" and "resource" somewhat troubling. If we read "resource" as "commodity" and "source" as "ground of value," as I think his texts invite us to do, then we seem to have slipped imperceptibly into one of the varieties of dualism that tend to lurk behind most varieties of idealism. Put in terms of some of the older idealisms, the source becomes the real, the resource what is only apparent.

I have already drawn attention to the Pragmatists' attempts to bypass dualisms of this type by treating resource and source, commodity and ideal, and even instrumental and intrinsic, as relative to one another as *aspects* or *moments* within inquiry, and not as ontologically distinct from one another. Especially in the work of Dewey, it is instruments—tools and methods—that relate commodity and ideal to one another, to check them against one another as means are checked against ends and ends are checked against means.

To be fair, Rolston does not argue that intrinsic value is the only type of value: he argues that "there is nothing secondary about instrumental value."[27] "Excellence," he writes, "does not consist in what a thing is merely for itself, but in what it is for others."[28] And he even sounds a bit like Dewey when he writes that "excellence is not a matter of encapsulated being, but of fittedness into a pervasive whole."[29] But what Rolston means by "pervasive whole" seems to involve an ideal cosmic system already complete with an (ideal) history of "storied achievements," whereas what Dewey means by "pervasive whole" involves a deliberative situation in which harmony and balance have been restored. In the final analysis, then, Rolston's view of instrumental value is nested in an ideal system, "the historic system that carries value to and through individuals."[30] Dewey, on the other hand, because he was an evolutionary naturalist, rejected such ideal "historic systems" as something that could lie outside of, but yet at the same time somehow be determinative of, experience.

In short, I am suggesting that the positions of both of these environmental philosophers, Zimmerman and Rolston, tend to be idealistic in a sense that was adumbrated and criticized in Dewey's essay almost a century ago.

"Eaton" Gets the Last Word

Since "Is Nature Good?" is Dewey's own essay, Eaton the Pragmatist is given the last word. He points out that Moore, the idealist, has to assume some ultimate value beyond experienced values in order even to articulate his claim that some values are genuine and others illusory. But, he continues, it is not the search for some ultimate value beyond experienced values that motivates practical men and women. In their attempts to regulate their lives and avoid undesirable consequences, they have to deal with all sorts of conflicting values and possible courses of action they have to find intelligent ways of discriminating between means and ends. This was probably what motivated Aldo Leopold's famous remark about how an environmentalist can appeal even to "Rotarians."[31]

In short, we human beings experience inherent value only in the highly attenuated sense that certain things are unreflectively *valued*. But since nature retracts what is valued as quickly and as unpredictably as it proffers it, it is the job of intelligence, or technology, to ascertain whether what is valued is also *valuable*; and if it be found to be such, to work to secure it.

To Moore's spiritual cousin Stair, the mystic, Eaton replies in a similar vein, that communication with Being through "the moments of insight and joy that life provides" (MW 4.28) is little more than self-indulgence, since even mystics need to eat and be housed and it is usually left to unmystic persons (such as Eaton) to do this.

What would be the Pragmatist Eaton's response to the "last person" problem, the question as to whether the last person on Earth, facing death, would choose to destroy the planet when she dies? Are there grounds for her not to do so?

For the last person to destroy the planet would be wrong, from the viewpoint of Eaton the Pragmatist, but not on the grounds usually furnished by his idealist interlocutors. It is not that there is an absolute value beyond human experience that serves as the criteria for human valuation, but rather that morality is a matter of the best choices that can be made *given* the context of our experience.

Though the last person would lack human companionship, she will realize, if she is a Pragmatist, that what she is, including her thought and her language, is nevertheless the product of a social world. Her refusal to destroy the planet would therefore probably be based more on her own integrity than something outside her culturally and historically constructed experience of nonhuman nature. Her evolutionary naturalism would lead her to honor the observable historical and genetic continuities between human and nonhuman animals. She might, for example, be concerned about the fate of Washoe, Nim Chimsky, and the other chimpanzees whose lives have intertwined both emotionally and cognitively with those of human beings (and with whom, as she knows, she shares more than 98 percent of her genetic material). Her environmental naturalism would also lead her to take into account the well-documented social lives of other nonhuman animals, including pets, which have entered into the cultural lives of human beings and each other. They are part of a cultural matrix which she honors. To diminish them would mean that she would die as a diminished person.

In order to understand her Pragmatic response to the "last person" problem, we must therefore take a step back from the question as it is usually stated in order to reconstruct it. The question for a Pragmatist is not "Why not destroy the earth?" but rather "What kind of a person would choose to do so?" The Pragmatist would answer that such a person would be one whose malice or insensitivity to other forms of life would itself reveal a lack of integrity, a life out of balance, in short, a failure to do what is moral. At least in this regard, the Pragmatist shares certain positions with the "virtue" ethicist: the moral individual is a construct, a well-articulated *artifact*, a finely honed *product* of factors that are uniquely individual entering into dynamic relationships with those that are cultural and historical. The moral and the technological are thus in her view inextricably linked, because the production of artifacts, including the artifact she knows as "nature-as-culture," is through and through a moral enterprise. But of course the Pragmatist also shares certain positions with the "consequentialist" as well, including concern for nonhuman sociality. The Pragmatist locates her own moral position within an historical context, looking both backward and forward in time.

Incidentally, by making this type of response to the "last person" problem the Pragmatist would avoid the criticism of those such as Bertrand Russell who have claimed that Pragmatic ethics involves a bare utilitarian consequentialism, a vulgar form of instrumentalism, or a gross commitment to "efficiency."

John Dewey is to my knowledge the only philosopher to have advanced a critique of technology as part of a broad philosophical program, including social and political philosophy, educational philosophy, ethics, and logic, or the theory of inquiry. No other philosopher of technology, so far as I know, has done this. Heidegger's work notoriously lacked a coherent social philosophy, and it exhibited nothing in the way of a philosophy of education. Dewey thought of all of these elements as playing pivotal roles within a comprehensive critique of technology. This is not to say that Dewey advanced what was known in the nineteenth century as "a philosophical system." He disliked systematizing, and made that dislike quite clear. Nevertheless, because he regarded philosophy as an attempt to understand and ameliorate experience as we find it—to foster growth and the enrichment of the meanings of human experience—he thought that insofar as it is possible a philosopher ought to have an *integrated* philosophy.

Dewey's critique of technology thus offers positive contributions to current debates within environmental philosophy. This applies not only to the work of philosophers such as Callicott and Norton, who have intentionally or unintentionally followed in his footsteps, but also to the work of the contemporary idealists and even mystics, whose arguments recapitulate many of those of the idealists and mystics toward which Dewey directed his criticism.

PART FOUR

CLASSICAL PRAGMATISM

TEN

WHAT WAS DEWEY'S MAGIC NUMBER?

Abraham Kaplan once suggested that Dewey's "magic number" was two. Unlike nihilists, whose magic number is zero, and also unlike monists, trinitarians, squares (whose magic number is four), pluralists (whose magic number is more than four), and radical pluralists (whose magic number is infinity), Kaplan thought that Dewey was particularly interested in the number two.[1] In support of his thesis he recalled the titles of Dewey's books, from *The School and Society* and *The Child and the Curriculum* to *Experience and Nature* and finally to *Knowing and the Known* (LW 10.xi–xii).

In making this observation, however, Kaplan hedged a bit. Perhaps it would be better, he added, to say that Dewey had *two* magic numbers; that he looked for twos to turn them into ones. "Dewey resolves dualisms," Kaplan wrote, "not by refusing to countenance the distinctions being drawn by dualists, but by reinterpreting differences thought to be substantive and intrinsic as being instead functional and contextual. It is a technique of cross-cutting, superimposing new distinctions perpendicular to the old ones" (LW 10.xii).

But even if Dewey often dealt with dualities by "crosscutting," as Kaplan suggested, that was only one of his many strategies. Sometimes he simply united two ideas, as in his discussion of democracy in the 1932 *Ethics*, for example (LW 7.349). And in his discussion of the moral self, also in *Ethics*, he rejects egoism and altruism (along with any combination of them), then reconstructs them as "secondary phases of a more normal and complete interest: regard for the welfare and integrity of the social groups of which we form a part" (LW 7.298–99). This strategy—reconstructing the poles of an unstable dyad as *phases* of a new unity or whole—was one of Dewey's favorites.

Considered in terms of Dewey's de-hypostatized and functionalized essences, the wholes that succeed unstable dyads may be said to be the pivot point of his thought. Since his notion of essences is dynamic, such new wholes tend to break down into new dualities. Considered in terms of method, however, Dewey's thought regularly returns to threes, which tend to be more robust and enduring than his ones. As Michael Eldridge has suggested, Dewey is probably best described as a dynamic pluralist with a triadic procedure.[2]

Some of these cases seem inspired by Hegel's dialectic. Others recall the categories of C. S. Peirce—especially as they are related to Peirce's method of fixing belief. By understanding Dewey's magic number, the structure and content of his work become a bit clearer, as do his debts to his predecessors. The three examples I have chosen are taken from Dewey's discussions of the arts, ethics, and inquiry.

The Arts

In chapter 9 of the 1925 *Experience and Nature* (LW 1.273), Dewey discusses three cases in which an art-object functions as "merely" fine. By "fine," Dewey meant the object is *final* because it is not part of the give-and-take of a world in which aesthetic experiences also function as the *means* of enrichment. These three cases involve art-objects whose sole or dominant feature is 1) self-expression (as apotheosis of some *quality* of the artist's experience), 2) experimentation with new techniques and tools (as *reaction* against some existing technique), and 3) emblematic of ownership or part of commercialized industry (as a failed attempt at *mediation* between the art-object and external, prosaic interests).

It is possible to see in this account a highly generalized application of Peirce's categories. Some careful reader of Peirce might object that the first case, artistic self-expression, is already too well defined to count as a case of Firstness, or *quality*, since it obviously involves Secondness in the sense of *reaction* to and among artistic materials and Thirdness in the sense of some form of *mediation,* that is, in the sense in which any completed art form points beyond itself in *some* way (see volume 1, section 530 [1.530] of Peirce's collected papers).[3] But Peirce's language in 1.306, 1.307, and 1.310 seems to allow for this type of generalization. He speaks of Firstness, for example, as what it is "regardless of anything else." And Dewey's claim about cases in which a work of art does not transcend self-expression is precisely the claim that the dominant *quality* of such art is that it is narrow and uninformed: that it does not take anything beyond the artist himself or herself into account and is therefore highly attenuated.

So first there is the self-absorbed artist whose preoccupation with self-expression renders his or her work isolated, autistic, and solipsistic, which is to say, more or less just as it is regardless of anything else. Second, there is the reactionary artist whose preoccupation with the rejection of accepted practice takes up all the space that a more relevant and vital content might have otherwise occupied. And third, there is the rule- or formula-driven artist whose work reflects the mediation of political, religious, or commercial concerns in ways that displace concern for the expression of his or her materials.

On a more positive note, Dewey thought that wherever means and ends come together in the arts there is also a triad at work. "Any activity that is productive of objects whose perception is an immediate good," he wrote, "and whose operation is a continual source of enjoyable perception of other events exhibits fineness of art" (LW 1.274). There is a conjunction of three characteristics or dominant *qualities* of a truly fine art-object in this statement. First, the object must afford perception of an immediate good—immediate in the sense that it requires nothing else for its enjoyment. Second, the object must be operative, as opposed to static—it must *react* to and eventually displace commonplace ways of experiencing. And third, the object must be meaningful in the sense that it points beyond itself and increases the enjoyment of other objects and events—it must *mediate* in the sense that it relates its appreciator to some third thing, carrying him or her beyond the art-object itself (but not allowing the third thing to dominate or define the art-object itself). Here again we have a highly generalized application of Peirce's three categories.

In yet another triad in the same chapter, Dewey contrasts his own view of art to what he regards as the extremes of romanticism and classicism. In a typical move, Dewey carefully culls what is best from both extremes, discards the rest, and then treats the salvaged elements as *phases* of something else. What is good in romanticism is that it excites a sense of possibilities. Romanticism turns bad when it goes too far, honoring possibilities beyond their "effective attainment in any experience." The objects of romanticism are not so much expressions as arousals of "a predetermined type of appreciation" (LW 1.282). As for classicism, what is good in it is that it emphasizes objective achievement. Classicism turns bad when it goes too far, treating achievements as if they were eternal. The objects of classicism are not so much expressions as rehearsals of fixed and finished forms.

Dewey turns an impasse to his advantage in the next stage of this typical strategy, by treating the spontaneity and possibility of romanticism and the satisfying achievement of classicism as *phases* in the process of making art, which involves the construction and the appreciation of the art-object. Reminiscent of the flights and perches of birds, to recall James's pregnant metaphor, these phases of aesthetic production are also identified as the phases of all productive inquiry.

Even in the cases of flight and perch, excitement and consummation, possibility and actuality (each pair, obviously, a dyad), Dewey retains his commitment to triads by emphasizing the dynamic qualities of the context in which they occur. Aesthetic production, as other types of inquiry, is never finished. For each perch brings a previous flight to a close at the same time that it anticipates the next flight. Excitement is the termination and disruption of a previous consummation, as well as the condition that generates a subsequent one. And possibility, if it is to be intelligible, must be referred to some prior actuality, even though under the pressure of events possibility also tends to become condensed into something that is newly actual at the same time that it is also generally applicable to further cases.

This, then, is the pattern of production in the arts. As Dewey puts it, "In complete art, appreciation follows the object and moves with it to its completion. . . . Art free from subjection to any 'ism' has movement, creation, as well as order, finality" (LW 1.282). More generally, this is also the pattern of organic behavior (of which inquiry is but a special type) that runs through the writings of the Pragmatists from Peirce to Dewey.

Ethics

In Dewey's essay "Three Independent Factors in Morals" (1930) we get another highly generalized application of Peirce's categories. Generally speaking, ethicists have tended to emphasize one of three broad approaches to the subject at the expense of the other two. Those who have been interested in the choice between competing *goods* have focused on the role of desire and purpose in choice, primarily as it relates to an individual. Those who have been interested in competing *rights* and obligations have tended to focus on the authority of laws, especially as they come into play when the good of one individual or group comes into conflict with the good of another. And those who have been interested in competing *virtues* have tended to focus on how goods and rights function within a broader context, namely approbation in terms of the received tradition of a particular community.

As Dewey notes, however, goods compete with other goods, rights compete with other rights, and virtues compete with other virtues. It is also the case that goods, rights, and virtues usually compete among themselves whenever significant moral problems are encountered.

What may be good from the standpoint of desire may be wrong from the standpoint of legal institutions, and what is right from the standpoint of legal institutions may not be acceptable from the standpoint of a given tradition of civic virtue. Working from the other direction, what is regarded as virtuous by a given community may not be legal, and what is legal often runs counter to the purposes and desires of an individual.

Dewey regarded each of these independent factors in morals as a tool or instrument for an inquiry in which "facts-of-the-case" and "ends-in-view" are reciprocally determined, developed, and tested. He thought such tools can be sharpened or even modified as processes of inquiry themselves require, and that progress in moral behavior and ethical theory alike depends on such improvements.

In making this point Dewey leads his reader beyond the most obvious triad in his essay: the goods of individuals, the rights of one individual or group against another, and the virtues of a community. This flat-footed triad (flat-footed because it comprises independent but intertwined factors) gives way to a dynamic, underlying triad that is present in one form or another in much of his written work: the triad of *conflict*, *deliberation*, and *resolution*. Even though goods, rights, and virtues are important as independent factors in morals, ethical theories that treat one of them as a definitive moral principle are faulty. Such theories lead easily to the conclusions that moral decisions involve choices between good and bad, right and wrong, virtue and vice; that the alternative courses of action are adequately defined from the outset; and that to be good, right, or virtuous just involves an exercise of will.

Dewey argues that such moral theories go wrong at the outset precisely because they ignore the most important phase of moral decision-making. "The essence of the moral situation," he writes, "is an internal and intrinsic conflict; the necessity for judgment and for choice comes from the fact that one has to manage forces with no common denominator" (LW 5.280). Since goods, rights, and virtues have different origins, moral decision-making is dynamic and evolutionary. One of Dewey's dynamic triads is at work in this passage:

internal and intrinsic conflict, a deliberate attempt to manage the various forces, and a judgment made. Dewey's naturalistic ethics thus employs a process that abstracts from an organic, triadic rhythm: conflict, deliberation, and resolution.

Inquiry

The cases I have so far discussed include some highly generalized applications of Peirce's categories, as well as a type of synthesis that might be called broadly Hegelian. But in chapter 7 of *Experience and Nature* (LW 1.198–200) Dewey relates three triads in a manner that has more obvious connections to Peirce's semiotic.

In this chapter Dewey discusses the evolutionary passage from the psycho-physical activities of complex nonhuman animals to the mental activities of human beings. The primary triad consists of feeling or sensibility, sense or meaning, and significance. A second triad consists of three ways in which complex nonhuman animals have "feelings which vary abundantly in quality, corresponding to distinctive directions and phases." Feelings are sensations; they are qualitative, and thus recall Peirce's Firsts. But what are the "directions and phases" that Dewey thinks furnish the basis for categorizing such sensations? The second triad categorizes the activities of the animal in terms of initiation, mediation (struggle to adjust), and completion (either fulfillment or frustration). The activities under discussion are neither random nor ad hoc. As Dewey puts it, they are "bound up in distinctive connections with environmental affairs" (LW 1.198).

So this is an account in which complex nonhuman animals are involved in action that leads to some sort of completion (on analysis, a Third). Looking backward from the completion (the Third) to the action (the Second), we as sign-users can see that there are sensations (Firsts) of three types: those associated with the initiation of the action (a First), those associated with mediation[4] of the action underway (a Second), and those associated with the outcome of the action (a Third).

Dewey's point is that it is not until these three distinct qualities of feeling or sensation are discriminated by sign-users that they become more than mere sensations. When they are discriminated, however, they begin to make sense. "Sense is distinct from feeling [or sensation]," Dewey tells us, because "it has a recognized reference; it is the qualitative characteristic of something, not just a submerged unidentified quality or tone" (LW 1.200).

So there is a third triad at work in this material, namely sensation, sense, and significance as they pertain to the mental life of human beings (as sign-users). It is only as sensations make sense that objectification can take place. What was an undifferentiated sequence of events in which certain organic activities merely took place becomes differentiated as, say, hunger and food. Although non-sign-using animals must eat, for example, food is not for them an object per se. Objectification of the qualities of sensation, in which the organism differentiates this from that, leads directly to the notion that what has been objectified can stand in some way to someone, a situation that recalls Peirce's Thirds.

If sense (a Second) is different from sensation (a First), then, it is also different from signification (a Third). Signification, Dewey tells us, "involves use of a quality as a sign or index of something else, as when the red of a light signifies danger, and the need of bringing a moving locomotive to a stop. The sense of a thing, on the other hand, is an immediate and immanent meaning; it is meaning which is itself felt or directly had. When we are baffled by perplexing conditions, and finally hit upon a clew, and everything falls into place, the whole thing suddenly, as we say, 'makes sense.' In such a situation, the clew has signification in virtue of being an indication, a guide to interpretation. But the meaning of the whole situation as apprehended is sense" (LW.1.200).

Dewey is here demonstrating the "Janus-faced" function of sense. As mediating element in inquiry, a Second, it points in two directions. It points back to what was previously a "submerged unidentified quality or tone," or First, differentiating and sharpening what was only inchoate, making the raw material of sensation into an intermediate stock part, available for further use. But it also points forward in that it can be used as a clue in a process of signification, or the standing of something to someone in some respect (a Third).

In the final chapter of *Experience and Nature*, Dewey wrote that "Conscience in morals, taste in fine arts and conviction in beliefs pass insensibly into critical judgments; the latter pass also into a more and more generalized form of criticism called philosophy" (LW 1.300). In this exquisitely wrought passage we encounter a succession of three elements that captures Dewey's notion of philosophy as cultural criticism.

We all operate on a daily basis with what Dewey terms conscience, taste, and conviction. These are the bits and pieces, the traditions and the opinions, that are gleaned from here and there. Sometimes, perhaps even usually, they are adequate to the tasks they are called upon to perform. When more precision is demanded, however, we move imperceptibly from conscience, taste, and conviction into a space where critical judgments must be made. It is at this level that the methods and materials of science and technology, business, agriculture, law, the arts, and so on come together to create a given culture. The progress of a culture moves forward on the tracks of critical judgments made in these fields.

But this is not the end of the matter. Dewey thought that there was one further level at which criticism takes place, namely the level at which the methods and materials of science and technology, business, agriculture, law, the arts, and so on are related to one another and subjected to further criticism with respect to their ability to generate new meanings, which is to say, to generate more refined values.

Although some may be tempted to read these remarks as an attempt to install philosophy as a kind of "grand narrative," this is not Dewey's intent. He thought of philosophy as a kind of "liaison officer," a kind of go-between, helping the various disciplines and professions within a culture communicate more effectively. And although philosophy does not have a subject matter per se, it does have a unique relationship to inquiry. Logic—the theory of inquiry—is one of its main charges.

To put this in terms of yet another triad, as Dewey did in an early chapter of *Experience and Nature*, "[The] incorporated results of past reflection, welded into the genuine materials of first-hand experience, may become organs of enrichment if they are detected and reflected upon. If they are not detected, they often obfuscate and distort. Clarification and emancipation follow when they are detected and cast out; and one great object of philosophy is to accomplish this task" (LW 1.40).

ELEVEN

CULTIVATING A COMMON FAITH

Dewey's Religion

B orn in 1859 in Burlington, Vermont, John Dewey was already
seventy-five years old in 1934 when he published his lectures on
religious experience under the title *A Common Faith*.[1] Although this
is Dewey's only book-length treatment of the subject, it would be a
mistake to conclude that he had demonstrated little interest in religion up to that point in time. The religious influences on the young
Dewey were in fact quite varied. Dewey's mother was a conservative
evangelical; his pastor at the local Congregational church was a liberal
evangelical; his grandparents were Universalists; and his teachers
were liberal-progressives. During Dewey's first decade of teaching,
from 1884 to 1894 at the University of Michigan, he taught Bible
classes and was an active member of a local church. Of particular note
is the fact that during this period he used Christian terms to defend
his notions of science and democracy.

When Dewey accepted a position at the new University of Chicago
in 1894, however, he did not renew his church membership. Instead,

he refocused his energies in two areas. One was the work of Jane Addams's Hull House, which ministered to tens of thousands of immigrants as they sought to establish homes in the predatory environment of industrial Chicago. He also turned his attention with renewed energy to the problems and prospects of education. He founded an elementary school designed to serve as an experimental laboratory for pedagogy as experimental laboratories served chemistry, physics, and other sciences.

Was this forty-year period between 1894 and 1934, then, one in which Dewey sidestepped matters related to religious experience, or stopped thinking about them altogether? It appears so. Yet if we dig deeper, we find a different picture. During those forty years, the terms "religious" and its cognates were used thousands of times in his works. *The Quest for Certainty* (1929), for example, contains an extended treatment of religious experience.

A careful reader of Dewey's work cannot avoid the conclusion that from beginning to end he devoted painstaking attention to religious themes as he characterized them in *A Common Faith*. Moreover, if we look closely at the arguments that Dewey advances in that little book we will see that they restate some of the core themes of his Pragmatism. These were the very themes that Dewey had been developing and refining, constructing and reconstructing, for more than four decades.

What are these themes, and how does Dewey relate them specifically to religious experience? The first theme is that the actual experiences of human beings, if they are allowed to develop freely on their own account, are capable of generating the aims and methods by which further experience can grow in ordered richness. Now this may seem like a fairly simple point, but there is in fact a great deal packed into it that is of special importance for understanding the connections between religious experience and education.

If our experience of physical and social relations is to develop freely on its own account, if it will follow the thread of truth wherever it leads, then it must be freed from norms, ideals, and other constraints that are commonly used to regulate experience from "outside" of experience. This may seem an uncontroversial point, but powerful forces are arrayed against the free development of experience: ideologies, theologies, party platforms, prejudices, and even putative "oughts" are just a few of them.

More specifically, Dewey's Pragmatism turned the old Platonic formula upside down. Our experience does not have to conform to putative supernatural, ideological, or transcendental ideals or norms; experience itself—our experience in and of our cultural and historical contexts—is capable of generating the norms and ideals that allow it to grow and develop. Dewey's argument in *A Common Faith* is that this idea pertains to religious experiences no less than other ones. Dewey thought it crucial that religious experience be allowed to develop without external constraints.

Michael Eldridge has expressed this matter very clearly. "Ideals, then, are action-guiding possibilities. They arise, guide action, and are revised in an ongoing reconstructive process. Over time, some ideals, such as democracy, gain considerable stability. But as generalized *ends-in-view* they never escape their origins in temporal conditions. They are not outside of experience."[2]

To understand what this means for the matters under discussion, it is important to note that Dewey distinguished religion, *a* religion, and *the religious*. Regarding the first of these, he asked us to note the obvious fact that there is no such thing as religion in general or religion per se. Dewey's language here foreshadows Wittgenstein's a dozen or so years later in his discussion of "family resemblances." Wittgenstein noted the futility of looking for a common property shared by all games. For his part, Dewey told us that try as we might, we will find no one single element, no single universal property, that is common to all religions and at the same time distinguishes them *as* religions. It is now safe to say that the testimony of anthropologists and the research of scholars in the field of comparative religion provide unambiguous confirmation of Dewey's conclusion.

Because one cannot be an adherent to a religion *in general*, one must make a choice among the world's religions to be a member of one: some particular religion must be chosen from all the rest. At this point in his argument, Dewey makes a move that demonstrates the extent to which his treatment of religious experience is integrated into his wider philosophy. Since the choice of a religion depends on many things, including cultural background, personal temperament, and so on, and since the world's religions take us in many different directions, perhaps it would be best, he suggested, if we emancipated the "elements and outlooks that may be called *religious*" from their traditional institutional moorings, that is, from *any particular religion*. What does "religious" denote in this context? He tells us it does *not* denote any specifiable entity, whether institutional or doctrinal. It does *not* denote anything that can exist by itself, or that can be organized into a particular and distinctive form of existence. It *does* denote "attitudes that may be taken toward every object and every proposed end or ideal" (LW 9.8).

Seen from the viewpoint of institutional religions, this might be a very hard and unwelcome conclusion. It might be seen as a move toward a type of empty ecumenism that resorts to the lowest common denominator among religious institutions, or it might even be seen as a call to abolish religious institutions altogether. But clearly Dewey embraced neither position. He thought that truth claims of religious institutions could be tested, and that the effects of their various claims could be adjudicated.

Charlene Haddock Seigfried has offered an account of classical Pragmatism that clearly articulates the background thinking that led to Dewey's position with respect to religious belief. Pragmatism, she has written, is "a philosophy that stresses the relation of theory to praxis and takes the continuity of experience and nature as revealed through the outcome of directed action as the starting point for reflection." Moreover, "Since the reality of objects cannot be known prior to experience, truth claims can be justified only as the fulfillment of conditions that are experimentally determined, i.e., the outcome of inquiry."[3]

Dewey and the other Pragmatists held the view that truth is the result of inquiry into the materials of human experience; it does not spring from any other source. Dreams, insights, revelations, visions, and other such supposed sources of directly communicated truths are for the Pragmatists not so much final truths, but starting places for determining what is true. They are the raw materials that must be tested in the same way that a geologist would test a sample of ore to determine whether it contains a rare mineral. Despite their appearances, they do not carry their truth on their faces. Their truth must be established experimentally and publically.

Responding to Bertrand Russell in the 1940s, Dewey offered a technical definition of truth that precisely captures what he meant. He defined truth as "warranted assertibility" (LW 14.168–69). According to Dewey's Pragmatist view of truth, the *warrant* of a true judgment points backward to propositions affirmed and inferential rules formulated and deployed. That is, the warrant points backward to evidence already marshaled and constructive work already done.

The *assertibility* of a true judgment points to the future: true judgments point forward in a general way to possible applications. We can, as we say, *bank* on a true judgment. It affords a reliable basis for things we need to do. True judgments point back to the past and forward to the future, then, but they also do their work in the present. They function as stable and reliable platforms for our actions. Putting the same point somewhat differently, William James wrote that truth is not otiose, but something that *happens* to an idea as it is constructed and reconstructed within human cognition.

As part my discussion of global citizenship in chapter 2, I pointed out that the Pragmatic method is more or less the same as what has been loosely termed "the scientific method" or "the experimental method." I also pointed out that what we generally refer to as "the scientific method" is in reality a family of methods that exhibit repeatability, falsifiability, transparency, and objectivity. Unlike other methods, including those sometimes used by religious institutions, experimental methods produce results that are subject to public review and able to meet the demands of concrete, existential affairs.

This set of methods does not depend on correct content for its authority. Its claim instead comes from the fact that it is self-correcting. Ideas and hypotheses are treated not as truths to be defended at all costs, but as tools that may themselves be altered as they are applied to the materials of concrete experience. It is for this reason that the Pragmatic method rejects "absolute" or "timeless" truths.

The point Dewey wanted to make in all this is that the Pragmatic notion of truth-as-method can embrace a wide variety of viewpoints and activities, including religious outlooks and practices. But the Pragmatist would not just accept any outlook or practice that claims to be religious. Religious beliefs have consequences, so they can be tested.

In my discussion of global citizenship, I recalled the metaphor of the Pragmatic method as a hotel corridor. A number of rooms would open onto it, and inside those rooms there would be a wide variety of persons and activities. Applied to the current discussion, religious people as well as nonbelievers would be there, monotheists and polytheists, and physicists as well as philosophers. There would be many differences of culture, interest, and temperament among the people in the rooms at the Pragmatic hotel. There would be Buddhists, Roman Catholics, Baptists, Muslims, Confucians, and even atheists. But despite their other differences, all of these people would have one important thing in common. Each one of them would have passed through the corridor of the Pragmatic method to get to his or her room.

But there are some people who would not have a room in the Pragmatic hotel. Even though you would find religious people and secularists in the hotel, for example, you would *not* find humanists and religious fundamentalists there.

The reason for this lies in the nature of the Pragmatic method itself. The reason that you would not find fundamentalists there is that the primary method of fundamentalism is not experimental. It is the method of authority. Christian, Muslim, and other forms of fundamentalism, for example, rest on appeals to direct divine revelation and textual literalism in ways that close down inquiry rather than opening it up for participation by all concerned. And if the method of authority fails to achieve their goals, what then? In the absence of experimentalism, religious and other types of fundamentalists must fall back on the application of psychological, physical, or political power rather than the application of intelligence.

So the idea behind the Pragmatic method is that it serves as an alternative to nonscientific methods such as appeals to tradition and authority. In judging religious belief, Pragmatists hold the view that the meaning of an idea or experience is the difference it will make for your and my future experience.

The first of the two themes of Dewey's Pragmatism that I singled out as having a major impact on his treatment of religious experience and education, then, is that experience must be allowed to develop on its own terms without being trumped by intransigent institutional doctrines. Ideals, as generalized ends-in-view, arise from experience, and "they never escape their origins in temporal conditions. They are not outside of experience."[4]

The second theme is truth is a matter of having been tested in the laboratory of experience. Ideals—even those that accompany or stem from religious experiences—must put to objective tests in order to determine the extent to which they are valuable.

If we take these two themes together, then we get the following picture. He was in no way suggesting that religious institutions are unimportant or should be abolished. Quite the contrary. His writings on social and political philosophy emphasize the importance of religious institutions as "publics," groups of individuals with common interests and purposes that relate to and interact with other publics.

So Dewey was in no way attacking the existence of religious institutions. By distinguishing *a* religion from *the religious*, meaning religious experience, he was instead saying more or less what William James had said in his essay "The Will to Believe": the meanings of religious institutions, and any other institution, are in the work they do, in the effects they have on people, not in criteria that exist prior to or outside of experience. The meanings of religious institutions do not lie in their history, dogma, or any other form of authority. The upshot of this is that for Dewey's version of evolutionary naturalism, religious institutions have no particular privilege just because they claim to have some link to the supernatural. The burden of the history of the effects of the Enlightenment—or what has been called modernity—is that religious institutions will either stand or fail on the basis of what they do to effect a better adjustment of human beings to their environing conditions. Dewey is clear on this point: the only alternative to coming to terms with modernity that is available to religious institutions is to lapse into fundamentalism or other forms of debilitating sectarianism.

In terms of education, including religious education, Dewey's program means educating the whole person, fostering the virtues of love and faith, encouraging the pursuit of learning, and respecting the dignity and worth of every person. It demands educators who are ready to devote their lives to the development of a humanistic culture in which all of humankind can participate.

Once the full impact of this idea is recognized, then it is easy to see why James called Pragmatism "a new name for some old ways of thinking." He was alluding to a famous saying in the Christian Bible. In the parable of the fig tree related in Matthew 7:16–20, Jesus says: "By their fruits you shall know them." He does not say, "By their *roots* you shall know them." Nor does he say, "You shall know them only when you have compared them to a transcendent norm or hallowed tradition." In this passage Jesus makes a Pragmatic point: although the roots of the tree are planted firmly in the soil of nature (and not up in the heavens), the test of its value lies in what it produces. Jesus says that it will be necessary to take a bite of a fig if we are determine whether the fruit of the tree is valuable.

This brings us back to a point I made earlier about Dewey's use of the term "religious." Since the term is an adjective, it does not denote "anything that can exist by itself or than can be organized into a particular and distinctive form of existence. It denotes attitudes that may be taken toward every object and every proposed end or ideal" (LW 9.8).

This is tantamount to saying that those who think that there is a definite type of experience that is termed "religious" and that is marked off from experiences that are aesthetic, scientific, moral, and political—from experiences that involve companionship and friendship—for example, are in effect limiting and demeaning the notion of religious experience. They are selling religious experience short.

On the contrary, Dewey thinks that "the religious" is a *quality* of experience that may belong to all these types of experience. He thus wants to demonstrate how *expansive* the notion of the religious is, and at the same time how it is often curtailed and stunted by too close an association with this or that religious institution.

The religious is thus not a type of experience that can exist by itself. It is instead a quality that can leaven many types of experiences, making them richer and more satisfying.

Dewey thus reminds us of something both obvious and overlooked. The religious quality of experience is the lifeblood of religious institutions. The religious, as the quality of many types of experience, provides the energy that can maintain and reform religious institutions, that can let them grow and flourish even as environing conditions change. His implicit argument is that religious institutions depend for their vitality on the quality of the religious in experience, not the other way around. If we think of this or that religious institution as the custodian of the religious quality of our experiences, therefore, then we have gotten the cart before the horse. More specifically, the religious quality in experience is a better adjustment to life and its conditions, not the manner and cause of an adjustment. The *fruits*, not the *roots*, provide evidence of the religious quality in experience.

When we experience this religious quality or attitude, then we do not merely adjust to changed circumstances, we have a profound and important awakening—a reorientation of the whole person. Dewey makes this point clearly in *A Common Faith* in his discussion of what he calls the two poles of human experience.

The first is the pole of our experience that is concerned with the alteration or adaptation of relatively external circumstances. The other is the pole that is primarily concerned with accommodation to such circumstances. It involves the changes we make in ourselves in response to environmental conditions that we cannot change, or cannot easily change. Beyond these ordinary modes of adjustment is the life-changing experience that exhibits a religious quality.

In the first few pages of *A Common Faith* Dewey expressed this matter at length:

> While the words "accommodation," "adaptation," and "adjust-ment" are frequently employed as synonyms, attitudes exist that are so different that for the sake of clear thought they should be discriminated. There are conditions we meet that cannot be changed. If they are particular and limited, we modify our own particular attitudes in accordance with them. Thus we accommo-date ourselves to changes in weather, to alterations in income when we have no other recourse. When the external conditions are lasting we become inured, habituated. . . . The two main traits of this attitude, which I should like to call accommodation, are that it affects *particular* modes of conduct, not the entire self, and that the process is mainly *passive*. It may, however, become gen-eral and then it becomes fatalistic resignation or submission. There are other attitudes toward the environment that are also particular but that are more active. . . . Instead of accommodating ourselves to conditions, we modify conditions so that they will be accommodated to our wants and purposes. This process may be called adaptation.
>
> Now both of these processes are often called by the more gen-eral name of adjustment. But there are also changes in ourselves in relation to the world in which we live that are much more in-clusive and deep seated. They relate not to this and that want in relation to this and that condition of our surroundings, but per-tain to our being in its entirety. Because of their scope, this modi-fication of ourselves is enduring. . . . It is a change *of* will conceived as the organic plenitude of our being, rather than any special change *in* will. (LW 9.12–13)

Of course there are elements of accommodation and adaptation in most of what we do on a daily basis. Dewey calls our attention beyond them to cases of adjustment that are more profound, that result in a "generic and enduring change of attitude" (LW 9.13). This is a type of adjustment that does not simply *supervene* upon life, but *intervenes* within it, touching its every aspect, interpenetrat-ing all of its elements.

The aims and ideals that move us are generated through imagination. But they are not made out of imaginary stuff. They are made out of the hard stuff of the world of physical and social experience. . . . The new vision does not arise out of nothing, but emerges through seeing, in terms of possibilities, that is, of imagination, old things in new relations serving a new end which the new end aids in creating. . . . There are forces in nature and society that generate and support the ideals. They are further unified by the action that gives them coherence and solidity. (LW 9.33–34)

Despite all I have so far said, it might be asked how we are able to test these ideas and ideals in the absence of higher norms that are absolute or transcendent. In order to answer this question, I now turn to a matter that has been just barely below the surface of what I have said up to this point. I now turn more explicitly to the relevance of my discussion to the philosophy of education.

The implications for education of Dewey's Pragmatic account of religious experience are far-reaching and profound. He works out those implications in considerable detail in his 1929 essay "The Sources of a Science of Education." At first glance his statement appears so disarmingly simple that it is easy to miss his point. He writes that "education is itself a process of discovering what values are worth while and are to be pursued as objectives. To see what is going on and to observe the results of what goes on so as to see their further consequences in the process of growth, and so on indefinitely, is the only way in which the value of what takes place can be judged. To look to some outside source to provide aims is to fail to know what education is as an ongoing process" (LW 5.38).

Three aspects of this type of educational program are pertinent here. First, education must take into account the fact of change. It is a simple historical fact that when religious dogma and the results of scientific experimentation have come into conflict, religious dogma has suffered defeat and loss of face. The case of Galileo provides an example from the 17th century, and so-called "scientific creationism" and "intelligent design" provide examples from our own century (even though the practitioners of such faulty attempts at scientific rigor don't seem to know or care just how ridiculous their claims sound to practitioners of real science.)

But conflicts between science and religion need not occur. If education is in fact a process of "discovering what values are worth while and are to be pursued as objectives," then it will be prized as a body of improving methods and not as a body of unchanging facts. Moreover, insofar as the religious quality of experience that I have been discussing becomes a part of the educational experience, then education will be touched with the sort of intelligence and idealism that looks forward to change with eager anticipation for the possibilities that it holds. It will not fear what may come, because it is open to opportunities for growth and development.

There is no reason why religious institutions cannot be in the forefront of such efforts to foster such progressive educational programs. Dewey thought that this in fact occurs when it is recognized, as he put it, that "the values prized in those religions that have ideal elements are idealizations of things characteristic of natural association, which have been projected into the supernatural realm for safe-keeping and sanction" (LW 9.48). Dewey wanted to push education, including religious education, in the direction of fostering and improving our knowledge of things in their fullness, and opening up new vistas of human communication. He saw in education the primary means for the growth of individuals and communities. What Dewey meant in this regard for religious education in particular is the moral faith that ideals or ends-in-view can be realized must trump the intellectual faith that posits this particular existence or that particular existence.

The second point is that this text does not say, and in fact denies, that existing social conditions or traditions are to be the sources of the discovery of educational values. The same is true of educators themselves. Social conditions and traditions, far from providing the ultimate norms for valuation, are among the things that education is called upon to evaluate. And even the ideas and ideals of the educator himself or herself, as they are expressed in the form of syllabi, lesson plans, or directives, must be evaluated in terms of the broader educational processes that Dewey here characterizes.

Allowing existing social conditions to dictate educational practice results in precisely the type of education against which Dewey argued forcefully during his decade at the University of Chicago, from, 1894 to 1904, and then, afterward, during his years at Columbia University. He continually reminded his readers that rote rehearsal of received tradition, without opportunities to innovate through creative hypothesis-formation and testing, fails to be educative: it is little more than indoctrination and initiation into the traditions of existing norms.

And third, this passage implies that neither the methods nor the contents of the technosciences are *directly* applicable to education in the absence of concrete, experienced problems. They should not dictate educational practice any more than do existing social conditions or traditions. In other words, the methods and contents of the sciences are only *instrumental* to education, and not its *equivalent.* Allegedly scientific tests, such as those that are administered to assess personality or intelligence, are not where education begins, even though they may be useful educational tools on an individual basis. Nor does education begin with instructions about how to take standardized tests (though it does sometimes seem to end there).

Dewey also addressed these matters in a 1922 essay, "Mediocrity and Individuality." He began by assuring his readers that he had nothing against mental testing provided that such tests were administered and applied in a proper manner. The goal of constructing tests, he wrote, "is a method of discrimination, of analysis of human beings, of diagnosis of persons, which is intrinsic and absolute, not comparative and common. . . . The pity is that a scheme for testing tests which are ultimately to be employed in diagnosing individuality has been treated as if it already provided means of testing individuals" (MW 13.292).

Does *the religious*, then, have a place in education? Of course it does. In all of this, Dewey argued that a religious perspective can and should enter into education in the form of a moral faith. What is this moral faith? It is a type of faith that involves a "natural piety" that "is not of necessity either a fatalistic acquiescence in natural happenings or a romantic idealization of the world. It may rest upon a just sense of nature as the whole of which we are parts, while it also recognizes that we are parts that are marked by intelligence and purpose, having the capacity to strive by their aid to bring conditions into greater consonance with what is humanly desirable. Such piety is an inherent constituent of a just perspective in life" (LW 9.18).

This religious perspective can and should also enter into education as promoting understanding and knowledge. It can and should enter into education as a "faith in the continued disclosing of truth through directed cooperative human endeavor [that] is more religious in quality than is any faith in a completed revelation" (LW 9.18).

Far from proposing *a religion*, Dewey offers us a "common faith" that is built upon *the religious* as a quality of experience. It is a faith that must be at the core of educational practice if it is to be successful. And it is a faith that transcends religious organizations and institutions in ways that can serve to bring them together in common purpose, even while they continue to honor what is good in their historical and cultural differences.

It is now time to pull these diverse strands together. On reflection, I think that we would have to agree with Dewey's claim that there is no such thing as religion in general, that is, that there is nothing that all religions qua religions have in common. But given the wide variety of the world's religions, and given differences in cultural background and temperament, how is it possible to choose *a* religion from among them? What sorts of criteria are available? Rejecting claims that ideals must be grounded in absolutes, justified in terms of objects and events that transcend experience, or warranted by history or tradition, Dewey invites us to exhibit a particular type of moral faith. This moral faith, this common faith, would be one that takes experience seriously as a source of values, that tests values and ideals experimentally, and that honors the religious qualities of experiences of many types, including those that are aesthetic, scientific, and educational. It is this religious attitude, this common faith, that Dewey thinks can drive, inform, and refresh religious institutions, insuring their continuing relevance in a changing world.

The norms by which our values and ideals are tested are themselves generated and tested through processes that are best described as education. And this is because it is education that broadens our cultural and historical understanding, allowing us to enter into the lives of individuals and communities of the past, in other parts of the world, in novels and plays, and elsewhere. It is only by means of education that the growth of individuals and communities can be advanced. Moreover, a key component in education is the religious perspective that enters into experience whenever and where ever education functions as it can and should.

TWELVE

BEYOND THE EPISTEMOLOGY INDUSTRY

Dewey's Theory of Inquiry

J ohn Dewey did not develop a theory of knowledge in the usual
sense of "epistemology," but he did have a well-developed theory
of inquiry.[1] He was in fact highly critical of what he called "the epistemology industry" because of its tendency to treat knowledge as something separated from the contexts in which actual inquiry takes place.

He thought that when epistemologists start out by positing cases
of "certain" knowledge, or "justified true belief," as they sometimes
do, and then attempt to find out *how* it is justified, they tend to get
matters backwards. It is more productive, he suggested, to examine
how actual cases of inquiry are related to one another and how they
increase our stock of guides for future action. In other words, analysis
should be a tool for the production of satisfactory outcomes, not an
end in itself. Epistemology as usually practiced was in Dewey's view a
conflicted mixture of proven and relevant logical tools, on the one
hand, and irrelevant psychological and metaphysical preconceptions,
on the other. If such preconceptions could be jettisoned, he thought,

then epistemology would be freed to do its real work as a theory of inquiry. The terms "epistemology" and "logic" would then become synonymous.

Although he did in fact use the term "knowledge" quite frequently, Dewey thought that it had so many infelicitous connotations that it needed to be replaced. He tried to do this in two ways. First, for the reasons I just indicated, he often used the gerund "knowing" in place of the substantive term "knowledge" in order to emphasize the fact that knowing is always a part of a larger process of inquiry.

But even this did not entirely convey what he had in mind, so he invented the phrase "warranted assertibility." The two parts of this somewhat cumbersome but descriptive phrase point in different directions. "Warranted" points backward in time toward something that has been accomplished. What is warranted is the result of reflection that has been effective in the sense that some specific doubt or difficulty has been resolved. "Assertibility" points forward in time toward something yet to be done. What is assertible is something general, and therefore something potentially applicable to future cases that are relevantly similar to the one by means of which it was produced. Unlike the alleged knowledge (or justified true belief) studied by most epistemologists, however, warranted assertibility is claimed to be neither certain nor permanent. The best it can offer is a measure of stability in an otherwise precarious world.

Inquiry as Organic Behavior

The work of Charles Darwin exerted a profound influence on Dewey's thought from the time he was an undergraduate during the 1870s until his death in 1952. In 1909, on the occasion of the fiftieth anniversary of *The Origin of Species*, Dewey wrote an essay in which he characterized his own work as doing for philosophy what Darwin had done for biology. Just as Darwin had proved the notion of fixed biological species untenable, Dewey would seek to demonstrate that there are no fixed or certain truths. Contrary to the claims of some of his critics, however, this project was motivated by neither skepticism nor nihilism. It was based on a candid recognition of the observable fact that living beings must constantly adapt to changing environmental circumstances. Even though they require overlapping and interpenetrating patterns of stability for their continued existence, their lives are at bottom and in the long run highly precarious.

Dewey identified inquiry as the primary means by which reflective organisms seek to achieve stability through adaptation. It is by means of inquiry that humans are able to exert control over their own habit formation, thereby creating new instruments. In the short run, these instruments enable us to improve conditions that we deem unsatisfactory. In the long run, they enable us to influence the course of our own evolution.

Because inquiry is an organic activity, and because organisms encounter constraints as well as facilities, assertions must continually be tested and new warrants must continually be issued. Successful living requires an active and ongoing reconstruction of experienced situations. Dewey's notion of warranted assertibility, therefore, unlike the concept of knowledge as it has functioned in systems such as those of Plato, Descartes, and many contemporary philosophers, is not a matter of a spectator getting a better view of a fixed state of affairs that is already "out there" (or even "in there").

Dewey constantly reminded his readers that if contemporary science has taught us anything, it is that there is nothing "out there," in any permanent sense of "out there," of which we can get a better view. At the level of immediate or unreflective experience, what is "out there" is always changing. And at the level of reflective or organized experience, what we count as being "out there" at any given time is a result of the activity of human intelligence as it takes into account the materials it finds in immediate experience and the tools currently at its disposal. The aim of inquiry is therefore to reconstruct both found materials and available tools in ways that render them more richly meaningful.

Inquiry as Instrumental

Dewey rejected versions of naive realism which claim that things already are as they will eventually be for us, even prior to our taking them into account. He also rejected the version of scientific realism just described, which claims that there is a fixed reality that is simply discovered by scientists and to which scientific "laws" therefore correspond. As a result, some of his earlier critics read him as advancing one or another variety of idealism, such as the view that the laws of science—or logic—are wholly a matter of coherence within a human or divine mind.

More recently, some of Dewey's interpreters have argued that he held a type of relativism similar to that of some of the French postmodernists, according to which human beings as language-users are caught in an infinite web of metaphors or tropes, none of which are any more privileged or warranted than any other. Richard Rorty, for example, has claimed Dewey's authority in advancing the view that there is no real distinction between the sciences and the arts, but that both are just types of literature. Dewey regarded both of these views—scientific realism and extreme relativism—as flawed, and he vigorously opposed them.

His name for his own view was "Instrumentalism." In 1903 he and his students and colleagues at the University of Chicago published a collection called *Studies in Logical Theory* which announced Instrumentalism as a school of thought and attempted to work out its implications.

Seen in the context of his Instrumentalism, warranted assertibility results from the experimental manipulation of tools, materials, and conditions as they are experienced. And the whole point of experimentation is to see whether we can make things better by finding out how experienced situations (which of course include ourselves as components) can be reconstructed.

Contrary to the position advanced by much of traditional philosophy, Dewey was convinced that the tools that we use in inquiry are not given to us a priori. They are instead instruments that have been developed in the course of inquiry that has proven successful. Inquiry is thus a reflective activity in which existing tools and materials (both of which may be either tangible or conceptual) are brought together in novel and creative arrangements in order to produce something new. The by-products of this process often include improved tools and materials which can then be applied to the next occasion on which inquiry is required.

To miss this point is to misunderstand the radical nature of Dewey's theory of inquiry. His view was that logical forms *accrue* to inquiry as a result of the subject matter it takes up and the conclusions it finds warranted. He put this matter very precisely in 1938, in *Logic: The Theory of Inquiry*: "logical forms accrue to subject-matter in virtue of subjection of the latter in inquiry to the conditions determined by its end—institution of a warranted conclusion" (LW 12.370).

One of the things that makes this claim so controversial is that traditional logic had claimed just the opposite—that logical forms are *imposed* upon the subject matter of inquiry. Dewey thus turned traditional logic on its head. This is an extremely important point, so I shall return to it later in the chapter.

The Role of the A Priori in Inquiry

Especially since Kant, the concept of the a priori has played an important role in philosophical discourse. It is therefore important to understand the two senses in which Dewey employed the term. What he called the "external" a priori corresponds to the way the term was used by Kant and subsequently in much of Anglo-American analytic logic and epistemology. What is a priori in this sense is strictly speaking prior to *any* experience. In Kant, for example, what is a priori provides the very conditions under which any experience is possible. Kant thus treats space and time as a priori forms that must be imposed on what is perceived in order for there to be any experience at all. Dewey denied that there is any such thing as an a priori in this sense. In his view, for example, space and time are not forms that are brought *to* experience, but conceptions that are constructed *on the basis* of experience.

Dewey did allow, however, the "operational" a priori. In inquiry, he observed, we develop habits of action that are known as "laws of inference." Because these are habits, rather than specific actions, they are general. Like other sorts of habits, they have been adopted (and they continue to be adapted) over time because they have been found to produce successful consequences. Dewey used the term "successful" in its precise Instrumental or Pragmatic sense. The laws of inference, he wrote, are successful when they are "operative in a manner that tends in the long run, or in continuity of inquiry, to yield results that are either confirmed in further inquiry or that are corrected by use of the same procedures" (LW 12.21).

He provided several excellent examples of what he meant by this. Take a logical postulate, he suggested, such as the "law" of the excluded middle (also called the "*tertium non datur*," which states that a thing is either A or not A, say, either a liquid or a non-liquid but not some third thing). This is a logical "law" in the sense that if we are going to reason at all, then we must take it (as well as other logical laws) into account. But there is nothing a priori in the external, or Kantian sense, about these laws. Dewey called such "laws" stipulations, or "formulations of formal conditions . . . to be satisfied." As such, he said, they are "valid as directive principles, as regulative limiting ideals of inquiry" (LW 12.345). Dewey called our attention to the obvious fact, for example, that at a certain temperature near the freezing point, water is neither precisely a liquid nor precisely a non-liquid.

Dewey argued that these "laws" are stipulations in much the same sense that the laws of contracts are stipulations that regulate business arrangements. If we are going to do business at all, then we must take into account as "directive principles" certain forms that have *proven* to be successful, that is, that have been *proven* to regulate a wide range of particular transactions in ways that keep the business community functioning. And if we are going to engage in inquiry at all, then we must take into account, again as "directive principles," certain logical forms that have been *proven* to be successful in precisely the same sense.

But these "laws" are not a priori in the sense that they are applicable regardless of subject matter. They accrue to inquiry *in virtue of* its subject matter. They arise out of subject matter, and they are returned to subject matter as tools for testing our conceptions of it: as such, they are conditions to be satisfied. In his treatment of the law of the excluded middle, for example, Dewey pointed out that the "fact that disjunctions which were at one time taken to be both exhaustive and necessary have later been found to be incomplete (and sometimes even totally irrelevant) should long ago have been a warning that the principle of excluded middle sets forth a logical condition *to be* satisfied in the course of continuity of inquiry. It formulates the ultimate *goal* of inquiry in complete satisfaction of logical conditions. To determine subject-matters so that no alternative is possible is the most difficult task of inquiry" (LW 12.344–45).

What is operationally a priori, then (and this is the only kind of a priori that Dewey admitted), is what has been brought to current inquiry as a byproduct of prior inquiry. There is nothing that is a priori in the Kantian sense. There is no a priori that is absolutely prior or external to experience.[2]

Common Sense and Science

Dewey thought that the splits within experience posited by most philosophers, especially since Descartes, were not only unwarranted but debilitating. He thought that the split between scientific inquiry and common sense which resulted from these philosophers' penchant for skepticism was no exception. Dewey characterized common sense as the part of experience in which humans make required behavioral adjustments as a response to "direct" involvement with the circumstances of their environing conditions. In other words, common sense involves ordinary use and enjoyment, and it is concerned with what is *practical*.

Dewey rejected the common notion that there are metaphysical or ontological differences between common sense and science. He did think, however, that there was a *logical* difference between these two types of inquiry: they use different logical *forms*. Science grows out of common sense as its tools of inquiry become more refined. But science is not final in the sense of being the end or point of inquiry. It does not tell us how the world really is in any final sense, and it is not the paradigm for all other forms of inquiry. It is not, to use Jean-François Lyotard's phrase, a "grand narrative." Scientific inquiry is in Dewey's view inquiry *for*. It is a theoretical enterprise that must ultimately return to the world of use and enjoyment in order to check its results.

Historically, one of the great philosophical errors has been the treatment of objects produced by abstraction from common sense experience as if they were prior to and independent of the experience from which they were abstracted. They are then said to exist in a realm that is separate and superior to common sense. Having then created this fracture within experience, some philosophers have spent inordinate amounts of time attempting to show how the two realms might be related.

Dewey thought this utter nonsense, and referred to it as "the philosopher's fallacy." His suggestion was that once it is recognized that there is a continuity between common sense and science, the purported fracture between these areas of inquiry will be recognized for what it is—nothing more than a difference of logical form. Metaphysical or ontological fractures will never open up in the first place.

Logical Objects

In 1916 Dewey gave a talk to the philosophy club at Columbia University in which he shed a good deal of light on these matters. The subject of his remarks was what he called "logical objects" or "logical entities." These were said to include such items as "between," "if," numbers, and essences. Historically, Dewey observed, these entities have been treated as 1) physical properties of objects, 2) mental or

psychical properties, or 3) some sort of "tertium quid" which is neither physical nor mental but "metaphysical."

Dewey rejected all three of these views. He argued instead that logical objects are just that—logical. By this he meant that they are the
by-products of inference. They are thus "things (or traits of things)
which are found when inference is found and which are only found
then" (MW 10.90).

The key to understanding Dewey's radical innovation on these
matters lies in his argument that what is logical must be separated
from what is purely mental or psychical. Of course Dewey did not
wish to deny that inquiry involves mental processes, or that there are
psychological factors that are present in inquiry. His point was rather
to insist that inquiry is always a behavioral response of a reflective
organism to its environing conditions. As such, he wrote, it belongs
to "action, or behavior, which takes place in the world, not just
within the mind or within consciousness" (MW 10.90). This means
that whatever mental processes may accompany a particular inquiry,
it is its behavioral results, and not some accompanying psychic or
mental process, that identifies it as inquiry. Inquiry, just as much as
walking or eating, is what Dewey termed an "outdoor fact."

Dewey's treatment of this subject was typical of his broader philosophical outlook. He undermined the customary ontological approach to the problem of logical objects (which relied on sorting
them into pre-existing categories) and then he argued that they
should be treated in functional terms. He thus identified inquiry as
an art, and its products and by-products (including logical connec-
tives such as "and," "or," and numbers) as manufactured articles.
Such artifacts, he reminded us, are manufactured for some purpose;
or at least they are connected to some process. To treat them as having existence apart from such purposes and processes is to fall back
into the older practice of giving them a spurious ontological status.

Geometrical points, temporal instants, and even logical classes
provide excellent examples of what Dewey had in mind. They refer to
a kind of reality that is neither physical, psychical, nor metaphysical.

The reality to which they do refer is no more or less than the behavioral reality of controlled inquiry. To treat them as something apart from inquiry, as has traditionally been the case, would be to make the same type of mistake that a biologist would commit if he or she were to infer from the conditions of a fish in water to those of a fish out of water (MW 10.95).

Abstraction

That Dewey used this particular figure of speech as a part of his discussion of abstract objects was perhaps occasioned by his reading of William James. James had observed that anyone who looks up through the side of an aquarium can see an object across the room, such as a candle, reflected from the bottom of the water's surface back down into the water. The water, he suggested, is like the world of sensible facts. And the air above it is like the world of abstract ideas.

> Both worlds are real, of course, and interact; but they interact only at their boundary, and the *locus* of everything that lives, and happens to us, so far as full experience goes, is the water. We are like fishes swimming in the sea of sense, bounded above by the superior element, but unable to breathe it pure or penetrate it. We get our oxygen from it, however, we touch it incessantly, now in this part, now in that, and every time we touch it, we are reflected back into the water with our course re-determined and re-energized. The abstract ideas of which the air consists are indispensable for life, but irrespirable by themselves, as it were, and only active in their re-directing function. All similes are halting, but this one rather takes my fancy. It shows how something, not sufficient for life in itself, may nevertheless be an effective determinant of life elsewhere.[3]

In his own treatment of abstraction, Dewey elaborates on James's simile. First, there is a living relation of transaction between the abstract and the concrete. Just as the fish draw their oxygen from the air above their everyday environment, human experience draws nourishment from abstract entities and relations. When this living relation is ignored, abstraction tends to become something negative and even the subject of parody. It becomes something arbitrary and aloof from everyday experience.

Second, the living relation between abstract and concrete is maintained by means of experimentation. Abstraction is not an end in itself, but instead a tool for developing new meanings that can be brought back down into the realm of concrete, existential experience. Inquiry always involves abstraction, since it always involves hypotheses that articulate alternative courses of action. It also relies upon relations (and relations of relations), which are the by-products of previous inquiries. Ultimately, however, inquiry is undertaken for the sake of effecting change in a concrete, existential world; it is there and only there that abstractions are determined to have succeeded or failed, that is, to have been useful or not.

Third, and contrary to the long tradition of Western philosophy, abstractions do not belong to a metaphysical or ontological order that is higher or more noble than that of concrete experience. James uses the term "superior" in his analogy to designate spatial location, not metaphysical preeminence, and Dewey's account makes it clear that abstract and concrete are coequal phases or moments within inquiry. In his account of the history of abstraction, Dewey reminds us that Socrates rendered a great service to his fellow Athenians by urging them to avoid excessive reliance on the concrete, that is, to avoid reasoning by simple enumeration of examples. Socrates's attempts to get his fellow Athenians to engage in hypothetical reasoning constituted a great step forward in the history of inquiry. But Plato made the opposite mistake: when he began to treat abstractions as metaphysical entities, he set an unfortunate course for 2,500 years of Western philosophy.

One of the reasons why philosophers since Plato have tended to think of abstractions as higher and more perfect than concrete experience is that they are said to afford a level of "certainty" that ordinary experience does not. The mathematical proposition "$2+3=5$" has, for example, been treated as a timeless truth, metaphysically superior because applicable everywhere and everywhen. But Dewey saw matters differently. The reason why mathematical propositions are often taken as timeless truths is that *qua* mathematical, [they] are free from the conditions that require any limited interpretation. They have no meaning or interpretation save that which is formally imposed by the need of satisfying the condition of transformability within the system, with no extra-systemic reference whatever. In the sense which "meaning" bears in any conception having even indirect existential reference, the terms have no meaning—a fact which accounts, probably, for the view that mathematical subject-matter is simply a string of arbitrary marks. But in the wider logical sense, they have a meaning constituted exclusively and wholly by their relations to one another as determined by satisfaction of the condition of transformability. (LW 12.395–96)

In other words, mathematical propositions may be meaningful in either of two senses. In terms of their relation to other elements of a formal system, they are meaningful in virtue of satisfying certain conditions of transformability within a system. It is in this sense that they *appear* to be true everywhere and everywhen. Their place in the formal system is secure, and results of transformation within the system that depend on them are uniform and dependable within that limited scope. In this sense, mathematical propositions refer to *no* existential individuals.

In a second sense, however, the sense in which mathematical propositions refer to *some* existential individual or another, they are not dependably applicable. Experimental science, as well as everyday experience, is replete with cases in which abstract mathematical propositions are too "thin" to apply to experience in all its robustness. It is important to note that Dewey does not think that mathematical propositions, or any other type of propositions, for that matter, are true or false. I shall discuss this matter in more detail later, in the section on propositions.

Matter and Form in Inquiry

It is now time to return to the matter of the relation of form and matter within inquiry. According to his critics, one of the scandals of Dewey's *Logic: The Theory of Inquiry* was its paucity of symbols. How, they asked, in a time when logic was increasingly symbolic, could they be expected to take seriously a book about logic that contained so few symbols?

Dewey addressed this question in the introduction to his book. Many of the problems of logic, he argued, have been the result of the separation of form and matter. This has in turn been the result of a rush to symbolize in the absence of a "general theory of language in which form and matter are not separated" (LW 12.4).

Dewey thought that logical forms are *disclosed* as inquiry is undertaken, but even more importantly, he thought that they *originate* as the by-products of inquiry. In order to understand this point it is necessary to differentiate inquiry, which Dewey sometimes calls "primary" inquiry, from logic, which he terms the "theory" of inquiry. "Primary inquiry," he writes, "is itself *causa essendi* of the forms which inquiry into inquiry [or logic] discloses" (LW 12.12). It is the function of (primary) inquiry to arrange its subject matter into settled forms. It is the function of inquiry into inquiry (logic) to take account of those forms, disclosing their relations to other forms and arranging them in ways that facilitate their use in further inquiries. When these things (settled forms) are used in further inquiries, they become the *means* to further results. But viewed retrospectively, they become *objects*. Dewey thus makes a radical move: he functionalizes objects by characterizing them in terms of their roles in continuing inquiry. "Objects," he writes, "are the *objectives* of inquiry" (LW 12.122).

Once established, objects (or settled forms) tend to persist long after their originating subject matter has been altered. Old forms are imposed on new subject matter. In some cases this works well enough, but in other cases the old forms are not really relevant to the new subject matter. Their use results in error and confusion. Dewey thought that this is precisely what had happened in the case of the Aristotelian syllogism. "The perpetuation of the forms of the Aristotelian tradition," he argued, "with elimination of the subject-matter of which they were the forms, also ruled out inquiry (which is effective reflection) from the proper scope of logic. The syllogism in the original logic was in no way a form of inferring or reasoning. It was immediate apprehension or vision of the relations of inclusion and exclusion that belong to real wholes in Nature" (LW 12.93).

Dewey freely admitted that logic has to do with formal relationships, and he accepted the widely held notion that this is what sets logic off from other sciences. But he also noted that logicians have tended to disagree about what this means. Their debates have been particularly sharp regarding the question of how logical form is related to subject matter. Logical formalists, for example, tend to hold that there is no relation between logical form and subject matter. But they disagree among themselves about how this tenet is to be interpreted. Some of them argue, for example, that forms constitute a separate realm of metaphysical possibilities (possible worlds). Others, exhibiting a less mystical temper, hold that logic is the study of the formal syntactical properties of sentences or propositions. Still other logicians, of a more realistic bent, oppose both types of formalism. They argue that logical forms are abstracted, rather like Aristotle's "intelligible species," from pre-existing materials.

Dewey rejected each of these views. As I have already indicated, he argued that "logical forms accrue to subject-matter in virtue of subjection of the latter in inquiry to the conditions determined by its end—institution of a warranted conclusion" (LW 12.370). In other words, logical forms accrue to subject matter in the process of inquiry. The subject matter does not have the logical forms prior to inquiry.

Dewey illustrates these points by drawing our attention to the history of jurisprudence. He observes that there have been numerous occasions on which

> forms of procedure had become the controlling factor at the expense of substance. In such cases, they ceased to be forms-of-matter and were so isolated that they became purely formalistic—a fact which perhaps contains an instructive lesson for logic, since it is clear that legal forms should be such as to serve the substantial end of providing means for settling controversies. . . . These rules of law provide multifarious examples of the ways in which

"natural" modes of action take on new forms because of subjection to conditions formulated in the rules. As new modes of social interaction and transactions give rise to new conditions, and as new social conditions install new kinds of transactions, new forms arise to meet the social need. When, for example, a new type of industrial and commercial enterprise required large capital, the form known as limited liability supervened upon the forms constituting the legal rules of partnership. (LW 12.370–71)

It is the business of controlled inquiry, then, to manipulate its subject matter in ways that allow new forms to accrue to it. After these new forms originate, it is the business of logic (as the theory of inquiry) to disclose the ways in which they are related to one another and to determine their potential use in further inquiry.

Judgments

Books about logic often begin with a discussion of terms. They then take up the various ways in which terms are joined to make propositions or judgments, and the various ways in which propositions or judgments are combined to make arguments. Aristotle, for example, combined terms into four forms of judgment: All S is P, Some S is P, No S is P, and Some S is not P. He demonstrated that when these judgments are combined into forms consisting of two premises and a conclusion (a syllogism), some of the arguments thereby constructed are valid, while others are invalid.

Dewey begins differently. In his view, terms and propositions can only be understood as *correlative* with judgment, which he terms the "settled outcome of inquiry" (LW 12.123). As already indicated, inquiry begins when a situation is doubtful or problematic. Tools and materials are then brought to bear on the situation in question. Hypotheses are formed and then tried out in what he calls "dramatic rehearsals" with a view to alleviating the undesirable circumstances of the situation. Along the way appraisals are made. Finally, where inquiry is successful, the situation is reordered in a way that renders it stable and unproblematic.

In Dewey's usage, therefore, a judgment is not the same as a proposition. A proposition is just that—a proposal which is only intermediate within inquiry. A judgment, on the other hand, carries what he calls "existential import." Whereas propositions *affirm*, judgments *assert*. Dewey uses a baseball metaphor to clarify this point. Drawing on the slang of his day, he writes that "a pitched baseball is to the batter a 'proposition'; it states, or makes explicit, what he has to deal with next amid all the surrounding and momentarily irrelevant circumstance" (MW 10.356). Continuing this analogy, we could say that a judgment is what is made by the batter as a result of (rapid) deliberation about whether he or she will swing the bat at the ball. The pitched ball is thus the proposition and the swing of the bat is the judgment. In this case, as others, deliberation takes into account observed conditions as well as established rules, such as those established to determine strike zones.

Switching to a different analogy, we might say that a proposition in a court of law is what is affirmed by one of the parties to a dispute, whereas a judgment is the assertion that is handed down by the court as a result of deliberation with respect to the evidence and its relation to established legal precedent. Of course intermediate judgments, or what Dewey calls "*appraisals*," such as those that determine the admissibility of evidence, are also a part of the overall process of inquiry that eventuates in a final judgment or settlement of the affair before the court. But whereas both propositions and intermediate judgments (appraisals) are intermediate, propositions are less determinate than are intermediate judgments.

Many logic texts treat the subject of a proposition as something given in a determinate fashion to the senses, and the predicate of a proposition as something conceptual that is attributed to the already determinate subject by means of an act of judgment. Dewey rejected this view. He argued that the subjects and predicates of judgments are determined correlatively to one another as a part of the process of inquiry (LW 12.128). The subject of a proposition is not given as already determined, he argued, since if it were there would be no occasion for inquiry in the first place. Since the point of inquiry is to *find out*, it follows that the subject of a proposition is something vague that requires further definition.

It may well be that what is taken as the subject of a proposition will have received determinate form in a *prior* instance of inquiry; but that does not insure that it will be relevant *as such* to the inquiry at hand. Progress in the sciences, as well as in common-sense inquiries, requires that the results of prior inquiries be treated as raw materials for further inquiries, and not as determinate results, established once and for all.

It is sometimes argued that pure reference can be established for the subject of a proposition merely by pointing to something and by referring to it as "this." But Dewey argues that there is no such thing as pure referentiality. He makes the point (later taken up and capitalized upon by Quine in his famous remarks on "rabbit stages") that even the act of pointing does not establish pure reference, since any of several sensory traits of an object (including its temporal stages) may be the object of the pointing. The fact is that subjects and predicates of propositions are determined correlatively to one another. Their definitions are refined as they are checked against one another. To establish a "this" in the first place is to establish it in terms of a predicate, that is, as *provisionally* one instance of a particular kind. A proposition, which associates a subject and a predicate, is therefore indefinite. It is an indication of tests to be made—of operations to be performed.

Dewey's view also differs from mainstream theories of logic in terms of what judgment can accomplish. It is a commonly held view that the point of judgment is to make a difference in the mental states or attitudes of the judging subject. But Dewey thought that this view yields too much to subjectivism. According to his own view, the point of a judgment is to make a difference in the existential conditions which gave rise to the inquiry of which the final judgment is the termination. Changes in wider existential situations may involve alterations of mental states and attitudes, to be sure, since mental states and attitudes are also existential. But to ignore the wider existential situation and to focus exclusively on mental states and attitudes is to open the door to the prospect of pure fantasy (LW 12.162).

This is particularly apparent in the case of what Dewey calls "judgments of practice," or judgments which involve considerations of value. The point of a moral decision is not to choose from among certain pre-established ends and thereby to change one's mental state. The point of a moral decision is to assess an existential situation, to bring the best instruments currently at one's disposal to bear upon it, and to arrive at a judgment which changes the "indeterminate situation into one that is so determinate in its constituent distinctions and relations as to convert the elements of the original situation into a unified whole" (LW 12.108).

Propositions and their Relations

As I have already indicated, Dewey characterized propositions as different from judgments in the sense that propositions are intermediate, that is, instrumentalities for the final settlement (judgment) of a particular case. Beyond that, however, Dewey divides propositions into two distinct but correlative types. What he calls *existential* propositions have to do with "actual conditions as determined by experimental observation," whereas what he calls *ideational or conceptual* propositions have to do with "interrelated meanings, which are non-existential in content in *direct* reference but which are applicable to existence through the operations they represent as possibilities" (LW 12.283–84). As we would expect, given the foregoing discussion of his treatment of abstraction, Dewey indicates that these two types of propositions are related not as inferior and superior, but as equal partners. He suggests that they represent a "division of labor" within inquiry.

From the viewpoint of some logic textbooks, Dewey's contention that propositions are neither true nor false is nothing short of scandalous.[4] But his point becomes clear enough when it is remembered that he views propositions as means rather than ends. As such, they may be said to be effective or ineffective, strong or weak, or even relevant or irrelevant; they are not, however, said to be true or false. Propositions that are effective, strong, and relevant with respect to the advancement of inquiry are said to be "valid." Propositions that are ineffective, weak or irrelevant are said to be "invalid." Judgments are said to be true or false to the extent that they involve warranted assertibility. And arguments are said to be formally correct or incorrect. This usage has been the occasion for great offense to some mainstream logicians who are accustomed to characterizing propositions as either true or false and arguments as either valid or invalid.

In an attempt to clarify these matters, Dewey provides the following example. "The syllogism 'All satellites are made of green cheese; the moon is a satellite; therefore, it is made of green cheese' is formally correct. The propositions involved are, however, *invalid*, not just because they are 'materially false,' but because instead of promoting inquiry they would, if taken and used, retard and mislead it" (LW 12.287–88). In a sequence of inquiry in which the judgment that "the moon is made of green cheese" was accepted as settling the matter, then, such a judgment would be false in the sense that it would lack warranted assertibility.

Dewey's full treatment of propositions is quite complex, so a complete discussion of it is well beyond the scope of this chapter. Nevertheless, before concluding I want to call attention to several additional points of interest.

First, Dewey distinguishes "particular" propositions from "singular" propositions. Since they sometimes have the same grammatical form, he points out, these two types of propositions are sometimes confused. A *particular* proposition (such as "this is hard"), draws attention to some change, that is, to something taking place as a consequence of the operation of some sense organ (LW 12.289). Such propositions are particular in the sense that they have reference to a particular time and place; they do not in themselves allow further inference. Dewey tells us that particular propositions "represent the first stage in *determination of a problem*; they supply a datum which, when combined with other data, *may* indicate what sort of a problem the situation presents and thereby provide an item of evidence pointing to and testing a proposed solution" (LW 12.290).

Although a *singular* proposition may be of the same grammatical form as a particular proposition (as in the case of "this is hard," for example), the two types of propositions function differently within inquiry. Whereas a *particular* proposition merely indicates the presence of a change, thus possibly instituting a problem, a *singular* proposition determines the "this," to be one instance of a certain kind. The logical structure of singular propositions is more obvious in the case of "this is a diamond," which asserts that "what occurs at the time is being taken as evidence of the permanent traits which describe a kind" (LW 12.291). Since they assert inference beyond the here and now to "permanent" or "general" traits not immediately experienced at the moment they are asserted, singular propositions are thus said to have a certain representative quality.

Dewey introduces several technical terms to help clarify his treatment of these matters. When I merely notice at some moment that something is hard, he suggests, then I am aware of some *quality*. But since our experiences are complex and overlapping, many different qualities may be experienced in a given span of time. Some of these qualities are existentially *involved* with others. Mere recognition of existential involvement, however, does not do much to advance inquiry. There is still the need to discover *which* qualities are relevantly involved with one another (in terms of the problem at hand), and *how* they are so involved. As Dewey puts it, "reasoning and calculation are necessary *instruments* for determining definite involvements" (LW 12.277).

In other words, *inference* is required: inquiry intervenes with a view to determining which involvement-relationships are relevant to the solution of a particular problem. The proposition "this is a diamond," for example, enables reasonably safe inference to still other qualities, such as that the "this" in question is not metallic. Under such conditions, a quality becomes a permanently distinguishing *trait* or *character*. Inference thus allows translation of existentially involved qualities into a form in which they can become useful in inference. They are taken as signs of something not present.

Generic propositions, such as "things that are diamonds are among the things that glass cannot scratch" are expressions of relations among kinds. Rather than proposing that something is one instance of a certain kind, as do singular propositions, generic propositions propose membership of one kind in another, more inclusive kind. Dewey's point here is not simply to construct a taxonomy of types of propositions. His point is rather to demonstrate how different types of propositions function differently within inquiry in ways that render judgment possible.

Generic propositions widen the scope of inference. They enable inference from traits of one kind to traits of another. And even more importantly, they provide the logical grounds for singular propositions. To say that something is one of a certain kind is unintelligible in the absence of a further condition, namely that "there are other kinds related to the one specified" (LW 12.294).

Unlike generic propositions, which are existential, *universal* propositions are conceptual. They formulate possible actions which may or may not be executed. As such, they do not even pretend to have direct existential import; they are instead relevant to inquiry *into* existence (LW 12.303). Here, as elsewhere, grammatical form may be misleading. The term "all" (and its correlate "anything") may indicate an existential relationship between the terms of an existential proposition that expresses a high level of probability, such as is the case with "All diamonds are crystals." On the other hand, it may express "a necessary relation which follows, by definition, from analysis of a conception" (LW 12.296), such as is grammatically more evident in the form "if anything is a diamond then it is a crystal." In the first case, the proposal is generic because it concerns existential singulars of a certain kind (this diamond, that diamond, and so forth) as belonging to a more inclusive kind. In the second case, the proposal concerns relations between meanings which may or may not have to do with existential affairs. If all diamonds were to disappear, and all crystals too, we might still (theoretically) make such a judgment. Universal propositions express meanings in terms of a system of related meanings. Rather than asserting existential relations, they advance procedures for finding out certain things about existential affairs. Generic and universal propositions are thus what Dewey calls "conjugate." They interact as partners within a sequence of inquiry, as inquiry moves back and forth between them.

Universal propositions exhibit *implication*. After qualities experienced as existentially involved with one another have been taken as traits and characters (by means of the formulation of singular and generic propositions and in ways relevant to the inquiry at hand), such traits and characters may be further abstracted. "This is a diamond" becomes a dependable sign of other, conjoined characteristics, such as "This is a crystal." Alternatively, "If anything is a diamond then it is a crystal." Once abstracted in this manner, what formerly functioned as a trait or character, allowing reasonably secure inference, is then termed a *property*.

Whereas existential things or qualities are *involved*, and whereas the determination of a thing as one of a certain kind is a matter of *inference*, fully abstracted (nonexistential) properties are related as signs within a given conceptual system by means of *implication*. As Dewey notes, however, such systems do not come to us "from the blue." They are "evolved and explicitly formulated in terms of conditions set by the need of dealing with actual cases of human action" (LW 12.278).

Dewey recognizes two logical types of universal propositions: those that may have quasi or limited existential import, and those that have no existential import. An example of a universal proposition of the first type is Newton's law of gravitation. Even though it relates abstract characters such as mass and distance, Dewey tells us, it is "framed with reference to the possibility of ultimate existential application [and so] the contents are affected by that intent. Such hypothetical universals do not exhaust the possible existential affairs to which they may be applied, and as a consequence *may* have to be abandoned in favor of other hypothetical universals which are more adequate or appropriate to the subject at hand. This is illustrated by the change from the Newtonian law of gravitation to the Einsteinian formulation" (LW 12.395).

A second type of universal proposition is illustrated by a mathematical formulation. The proposition "$2 + 2 = 4$" is purely a relation of meanings within a constructed system of meanings, and is therefore free of any "privileged interpretation" (LW 12.395). Technically speaking, it has no extrasystemic reference whatsoever.

One final logical relation needs to be discussed. In addition to involvement, inference, and implication, ordered logical discourse includes what Dewey calls "*reference.*" As opposed to the logical formalists, Dewey thought that the point of inquiry is to settle existential difficulties. He therefore thought that the "excursus" into deliberation that involves the manipulation of conceptual material, that is, the determination of implicatory relations between signs within universal propositions, needs to be completed and complemented by a "recursus" that brings the results of such abstract thinking back down to the existentially doubtful situation that originated the particular sequence of inquiry in question. This is possible because of the conjugate relation between universal and generic propositions. In other words, symbol relations used in inquiry may have *reference* to existential affairs. The point of inquiry, it should be recalled, is to reorder involvement relations in such a way that a problematic situation is brought to a final resolution in terms of a judgment that carries warranted assertibility. It is also interesting to note that whereas standard treatments of logic tend to *start out* with reference, claiming that the subject term of a proposition has determinate reference, Dewey's theory of inquiry *ends up* with determinate reference, namely as a name for how the results of inquiry are applied to and checked against existential affairs. Reference is thus for Dewey a relation within inquiry as it comes to a close, and not something separate from inquiry that initiates it.

Inquiry as Social

Given the fact that he characterized propositions as being of two types, namely those that are existential and those that are conceptual,

Dewey recognized that his readers might wonder which comes first: the constitution of abstract meaning relations in discourse, or the constitution of existential significance relations. His answer to this question has two parts. First, because the existential and conceptual propositions work together as conjugate aspects of inquiry, he suggests that the question remains "rhetorical." He thus emphasizes what I have called the "excursus" and "recursus" movements within inquiry. As he puts it, the

> ability to treat things as signs would not go far did not symbols enable us to mark and retain just the qualities of things which are the ground of inference. Without, for example, words or symbols that discriminate and hold on to the experienced qualities of sight and smell that constitute a thing "smoke," thereby enabling it to serve as a sign of fire, we might react to the qualities in question in animal-like fashion and perform activities appropriate to them. But no inference could be made that was not blind and blundering. Moreover, since *what* is inferred, namely fire, is not present in observation, any anticipation that could be formed of it would be vague and indefinite, even supposing an anticipation could occur at all. (LW 12.61–62)

Even if the question of priority is "rhetorical," however, it leads to a consideration that is itself quite fruitful. The context in which these conjugate aspects of inquiry work together is profoundly social both in origin and in import. The fact that existential things have signifying power is not a fact of nature per se, but a fact of a culture which supervenes upon it. Communication, which includes all the aspects of inquiry so far described in this essay, is the result of conjoint activities—both cooperative and competitive—among reflective beings. Culture is thus both a condition and a product of language (LW 12.62).

Inquiry promotes cooperation among reflective organisms because it allows them to "rehearse" or try out activities before making a final irretrievable commitment to some overt action. At a very primitive level, the threatening gesture supplants and obviates the attack. At a higher level of organization, two friends "talk over" some disagreement rather than risking a rupture of their relationship. At a still more sophisticated level, complex political and economic plans of action are deliberated by a democratic electorate and orderly change ensues. These are among the developmental stages of inquiry. As Dewey puts it, "The habit of reasoning once instituted is capable of indefinite development on its own account. The ordered development of meanings in their relations to one another may become an engrossing interest. When this happens, implicit logical conditions are made explicit and then logical theory of some sort is born" (LW 12.63).

It should by now be clear that Dewey rejected the notion of inquiry as an end in itself, and he also rejected the notion of the theory of inquiry (logic) as a strictly formal discipline complete in itself and devoid of relevance to the affairs of daily life. It was for these reasons that he thought that the next great scientific-technological revolution, if it should occur, will involve advances in the social sciences. Inquiry, and the theory of inquiry, were in Dewey's view among the most important tools at our disposal for learning to live together in ways that take into account the constraints of our environing conditions, as well as the full range of human needs and aspirations.

THIRTEEN

THE *HOMO FABER* DEBATE IN DEWEY
AND MAX SCHELER

I t would be difficult to find two contemporaneous philosophers
whose style and temper appear less similar to one another than do
those of John Dewey and Max Scheler.[1] Dewey was a Protestant Yan-
kee, Scheler was a German whose mother was a Jew and whose father
was Catholic. Dewey's style was calm and measured, Scheler's was
deeply passionate and at times frantic. Apart from reviews and replies, Dewey seldom mentioned his opponents by name, and he usually found something of value even in those views to which he was
most opposed. Scheler not only mentioned his adversaries by name
but often characterized their views in terms that were quite caustic.
Dewey's academic career was long, distinguished, and honored.
Scheler, already in his forties when he obtained his first academic ap-
pointment, was always an academic outsider. Dewey's work has been
characterized as holistic and integrative. Scheler's work seems at
times almost rent asunder by his attraction to two competing approaches to philosophy: the "life philosophies" of Nietzsche, Dilthey,

and Bergson, on one side, and phenomenology, on the other, which he and Husserl share the honor of founding.

It does not appear that Dewey ever mentioned Scheler by name. Dewey's student Sidney Hook did, however, in his book *The Metaphysics of Pragmatism*,[2] which he published in 1927. Scheler not only singled Dewey out, but had a great deal to say about what he took to be positions held by him and the other Pragmatists. One of Dewey's doctrines stands out for Scheler as particularly interesting. It is the same topic that was the occasion of Hook's citation of Scheler. It is what both called the doctrine of *"homo faber."*

In his reference to Scheler,[3] Hook indicated that he owed his own formulation of the *homo faber* doctrine to Bergson. What Hook probably had in mind was Bergson's remark in his 1911 *Creative Evolution*: "If we could rid ourselves of all pride, if, to define our species, we kept strictly to what the historic and the prehistoric periods show us to be the constant characteristic of man and of intelligence, we should say not *Homo sapiens*, but *Homo faber*. In short, *intelligence, considered in what seems to be its original feature, is the faculty of manufacturing artificial objects, especially tools to make tools, and of indefinitely varying the manufacture.*"[4]

It may be helpful to recall that during Dewey's twenty-six months in China (1919–21), he had presented a lecture on Bergson's *Creative Evolution* (MW 12.211ff), in which he summarized Bergson's position on the difference between humans and the lower animals in three points. First, and most important, animals operate upon life by means of instincts. Human beings compensate for their lack of instincts by adopting something much more chancy, something much more open to failure, to wit, intelligence. Second, humans are able to make tools that are separate from themselves. Their tools are among the ways that they supplement their instincts by using intelligence. Third, whereas the lower animals are at a disadvantage because they cannot use intelligence, human beings are at a disadvantage because they have not been able to develop their instincts. The active cooperation in human life of instinct and intelligence would overcome this debility.

Dewey alluded to Bergson's view that human life is continuous with that of the lower animals. Such continuity, or "transformism" as it was then called, was a matter of considerable debate during Bergson's time (as it continues to be under different names such as "creation science" and "intelligent design" in our own). *Creative Evolution* contains a lengthy discussion of the grounds of Bergson's acceptance of this view as a working hypothesis.[5]

Even though Bergson had identified human intelligence with the manufacture and use of tools, he did not think that such intelligence could grasp "the meaning of life." Such a task is the proper aim of the development of instincts. Dewey thought this insight a very great contribution to philosophical understanding. He paraphrased it by saying that "the meaning of life cannot be grasped through knowledge," and that "we can understand life only by living it. Behaviors cannot be the objects of knowledge; they can be understood only through behaving or acting" (MW 12.235).

Nevertheless, it was Bergson's view that tools and instruments are among the means by which human beings continue to effect open-ended self-creation. His enthusiasm with respect to the invention and development of the steam engine, for example,[6] was prodigious. He saw arising in its wake important new ideas and the flowering of new feelings. But he voiced a regret that is increasingly heard in our own time, namely, that "it takes us longer to change ourselves than to change our tools."[7] He further observed that "our individual and even social habits survive a good while the circumstances for which they were made, so that the ultimate effects of an invention are not observed until its novelty is already out of sight."[8]

Even though Bergson argued for transformism, it was, I suggest, a weak form of that thesis. Implicit in his transformist hypothesis are three elements. From the standpoint of history there is emergence, and from the standpoint of scientific explanation there is continuity. But in terms of valuation and the prescription of activities, Bergson thought he saw a gap that all but vitiated the significance of the other two elements. He thought that historical emergence and explanatory continuity have not been appropriated in ways that allow the integration of the bequest of the lower animals into the lives of humankind.

For his part, Hook recognized the *homo faber* doctrine as extremely important, and he used it as a tool to initiate his discussion of some of the differences between Dewey's version of Pragmatism, which he termed "Instrumentalism," and the views of its critics. He even went so far as to characterize Instrumentalism in terms of the *homo faber* thesis: he suggested that Instrumentalism was "the culminating expression of one of the great philosophical *motifs* in the history of thought," by which he meant the *homo faber* doctrine.[9] It was in this connection that Hook mentioned Scheler.

Hook's remarks followed the publication of Scheler's important essay "Mensch und Geschichte"[10] by just one year and preceded the publication of his book *Man's Place in Nature*[11] by a like period. In those works Scheler outlined, then criticized and rejected, what he regarded as the primary features of the *homo faber* doctrine: humankind is uniquely a sign-making animal (*ein Zeichentier*), a tool—or instrument—using animal (*ein Werkzeugstier*), and "brainy" (*ein Gehirnwesen*). In other words, human beings are able to make signs and tools, and they have a larger and more powerful cortex than do the lower animals.

For the proponents of the *homo faber* doctrine, Scheler suggested, signs, words, and even concepts are highly "psychically" refined tools.[12] He identified this view of humankind with the evolutionists of the "Darwinian-Lamarckian school"[13] or what we today call "evolutionary naturalists." He contrasted their view with the *homo sapiens* doctrine. This view, he suggested, "would reserve intelligence and choice for man and deny them to the animal."[14] He associated the *homo sapiens* doctrine with the ancient Greeks, particularly Anaxagoras, Plato, and Aristotle, whom he thought had argued for a radical break between human beings and lower animals.[15]

Scheler rejected both of these views. He favored the "discontinuity" thesis of the *homo sapiens* doctrine, but argued on the basis of his careful reading of Wolfgang Koehler's study of higher primates that what the *homo sapiens* doctrine took to be unique to mankind—

technical intelligence and the ability to choose—is exhibited by the higher primates as well as human beings. He argued that what is unique to humankind "goes far beyond the capacity for choice and intelligence and would not be reached even if we were to enlarge these powers [in the lower animals], in a quantitative sense, to infinity."[16] He even suggested that "between the clever chimpanzee and an Edison, taking the latter only as a technician, there is only a difference in degree—though a great one to be sure."[17]

Scheler rejected the three planks of Bergsonian transformism: historical emergence, explanatory continuity and the desirability of integrating the instincts. He argued that human beings have a distinctive ontological status that goes beyond technical intelligence and the ability to use tools. What is unique about humankind is not in any way continuous in the evolutionary sense with nonhuman life, but is rather a "genuinely new phenomenon"[18] which he called "spirit." Spirit is for Scheler what frees human life from the bondage of natural sequences and even from its own instinctual drives, and allows it to become self-conscious. It is what allows human beings to create their own environment by experimentation, rather than just reacting to environmental conditions as an entire organism.

The irony of Scheler's position with respect to the Instrumentalism of Dewey and Hook is that he took the continuity between human beings and the higher primates much more seriously in concrete terms than they did, cheerfully admitting the involvement of the higher primates in symbolic behavior and their use of simple forms of language. Dewey, on the other hand, a self-described evolutionary naturalist or transformist, argued precisely the opposite view in *Reconstruction in Philosophy*: what differentiates human beings from the lower animals is human sign-use.

Dewey thus argued that intelligence in human beings is not discontinuous with nonhuman nature in an evolutionary sense, but that it reflects an increased order of complexity that is not different in kind from the adaptive behavior of the lower animals. But he also held that such intelligence is unique insofar as it generates meanings and language through social interaction and cooperation, even though it does not have special ontological status. For Dewey, humanity comes to its unique self-consciousness not because it exhibits something that constitutes a new ontological category, but because of the development of a greatly augmented ability to adjust to an ever larger and more meaningful environment—an environment which human beings themselves are always actively creating.

Scheler saw matters quite differently. He thought that human beings are only quantitatively, not qualitatively, different from the higher primates in terms of their shared ability to use signs. His view was thus much more transformist than Dewey's when taken just that far. What really distinguishes human beings from the higher primates is for Scheler not, as it was for Dewey, the functional feature of greater organizational ability, but the ontological fact that human beings exhibit "spirit." Complicating matters even further, Scheler held that even though human beings are in a different ontological category because of spirit, spirit is itself nothing substantial. It is functional in much the same sense that "mind" was functional for Dewey.

Beyond this odd difference regarding the transformist theses, the views of Dewey and Scheler exhibit some remarkable similarities. For Dewey, as for Scheler, humankind constitutes continuously new and open-ended environments by means of active experimentation, which requires the use of tools. Dewey treats language, and even ideas, as tools. In certain places Scheler seemed inclined to do this as well, although he generally wrote of tools in their more conventional sense as hardware. Thus though Dewey and Scheler had remarkably similar descriptions regarding what it is that human beings *do* that exhibits their uniqueness, they held very different views about the source of such activities. It is remarkable that over a half century after Darwin's influence came to be felt, Scheler could have still rejected evolutionary naturalism. For Dewey, evolutionary naturalism was a central feature of his understanding of the role of tools in the human project. It was not that Scheler denied the use of tools as an important human activity, but just that he thought that tool-use was not sufficient to account for human uniqueness.[19]

The Pragmatists' acceptance of transformism or evolutionary naturalism was not the only problem that Scheler had with their *homo faber* doctrine. Another was his perception (which was in fact a misperception) that an essential component of their version of the *homo faber* thesis included what we might call the "cortex" thesis, that is, the idea that what accounts for the human use of tools is heightened cortical prowess. "It is the entire body," he wrote, "and not only the brain, which has become the physiological field corresponding to psychic processes."[20] Scheler's view was that the difference between the psychological and the physiological in humans is not ontological, but phenomenological.[21] But even where these aspects of human life are so differentiated, he argued, it is obvious that neither the physiological nor the psychological aspect of life is mechanical, and both aspects of the organism are oriented towards goals and toward wholeness.[22] In short, "psychophysical life is one."[23]

This view led Scheler to dismiss the traditional dualism between mind and body. He put this quite acutely: "We may say that the mind-body problem has lost the metaphysical significance it has had for centuries. Instead, the dualism which we encounter in man and which we experience ourselves is of a higher order: it is the antithesis between spirit and life."[24] In other words, there are psycho-physical life processes present in humankind as well as nonhuman animals. But in humankind there is something more, namely a spirit that transcends those processes and objectifies them. Spirit is not an object itself, but what objectifies. It draws upon the energies of life processes and is "embedded" in them.[25]

The extent of Scheler's misreading of the Pragmatists is evident when we consider Dewey's remarks in chapter 7 of *Experience and Nature* some years earlier. Dewey also thought the traditional dualism of mind and body untenable, but he refused to replace it with another. He not only argued that the "psychophysical life is one," as Scheler later put it, but that where there are grounds for differentiating between physical and psychological functions of organisms such grounds are not ontological but instrumental. The grounds for distinguishing the physical from the psychological are just those that allow a description of the "increasing complexity and intimacy of interaction among natural events" (LW 1.200).

Dewey held that mind arises as a complex tool out of such natural interactions as a result of increasing levels of complexity. It is not increased cortical power that leads to extended tool-use. In Dewey's broad sense of "tool," the cortex is itself a kind of tool that is used by a complex organism in order to undertake more effective control of its environment. "To see the organism *in* nature," he wrote in *Experience and Nature*, "the nervous system in the organism, the brain in the nervous system, the cortex in the brain is the answer to the problems which haunt philosophy. And when thus seen they will be seen to be in, not as marbles are in a box but as events are in history, in a moving, growing never finished process" (LW 1.224).

Dewey came close to speaking of "spirit" in terms that would probably have been acceptable to Scheler. Although he thought that the term carried too much "traditional mythology and sophisticated doctrine," he nevertheless wrote of spirit as "living," of spirit as informing, of spirit as a "moving function" (LW 1.224).

At the level of phenomenology, Dewey and Scheler at times wrote like twins. For Scheler spirit involves the selection of certain features of resistances within the environment which it, spirit, then condenses into objects. Spirit is the referral of such concentrations to the purposes for which they are effected and to the center of the action of concentration and goal—direction which we call the self. This could be a paraphrase of portions of Dewey's introduction to his 1916 *Essays in Experimental Logic* and his 1938 *Logic: The Theory of Inquiry*. In the latter book he described the "taking" of an aspect, phase, or constituient of an existentially present situation. Scheler's term "condensation" would probably have served quite as well in this context. In *Experience and Nature* Dewey wrote of mind as a "constant luminosity," a backdrop against which consciousness intermittently operates. His talk of mind as a center of action and of goal-direction is also well known.

Spirit was for Scheler neither object nor substance, but a "continuously self-executing, ordered structure of acts." He did not reify spirit, as had Hegel, but functionalized it instead, as Dewey had mind. He rejected theism, as did Dewey, and the idea of an eternal spirit creating the world according to a divine plan. He argued instead for a "co-creation of ideas, essences, and values, all undertaken by human beings in league with an eternal *logos*." He found it wonderful that even the most abstract of mathematical discoveries is capable of application to the world of real, empirical things.

Dewey, of course, had de-hypostatized both spirit and *logos*: neither was for him eternal and neither was transcendental. He was specifically concerned to strip *logos* of its mystic sense and to locate it with a small L in developing human linguistic communities (LW 1.134). With respect to the objects of mathematics and logic, he wrote in 1916 that they are just instruments of a highly refined type and that they are thus applicable to the real world of empirical things precisely because they are tools that have been generated in the course of inquiry much as agricultural tools have been generated by agricultural practice (MW 10.92–93).

It was on this point that Scheler criticized Dewey and other Pragmatists, including James, Peirce, and Schiller, by name. He accused them of a kind of vitalism that "has tried to derive the forms and laws of thought from the respective modes of human work and activity (*homo faber*)," which he identified with the drive for power. But this is an unfortunate reading of Dewey. (It may well be that, as my colleague Kenneth Stikkers has suggested, that Scheler had perhaps not read Dewey at all, and that what he knew of the Pragmatists was from the work of William James in translation.) For Dewey's Instrumentalism it is not the will to power that is the engine for the increasing complexity and ever more sophisticated forms of adaptation that characterize human life, but a desire for appropriate and effective management of the environment that takes many forms: science, mathematics, religion, magic, and communication of all sorts. To reduce these many forms of management to "the will to power" would be to impoverish our understanding of human activity.

In sum, despite their enormous differences, Dewey and Scheler articulated remarkably similar views regarding the function of tools in intelligent adaptation. That Dewey held a version of the *homo faber* thesis that Scheler violently attacked should not obscure their fundamental agreements regarding the issues that vitalize that thesis.

FOURTEEN

PRODUCTIVE PRAGMATISM:
HABITS AS ARTIFACTS IN PEIRCE AND DEWEY

The real and living logical conclusion *is* [the] habit; the verbal formulation merely expresses it. . . . Action cannot be a logical interpretant, because it lacks generality.

—C. S. Peirce

The concept which is a logical interpretant is only imperfectly so. . . . [It is] inferior to the habit. . . . The deliberately formed, self-analyzing habit—self-analyzing because formed by the aid of analysis of the exercises that nourished it—is the living definition, the veritable and final logical interpretant.

—C. S. Peirce

The whole function of thought is to produce habits of action.

—C. S. Peirce

Moreover—*here is the point*—every man exercises more or less control over himself by means of modifying his own habits.

—C. S. Peirce

Critics of the classical Pragmatists seem never to have tired of accusing them of making action an end in itself.[1] Bertrand Russell misread them in this way, accusing Dewey of subordinating knowledge to action. Russell charged Pragmatism with saying that "the only essential result of successful inquiry is successful action."[2] He was later joined in this mistake by members of the Frankfurt School, including Max Horkheimer and Theodor Adorno.[3]

This misunderstanding has been more than a simple matter of the cultural differences between philosophers living on different sides of the Atlantic. Lewis Mumford, who should have known better, mocked Dewey's version of Pragmatism as being "all dressed up, with no place to go."[4] This charge has also been the occasion for the turning of Pragmatist against fellow Pragmatist. In 1902 Peirce charged William James with holding the view that "the end of man is action."[5] Even Richard Bernstein has labeled the Pragmatists' account of action as "vague." He has written that there is still "a great deal of confusion about what the pragmatists understood by 'action' and precisely what role action does or ought to play in understanding human life."[6]

Perhaps it was what both Peirce and Dewey characterized as his nominalism that led James to yield on occasion to the temptation to make action an end in itself. But the situation is quite different with respect to the work of Peirce and Dewey; their work exhibits elaborate safeguards against such a move. Dewey complained in his 1925 essay "The Development of American Pragmatism" that his critics had misunderstood him in just that regard. Earlier, Peirce, in his 1905 article "What Pragmatism Is," had already taken considerable delight in constructing a lengthy response to an imagined critic who had charged him with making "Doing the Be-all and the End-all of human life" (5.429).

The manner in which Peirce and Dewey treated action was neither vague, nor did it make action an end in itself. In their hands, practice was regarded as much more than simple action; both men characterized action as an instrument of production, and both adjudicated action in terms of its products. Their critiques of action were embedded in their critiques of production.

It is not at all difficult to demonstrate that Russell, Mumford, and Horkheimer misunderstood Peirce and Dewey, so I will leave that exercise aside. Beyond that, however, I wish to draw two conclusions from Peirce's and Dewey's treatments of cognition, action, and production. The first is that Peirce and Dewey were able to move beyond what are now called traditional "cognitivist" metaphysical positions, and even beyond the praxis philosophies of the Continental thinkers from Marx through Scheler to Heidegger (and beyond), thence to fashion a comprehensive philosophy of production. The second is

that what was to become Dewey's Instrumentalist version of Pragmatism is rooted firmly in the work of Peirce.

It is possible to see within the history of Western philosophy a kind
of tug-of-war between those who have sought to make theory dominant and those who have worked for the ascendancy of practice. Cognitivists, taking their cues from Plato and Descartes, have tended to
view the formation of correct concepts or ideas as the goal of philosophical activity. It is in this sense that much of contemporary linguistic analysis has been concerned with "getting clear" about various
issues by means of the analysis of concepts. The approach of the
praxis philosophers, following Marx and Heidegger, has been quite
different. Their emphasis has been more on doing than on thinking,
and their tendency has been to take into account a whole organism
in an environment rather than just a ghost in a machine (or a brain
in a vat). Don Ihde has captured this feature of the work of the early
Heidegger, for example, in his assessment that Heidegger's goal was
the practical knowing-involvement that comes through "such phenomena as moods and emotion and, what is more, bodily movement,
such that the human being as a totality is 'being-in' an environment
or world."[7]

After Peirce's sharp critique of Descartes in his 1877 and 1878 articles in *Popular Science Monthly*, even the most obtuse of critics would
have been reluctant to place him in the camp of the cognitivists. Consequently, exhibiting the unfortunate excluded-middle fixation found
so frequently in much of the history of philosophy, critics of the Pragmatists have tended to locate them inside the praxis camp. Bertrand
Russell, for example, was fond of lumping them together with Marx.

Pragmatism does in fact share many concerns and conclusions
with praxis philosophy. But both Peirce and Dewey in fact located
their own positions well outside of this cognitivist-praxicalist struggle, arguing that the positions of both camps are defective because
they are incomplete. Peirce and Dewey did this by subordinating both
theory and practice (cognition and action, thinking and doing), to
production or making; to what the Greeks had called *poietike*.[8] It is
not that they ignored either cognition or praxis, for they did not: it is

just that neither Peirce nor Dewey thought cognition or praxis to be the end of inquiry.

But if Pragmatism is concerned with production, what are its products? A general, though somewhat misleading, answer is that the products of Pragmatism are habits. The reason why this statement is a bit misleading is because the term "habit" is equivocal in the work of both Peirce and Dewey, and because of the presence in Peirce's work of what may be called "quasi-habits."

For Peirce, habits are associated with control, and control is linked to products and production. In the context of his remarks on critical common-sensism, Peirce outlined a continuum of levels of control which are correlated with the habits he calls "inhibitions and coördinations" (5.533). Moving from less to more control, there are habits that are unconscious, habits that are instinctive, and habits that are the result of training. Peirce was not reluctant to describe a stream cutting its bed as the unconscious formation of a habit (5.492). Ants and other insects which we do not normally count as trainable nevertheless operate according to instincts, which are another type of habit. And nonhuman animals, especially the higher primates, are capable of certain forms of training which habitualizes them to certain forms of responses.[9] In none of these cases is control self-conscious, but in each of them the level of complexity of control is linked to and consistent with the level of complexity of the entity or organism.

Among human beings, however, it is possible for an individual to be his or her own "training-master," and it is at this stage that control becomes self-control. Up to this point, habits have operated in Peirce's sketch as a *means* of control: as a *terminus a quo* of action (even though that action is not self-controlled). The habit that is the bed of the river controls its flow. Instincts genetically transmitted to insects control their activities. And the training instilled in a loquacious parrot controls its vocabulary.

Beyond this watershed, however, habit, in addition to being means of control, operates as a *goal* of control: in addition to being a *terminus a quo* of action, it also functions as a *terminus ad quem* of action.

In addition to self-training that involves gross motor functions, self-training may also be conducted in the imagination. Further, self-training may involve just a single insight or association rather than a repetition.[10] Peirce is not reluctant to speak of habits as being "produced" even in such circumstances (5.477).

In imaginative self-training, ideas and ideals often enter into the training process and serve as its norms. Among such ideals are the "leading principles" of Peirce's famous thought experiments. Moreover, at a certain stage of self-control, ideas and ideals are themselves the subject of improvement by means of control. This is a very high level of production which Peirce calls control over control of control (5.533).

Peirce thought that language itself is a "phenomenon of self-control" (5.534), but one in which two distinct levels are possible, corresponding to the grades of complexity with respect to which self-control is capable of being exercised. He was willing to admit that nonhuman animals use signs, but he thought that the difference between their form of sign use and the forms invented and developed by human beings is exhibited in the extent to which human beings are able to control signs *in their role as signs*.

Another way of putting this is that human beings are able to conduct themselves more productively than nonhuman animals. Habits are what allow nonhuman animals to produce certain things, and this is also true of human beings. But human beings are in addition capable of producing habits, and their greater organizational complexity—their greater powers of self-control—allow them to craft these habits so that they are increasingly sharper and more pertinent to their existential situations. Like nonhuman animals, human beings are just "endowed" with a store of habits. Unlike nonhuman animals, they are able to manipulate and improve old ones, and they are able to produce new ones.

Besides habits, Peirce thought that human beings produce what may be called "quasi-habits." Among these quasi-habits are what Peirce calls "hypostatic abstractions." In his 1905 remarks on common-sensism, Peirce lists several examples of hypostatic abstractions:

a collection (or a class qua extended, i.e., predicable of its members), a multitude (or an abstraction from the predicate of a collection, i.e., "intended," or taken as a subject for further predication), a cardinal number (or a predicate of a multitude), an ordinal number (or an abstraction by means of which cardinal numbers are placed in space with respect to one another), and so on. Each of these things is a product of strictly controlled sign-usage, or what Peirce calls a "logical interpretant," and the meaning of each is a habit, or general way of treating situations that may occur in the future.

Each of these things I have just listed, a collection, a multitude, a cardinal number, and an ordinal number, is also characterized by Peirce as an *ens rationis* or "being of reason." He follows the Thomists and Scotists of the thirteenth through the sixteenth centuries in this matter, adopting their technical term for an entity which is the result of the operation of the intellect in its interaction with its "data," literally whatever is given to it.

The scholastics had differed among themselves rather sharply regarding whether these *entia rationis* were invented or simply discovered as something pre-existing, and in this they anticipated the debates regarding the foundations of mathematics which were such an important feature of the intellectual life of the last decades of the ninteenth century and the first decades of the twentieth.[11]

Peirce thought that these *entia rationis* are produced, and that despite their name, they may sometimes be real. By calling some *entia rationis* "real," his terminology departed radically from that of the scholastics, although in terms of practical effects, his view reflects the position of one of the many factions that made up that movement. What Peirce means when he speaks of *entia rationis* being real is that once abstracted, once produced, they have effects that do not depend on what any one person thinks them to be.

Peirce has sometimes been misread on this point as being an epistemological realist of the sort who says that things are such as they are regardless of whether *anyone* ever knows them to be as they are. And there is a certain sense in which Peirce contributed to this misunderstanding by his use of the terminology employed by some of the "scientific realists" who contributed to the scientific revolution of the seventeenth century.

The early paragraphs of the seventh volume of the *Collected Papers* indicate the extent to which he took over that terminology (although he intermingles it with the terminology of evolutionary theory). There he tells us that science is not a body of knowledge, but "the concrete life of the men who are working to find out the truth" (7.50). He argues that this scientific passion is not separate from the process of organic evolution, but just a part of its emerging organizational complexity. "Given the oxygen, hydrogen, carbon, nitrogen, sulphur, phosphorus, etc., in sufficient quantities and under proper radiations, and living protoplasm will be produced, will develop, will gain power of self-control, and the scientific passion is sure to be generated. Such is my guess. Science was preordained, perhaps, on the Sunday of the *Fiat lux*" (7.50).

Peirce characterizes science as "storming the stronghold of truth" (7.51), and as "a mode of life whose single animating purpose is to find out the real truth" (7.54). Further, "Science is foredestined to reach the truth of every problem with as unerring an infallibility as the instincts of animals do their work" (7.77). The "infallibility" of science is due to its rationality, or what may seem somewhat paradoxical, to its procedures for detecting whatever is fallible. The rationality of science lies precisely in the fact that it is "self-criticizing, self-controlling and self-controlled, and therefore open to incessant question" (7.77).

Peirce's description of science might appear somewhat old-fashioned to many of us now. Some of us might have a tendency to wince at words like "real truth," "unerring infallibility," and "preordained." Taken by themselves, these terms might lead us to place Peirce among the cognitivists. But beneath these grand phrases, we can see Peirce at work constructing a kind of realism far different from the one that says things are such as they are regardless of their being known by anybody. His language is that of seventeenth-century science, but his message is Lamarckian and Darwinian: it includes as elements not only his doctrine of chance, his tychism, but also his view that the experimental method is the only one that is self-correcting.

For Peirce, scientific thinking, like thinking in general, is iconic. The difference between scientific reasoning and what he calls "sham" reasoning (1.57) is that the experimentalist must exercise the kind of self-control that proceeds from a commitment to follow the dictates of reasoned inference, regardless of where such inference may lead.

But the goal of technoscience—the goal of logic, the goal of self-control, the goal of production—is the finding out of what is before us, and this is only possible insofar as the investigator produces ever more finely wrought and powerful habits. We always produce more than we can consume, and it is the job of experimental technoscience to keep finding new patterns of consumption, and, thereby, new patterns of production. Habits are thus for Peirce both produced and productive. They are more or less the tools and instruments that Dewey was later to spotlight in the 1903 *Studies in Logical Theory* and in the 1916 *Essays in Experimental Logic*.

Now Peirce not only avoided the language of Dewey's Instrumentalism, but in fact criticized Dewey's instrumentalized theory of inquiry.[12] His response to Dewey's 1903 *Studies in Logical Theory* was to accuse Dewey of lack of self-control, adding that perhaps it was because Dewey had become corrupted by having lived too long in Chicago. But when Peirce speaks of the things he calls "real," he, like Dewey, does not take them to be independent of *all* thinking, but only independent of any particular way of thinking about them. In "How to Make Our Ideas Clear" he writes that "reality is independent, not necessarily of thought in general, but only of what you or I or any finite number of men may think about it . . . and . . . on the other hand, though the object of the final opinion depends on what that opinion is, yet what that opinion is does not depend on what you or I or any man thinks" (5.408). Understood in the context of his characterization of technoscientific methods, this just means that the result of an experiment, qua general, does not depend on it being replicated in any *particular* experimental situation, though it must be replicable in *some* experimental situations.

I passed rather too quickly over Peirce's contention that self-controlled inquiry is iconic, so let me return to that matter, for it is an essential part of Peirce's account of production. He argues that perception is generally *beyond* our control; that we do not choose what we perceive. After the production of the *entia rationis* which Peirce calls "hypostatic abstractions," a new iconic situation is present. This, in fact, is the point of the work that leads to the hypostatic abstraction. "All necessary reasoning without exception is diagrammatic. That is, we construct an icon of our hypothetical state of things and proceed to observe it. . . . We not only have to select the features of the diagram which it will be pertinent to pay attention to, but it is also of great importance to return again and again to certain features" (5.162).

After the construction of the diagram or icon, in other words, the experimenter is then able to perceive certain things about the new situation that were not theretofore present or (if it is later determined that they were present) were not obvious. But since perception is not generally a matter of self-control, since it is a matter of habits already autonomized, doesn't this mean that the task of the logician or scientist is just to be a keen observer rather than a "producer"? This is to a certain extent the case. But the qualifier "generally" is essential to understanding Peirce's position on this matter, since in certain circumstances perception is in Peirce's view linked to a kind of controlled conduct, a controlled product.

His example (5.183) is of what we today know as the favorite figures of the gestalt psychologists. Looking at a "duck-rabbit" or "face-vase," it is as if the perceiver gets "tired" or "bored" with seeing it one way, then switches ground and figure or sees the figure as rotated. Once this is done, such switching may be a matter of control, as it is for those of us who are familiar with the work of the gestalt psychologists (or the artists, such as M. C. Escher, who have been influenced by the gestaltists). In such cases, we can generally choose one percept over another, and this is where judgment and production enter into the situation.

Another way in which perception is linked to control lies in the transformation of the icons or diagrams. Peirce writes of "such a transformation of our diagrams that characters of one diagram may appear in another as things" (5.162).

The meanings of the hypostatic abstractions just discussed are thus habits. They mean that the person who interprets them will be inclined to do certain things under certain conditions. But they are also *produced* or manufactured. Peirce argues that the certainty of pure mathematics is "due to the circumstance that it relates to objects which are the creations of our own minds" (5.166). But what of the fact that mathematicians speak of "discoveries" rather than "products"? In one sense, self-control has led to the construction of the mathematical objects; but the mathematician may exhibit the surprise of discovery because weak or loose reasoning had led her or him to think such objects impossible or unlikely, or not even to think of them at all.

Now habits are for Peirce, as they were for Dewey, "Janus-faced" entities. This is what Peirce has in mind when he refers to them as inhibitions *and* coordinations. One face is their autonomy. William James characterized habit as the "flywheel" of society and of the inquiry undertaken by individuals. It is in this sense that a habit is a *terminus a quo*. It is the dead but lingering force of momentum—a flywheel.[13] In this sense a habit may function unconsciously, and this is the popular sense of some activity being called "habitual." This is the sense in which habits are "transparent" in use: they involve a certain autonomy. We do not have to think about tying our shoelaces or remember how to use the number two.

The other face of a habit involves the way in which it is formed. This is the function of habit as *terminus ad quem*. A habit has "to be formed" as a part of a successful piece of inquiry. A habit is in this sense a goal or ideal which is solidified as a part of the puzzle which Peirce thinks science continues to piece together. If action (of which inquiry is a species) is properly controlled, then its products are the habits he calls "final logical interpretants." Thus the "real and living logical conclusion" of a piece of reasoning is a habit (5.491). Logical interpretants are products in a way in which actions can never be, because unlike actions, they are general: they are general in the sense that they are enduring instrumentalities for future action, and they are general in the sense that they are able to operate not only with respect to this or that thing, but with respect to a whole class of things.

In 1952, George Gentry published an essay that shed a great deal of light on these logical interpretants. It was included in the first series of *Studies in the Philosophy of Charles Sanders Peirce*.[14] He pointed out that Peirce's writings have two very different kinds of logical interpretants. Early in his career, Peirce held the view that there is an infinite continuum of signs such that there is neither a "first" nor "last" object which is not a sign of something further. More specifically, in his early work Peirce rejected the view that there is a terminal logical interpretant, or a logical interpretant that requires no further interpretant of the same category, that is, a sign. In his early work, Peirce argued that the interpretant of every sign is itself a sign of something further, that it has a logical interpretant—and so on to infinity.

These logical interpretants of intellectual concepts are what are best termed "quasi-habits." Like habits, they are conditional. Peirce tells us that they are associated with a "conditional future," and that in mathematics "they are as plenty as blackberries" (5.483). Their conditionality also lies in the fact that they may or may not lead to action. But they are also like habits in that they are general. He tells us that they are "either general or intimately connected with generals" (5.482). They are not actions, which are particular, but ways of acting, which are general: they are rules of action.[15]

But Peirce eventually abandoned this view for another one. Or, put perhaps more accurately, he added something to his earlier view which made it function better. In addition to there being logical interpretants which themselves have further logical interpretants, Peirce began to write of logical interpretants that are "ultimate" or "final" or "veritable." He realized that what he had developed up to that point were just "quasi-habits" that lacked something that habits must possess: they must possess what Gentry called "ultimacy" or "*termi-nality* with respect to an interpretative transaction. A terminal, *i.e.*, an ultimate or final interpretant of the logical species, is, as Peirce conceived it, an interpretant characterized by both conditionality and generality, which *itself* does not presuppose or require an interpretant in the proper sense."[16]

Whereas concepts can still function as "ordinary" logical interpretants, such concepts are now subordinated in terms of their importance to "final" logical interpretants, which are habits in the full sense. As Peirce puts it in his "Survey of Pragmaticism,"

> The concept which is a logical interpretant is only imperfectly so. It somewhat partakes of the nature of a verbal definition, and is as inferior to the habit, and much in the same way, as a verbal definition is inferior to the real definition. The deliberately formed, self-analyzing habit—self-analyzing because formed by the aid of analysis of the exercises that nourished it—is the living definition, the veritable and final logical interpretant. Consequently, the most perfect account of a concept that words can convey will consist in a description of the habit which that concept is calculated to produce. But how otherwise can a habit be described than by a description of the kind of action to which it gives rise, with the specification of the conditions and the motive? (5.491)

The production of the final logical interpretant is a matter of self-control—the control that is exercised by means of judgments of perception insofar as that is possible, and the checking of consequences against certain habits of action which he calls "leading principles." The production of the final logical interpretant involves recourse to concepts and activities—to thinking and to doing. But the ultimate products of Peirce's Pragmatism are neither concepts nor activities: they are habits which are not themselves necessarily signs of something further.

Peirce thought that technoscience is a habit of changing habits, and he called this a "plastic" habit.[17] He argued that the Darwinian view, namely that "the whole gulf [between the simplest protozoa and human beings] has been bridged by imperceptible variations at birth," was inferior to the view of Lamarck, namely that "it is exercise and the consequent growth which by imperceptible steps has transformed the Moner into Man."[18] In short, some tychistic event occurs which is transformed by specialized and focused energy into new habits.

Peirce thought that evidence for the Lamarckian version of evolution was everywhere in the scientific-technological world.

> Some invention like that of writing, or printing, or gunpowder, or the mariner's compass or the steam engine, in a comparatively short time changes men very profoundly. It seems strange that we who have seen such tremendous revolutions in all the habits of men during this century should put our faith in the influence of imperceptible variations to an extent that no other age ever did. Is it because we have so little of Asiatic immovability before our eyes that we do not realize now what the conservatism of old habit really is?[19]

Technoscience thus presents for Peirce the clearest exhibition of the ways in which a habit is produced: "It is formed by the interaction of the two elements, a . . . mind of common origin with the universe, and facts which are selected by that mind as its suitable pabulum."[20]

Peirce's attention to the instruments of scientific technology offers a bridge to the second conclusion I wish to draw from his treatment of cognition, practice, and production. Very briefly put, it is that Dewey's Instrumentalism is happily rooted in the soil of Peirce's account of the production of habits. Like Peirce's habits, Dewey's instruments are *conditional, general,* and *final.* They are *conditional* in the sense that they are available for use if the proper situation presents itself. Like tools in a toolbox, it is not that they *must* be used, but that they are available for use. They are *general* because they are applicable to whole classes of situations, and those classes are defined by and further refine their associated tools. There is a class of objects to which a hammer can be applied; but if an object is included in that class to which the hammer is not fully applicable, then, given the proper motivation, the hammer can be redesigned. They are *final* because even though they may operate as signs of something further, there is no requirement that they do so: they terminate in action that is satisfactory, and that is all that can be asked. For Dewey, tools perform certain types of work, and if they perform satisfactorily there is no need to develop them further, to inquire into their extended meanings.

In sum, both Peirce and Dewey reached escape velocity with respect to the traditional and still-raging debate between the cognitivists and the praxicalists. They accomplished this by measuring human development and accomplishment in terms of neither ideas, nor activities, but in terms of habits produced. Their root metaphors went beyond theory and practice all the way to production.

Viewed from a slightly different angle, the insights of Peirce and Dewey into the nature and function of habits provides support for classical Pragmatic post-postmodern solutions to the two difficulties of "official" postmodernism that I identified in chapter 1. First, because of the ways in which Peirce and Dewey link the experimentalism of the technosciences to the quotidian production of habits, they can account for objectivity. Second, because of their arguments on behalf of what Peirce termed the final, veritable, logical interpretant of a sign, they have the means to terminate processes of infinite self-referentiality, redescription, and reinterpretation in ways that can produce reliable habits which can serve as platforms for action, should the need arise.

Notes

CHAPTER ONE
CLASSICAL PRAGMATISM
Waiting at the End of the Road

1. An earlier version of this chapter was presented at a conference in Great Barrington, Massachusetts, in July 2001, sponsored by the Behavioral Research Council, a division of the American Institute for Economic Research. A revised version of that presentation was published as "Pragmatism as Post-Postmodernism," in *Dewey, Pragmatism, and Economic Methodology*, ed. Elias L. Khalil (London: Routledge, 2004), 87–101. I am grateful to my conference respondent, Elise Springer, for the meticulous care with which she read this paper and her numerous helpful suggestions for its improvement.

2. Richard Rorty, *Consequences of Pragmatism* (Minneapolis: University of Minnesota Press, 1982), xviii.

3. Ibid., 207.

4. Ibid., 208.

5. Kwame Anthony Appiah, *In My Father's House: Africa in the Philosophy of Culture* (Oxford: Oxford University Press, 1992); James Livingston, *Pragmatism and the Political Economy of Cultural Revolution, 1850–1940* (Chapel Hill: University of North Carolina Press, 1994), 214ff.

6. Elise Springer has reminded me that Dewey did not subscribe to linear models of thinking, let alone linear models of progress, and that it is therefore important to emphasize that my characterization of his work as post-postmodern does not require any metaphor of this sort. My claim is a more modest one, namely that he anticipated and resolved some of the very problems now faced by postmodernist writers.

7. Elizabeth Deeds Ermarth, *Sequel to History: Postmodernism and the Crisis of Representational Time* (Princeton, N.J.: Princeton University Press, 1992).

8. Elizabeth Deeds Ermarth, "Postmodernism," in *Routledge Encyclopedia of Philosophy* (London: Routledge, 1998).

9. Appiah, *In My Father's House*, 143.

10. Ermarth, "Postmodernism."

11. Ibid.

12. Appiah, *In My Father's House*, 145.

13. See, for example, Marshall McLuhan, *Understanding Media* (New York: McGraw-Hill, 1964).

14. John Dewey, *The Correspondence of John Dewey, 1871–1952*, ed. Larry A. Hickman, rev. ed., vol. 1 (1871–1918) (Charlottesville, Va.: Intelex, 2005), 1893.05.10 (00478).

15. Dewey, *Correspondence*, 1891.05.31 (00069).

16. Metaphysics as system, of course, takes many forms. One interesting interpretation of what this might mean can be found in the essay on the subject by W. H. Walsh, "Metaphysics, Nature of," in the *Encyclopedia of Philosophy*, ed. Paul Edwards (Macmillan, 1967), 5: 302. According to Walsh, there are "three main features in the projected science of metaphysics. It claims to tell us what really exists or what the real nature of things is, it claims to be fundamental and comprehensive in a way in which no individual science is, and it claims to reach conclusions which are intellectually impregnable and thus possess a unique kind of certainty."

17. Richard Rorty, *Contingency, Irony, and Solidarity* (Cambridge: Cambridge University Press, 1989), 94.

18. T. Hugh Crawford, "An Interview with Bruno Latour," in *Configurations* (Baltimore: Johns Hopkins University Press, 1993), 254, http://muse.jhu.edu/journals/configurations/v001/1.2crawford.html.

19. I am grateful to Stanley Fish for suggestions regarding this paragraph. He reminded me that there are in fact individuals who are temperamentally disposed to belief in a literal soul—one that can either be saved or lost for eternity—as a part of their pressing need to come to terms with the events of *this* world. This is of course a point that William James also made.

20. If liberals expect that philosophy should have anything to say about cruelty and kindness, then that "expectation is a result of a metaphysical upbringing. If we could get rid of the expectation, liberals would not ask ironist philosophy to do a job which it cannot do, and which it defines itself as unable to do." (Rorty, *Contingency*, 94).

21. Ermarth, "Postmodernism."

22. Dewey, *Correspondence*, 1939.03.05 (08613).

23. Dewey, *Correspondence*, 1940.07.10 (14016).

24. Dewey, *Correspondence*, 1940.07.18 (14017).

CHAPTER TWO
PRAGMATISM, POSTMODERNISM, AND GLOBAL CITIZENSHIP

1. Earlier versions of this essay were published under the same title in *Metaphilosophy* 35, nos. 1 and 2 (January 2004): 65–81, and in *The Range of Pragmatism and the Limits of Philosophy*, ed. Richard Shusterman (Oxford: Blackwell, 2004): 63–79.

2. The term "postmodernism" is, of course, notoriously vague. There is an important sense in which American Pragmatism is a type of postmodernism, if by that it is meant that its founders rejected some of the central theses of modernist philosophers such as Descartes and supplanted them with conceptual tools that they viewed as more productive. In this essay, however, "postmodernism" will be used to refer to a set of views that emphasize difference and discontinuity and embrace cognitive relativism, as those two positions have been characterized by their proponents, whose work will be appropriately cited. For more on this subject, see the first chapter of this volume.

3. Onora O'Neill, "Foreword," to *Global Citizenship: A Critical Introduction*, ed. Nigel Dower and John Williams (New York: Routledge, 2002), xi.

4. This was in fact the model proposed by John Dewey in *The Public and its Problems* in 1927. (LW 2.235ff)

5. Nigel Dower and John Williams, eds., *Global Citizenship: A Critical Introduction* (New York: Routledge, 2002), 5.

6. William James, *Pragmatism*, ed. Frederick Burkhardt and Fredson Bowers (Cambridge, Mass.: Harvard University Press, 1975), 31–32.

7. There is, of course, a good deal of debate regarding what, if anything, constitutes scientific method. Although most philosophers of science would probably agree that there is no one method that can be identified as "the" scientific method, according to the position of the founding Pragmatists it is nevertheless possible to identify a general method of inquiry that can be termed "scientific," as opposed, for example, to methods of authority, tenacity, or a priori reasoning.

8. William James, *Pragmatism*, 32.

9. Charles Sanders Peirce, *Collected Papers*, ed. Charles Hartshorne and Paul Weiss (Cambridge, Mass.: Harvard University Press, Belknap Press 1935), 5: 258. Whenever possible I will also cite the new—but not yet complete—edition of Peirce's writings. In the present case: Charles Sanders Peirce, *The Writings of Charles S. Peirce: A Chronological Edition*, vol. 3, 1872–1878, ed. Christian J. W. Kloesel (Bloomington: Indiana University Press, 1986), 266.

10. William James, *Pragmatism*, 259.

11. Peirce, *Collected Papers*, 5:317.

12. Peirce had characterized truth as opinion that converges toward reality over time as the result of the efforts of a community of inquiry.

13. James, *Pragmatism*, 97.

14. Bertrand Russell had accused Dewey of attempting to substitute his notion of warranted assertibility for truth. Dewey replied that he did not wish to *substitute* warranted assertibility for truth, but to *define* truth as warranted assertibility (LW 14.168–88).

15. Stuart Sim, ed., *The Routledge Companion to Postmodernism* (London: Routledge, 2001), 5. As Stuart Sim has noted, "There is what amounts to a commitment to finding, and dwelling on, dissimilarity, difference, and the unpredictability of analysis among poststructuralist thinkers."

16. William James, *Essays in Radical Empiricism*, ed. Frederick Burkhardt and Fredson Bowers (Cambridge, Mass.: Harvard University Press, 1976), 26.

17. Ibid., 31.

18. The 1896 volume of the *Psychological Review*, for example, under "Studies from the Psychological Laboratory of the University of Chicago" contains several reports on experimental work by Dewey's departmental colleagues. In addition, Dewey was drawing on the experimental work of colleagues in other departments of the University of Chicago, such as the neurologist C. L. Herrick. See Thomas Dalton, *Becoming John Dewey: Dilemmas of a Philosopher and Naturalist* (Bloomington: Indiana University Press, 2002), 65.

19. Charles Haddock Seigfried, "Socializing Democracy: Jane Addams and John Dewey," *Philosophy of Social Sciences* 29, no. 2 (1999): 213.

20. Seyyed Hossein Nasr, *Science and Civilization in Islam* (Cambridge, Mass.: Harvard University Press, 1968), 27.

21. Elizabeth Deeds Ermarth, "Postmodernism," in *Routledge Encyclopedia of Philosophy* (London and New York: Routledge, 1998).

22. Ian Hamilton Grant, "Postmodernism and Politics," in *The Routledge Companion to Postmodernism*, ed. Stuart Sim (London: Routledge, 2001), 30.

23. Emrys Westacott, "Relativism of Autonomy," *The Philosophical Forum* 27, no. 2 (1996): 131. Thanks to John Hartmann for calling my attention to this wonderfully concise statement of the position.

24. David Wong, "Relativism," in *A Companion to Ethics*, ed. Peter Singer (Oxford: Blackwell, 1994), 442–50. David Wong reminds us that "almost all polemics against moral relativism are directed at its most extreme versions." He advocates a position that holds that there is no single true morality, but

at the same time he "does not deny that some moralities might be false and inadequate for the functions they all must perform." The position of this essay is that cognitive relativism is a form of moral relativism, since morality requires judgments. Moreover, it is an extreme form of relativism, since it provides no methodological basis for making such judgments. Wong, "Relativism," 446.

25. I am hardly the first to point out that the cognitive relativist appears to adopt a standpoint that he or she treats as privileged.

26. That true judgments are warranted means that substantive work has been done *in the past* to support them against challenges. That they are assertible means that they have a generality of application over relevant cases *in the future*. Their universalizability means that they are applicable anywhere, under relevant conditions, until successfully challenged. The judgment that a sample of pure tin melts at 232°C at one standard atmosphere is thus universaliz*able* in the sense that it *would be* applicable anywhere regardless of cultural differences, even if it is not universaliz*ed*, that is, actually practiced in a particular culture. That some cultures do not melt tin does not, therefore, militate against the universalizability of the judgment. The Pragmatists identified judgments of this type as habits of action in the sense that they provide the basis for future activities until replaced with something more appropriate.

27. See Martin E. Marty and R. Scott Appleby, eds., *Fundamentalisms and Society* (Chicago: The University of Chicago Press, 1993) and Vine Deloria Jr., *Red Earth, White Lies, Native Americans and the Myth of Scientific Fact* (New York: Scribner, 1995).

CHAPTER THREE

CLASSICAL PRAGMATISM, POSTMODERNISM, AND
NEOPRAGMATISM

1. An earlier version of this chapter was presented at the World Congress of Philosophy, Istanbul, Turkey, August 13, 2003. It develops some of the themes of my earlier essay "Art, Technoscience, and Social Action," published as the fourth chapter of *Philosophical Tools for Technological Culture: Putting Pragmatism to Work* (Bloomington: Indiana University Press, 2001).

2. Rorty's address was published as "Pragmatism, Relativism, and Irrationalism," in *Consequences of Pragmatism* (Minneapolis: University of Minnesota Press, 1982), 160–75.

3. The term postmodernism is, of course, notoriously vague. See the first and second chapters of this volume for a discussion of some of the meanings of the term.

4. Richard Rorty, *Consequences of Pragmatism* (Minneapolis: University of Minnesota Press, 1982): xviii.

5. Ibid., 207.

6. James Livingston, *Pragmatism and the Political Economy of Cultural Revolution, 1850–1940* (Chapel Hill: The University of North Carolina Press, 1997), 214.

7. Ibid.

8. It could also be argued that Pragmatism is a "post-postmodernism," that is, that it has come to terms with many of the problems that continue to bedevil official postmodernism. See chapter 1, "Pragmatism as Post-Post-modernism" for an extended discussion of this issue.

9. Emrys Westacott, "Relativism and Autonomy," *The Philosophical Forum* 27, no. 2 (1996): 131.

10. Alan Sokal and Jean Bricmont, *Fashionable Nonsense: Postmodern Intellectuals' Abuse of Science* (New York: Picador USA, 1998).

11. Jim Holt, "Fashionable Nonsense," *New York Times Book Review*, November 15, 1998, 8.

12. Rorty, *Consequences*, 51.

13. Richard Rorty, *Contingency, Irony, and Solidarity* (Cambridge: Cambridge University Press, 1989), 83.

14. Ibid., 13.

15. See chapter 4 of this volume for an extended Pragmatist critique of the work of Habermas.

16. Ralph Sleeper, *The Necessity of Pragmatism* (New Haven, Conn.: Yale University Press, 1986), 1.

17. Larry A. Hickman, *Philosophical Tools for Technological Culture: Putting Pragmatism to Work* (Bloomington: Indiana University Press, 2001), 98ff.

18. Konstantin Kolenda, *Rorty's Humanistic Pragmatism: Philosophy Democratized* (Tampa: University of South Florida Press, 1990), 37.

19. Richard Rorty, *Rorty & Pragmatism*, ed. Herman J. Saatkamp, Jr. (Nashville, Tenn.: Vanderbilt University Press, 1995).

20. Richard Rorty, *Philosophy and Social Hope* (New York: Penguin, 1999), 237.

21 Ibid., 238–39.

22. Steven Shapin, "Dear Prudence," *London Review of Books*, January 24, 2002, 25.

23. Hickman, *Philosophical Tools for Technological Culture.*

24. James Gouinlock, "What is the Legacy of Instrumentalism? Rorty's Interpretation of Dewey," in *Rorty & Pragmatism*, ed. Herman J. Saatkamp, Jr. (Nashville, Tenn.: Vanderbilt University Press, 1995), 72–90.

25. Ibid., 88.

26. Ibid., 89.

27. Richard Rorty, "Response to James Gouinlock," in *Rorty & Pragmatism*, ed. Herman J. Saatkamp Jr. (Nashville, Tenn.: Vanderbilt University Press, 1995), 92.

28. Ibid.

29. Ibid., 94.

30. Ibid., 93.

CHAPTER FOUR

CLASSICAL PRAGMATISM AND COMMUNICATIVE ACTION

Jürgen Habermas

1. This chapter first appeared as "Habermas's Unresolved Dualism: *Zweckrationalität* as *Idée Fixe*," in *Perspectives on Habermas*, ed. Lewis Edwin Hahn (Chicago: Open Court, 2000), 501–13.

2. Jürgen Habermas, *Toward a Rational Society*, trans. Jeremy J. Shapiro (Boston: Beacon Press, 1970), 91.

3. Ibid., 92.

4. Jürgen Habermas, *Theory and Practice*, trans. John Viertel (Boston: Beacon Press, 1973).

5. Herbert Marcuse, *One-Dimensional Man* (Boston: Beacon Press, 1964) as quoted by Habermas, *Toward a Rational Society*, 86.

6. Habermas, *Toward a Rational Society*, 87.

7. Jürgen Habermas, *Knowledge and Human Interests*, trans. Jeremy J. Shapiro (Boston: Beacon Press, 1971), 315.

8. Ibid., 316.

9. Habermas sometimes seems to sense that he may have gone a bit too far in championing this breach between scientific technology and the human sciences. He attempts to backpedal in a footnote to his essay "Reconstruction and Interpretation in the Social Sciences." "I should add," he writes, "that by distinguishing sciences based on hermeneutic procedures from those that are not, I am not advocating an ontological dualism between specific domains of reality (e.g., culture versus nature, values versus facts, or similar neo-Kantian dichotomies introduced chiefly by Windelband, Rickert, and Cassirer). What I do advocate is a *methodological* distinction between sciences that gain access to their object domain by understanding what is said to someone and those which do not. All sciences have to address problems of interpretation at the *metatheoretical level*. . . . Yet only those with a hermeneutic dimension of research face problems of interpretation

already at the level of *data generation* [emphasis in original]." Jürgen Habermas, "Reconstruction and Interpretation in the Social Sciences," in *Moral Consciousness and Communicative Action*, trans. Christian Lenhardt and Shierry Weber Nicholsen (Cambridge, Mass.: MIT Press, 1990), 41–42n. Habermas thus seems to want to avoid a dualism of fact and value by replacing it with a dualism of theory and metatheory.

10. Habermas, "Reconstruction and Interpretation in the Social Sciences," 26.

11. Hans Joas, "The Unhappy Marriage of Hermeneutics and Functionalism," in *Communicative Action*, ed. Axel Honneth and Hans Joas, trans. Jeremy Gaines and Doris L. Jones (Cambridge, Mass.: MIT Press, 1991), 101.

12. Alan Ryan, *John Dewey and the High Tide of American Liberalism* (New York: Norton, 1995), 357.

13. Habermas, *Knowledge and Human Interests*, 309.

14. Robert J. Antonio and Douglas Kellner, "Communication, Modernity, and Democracy in Habermas and Dewey," *Symbolic Interaction* 15 (1992): 277–97. See especially their comments on page 284. "In contrast to Habermas's sharp division between 'labor' and 'interaction,' Dewey treated technical and communicative activities as continuous, entwined spheres." And further, "Contrary to Habermas, Dewey's antidualistic naturalism opposes any effort to set off communication from other forms of understanding."

15. Habermas, *Knowledge and Human Interests*, 309.

16. Ibid., 310.

17. Jürgen Habermas, *The Theory of Communicative Action*, vol. 1, trans. Thomas McCarthy (Boston: Beacon Press, 1984), 288.

18. Jürgen Habermas, *The Past as Future*, ed. and trans. Max Pensky (Lincoln, Neb.: University of Nebraska Press, 1994).

19. Ibid., 101.

20. Ibid., 102.

21. Ibid., 101–2.

22. Hilary Putnam and Ruth Anna Putnam have also noted the fact that experimentation does not seem to play much of a role in Habermas's account of communicative action. See Hilary Putnam and Ruth Anna Putnam, "Education for Democracy," in *Educational Theory* 43, no. 4 (Fall 1993): 371: "Although Habermas does not actually deny the need for experiment in the establishment of norms, he rarely mentions it. His picture is one in which communities arrive at norms by mere discussion, while they arrive at 'facts' by experimentation. Moreover, (although Habermas has been moving away from this of late), the methodology that is supposed to guide the norm-producing discussion is itself derived *a priori*, via a 'transcendental pragmatics.'"

Dewey, we believe, would welcome Habermas's notion of an 'emancipatory interest,' but he would wish to break down all of the dualisms and reject all of the apriorism implicit in Habermas's scheme."

23. Antonio and Kellner, "Communication, Modernity, and Democracy in Habermas and Dewey," 280. "[Habermas's] Pragmatism is partial and contradictory, because of his nonhistorical standard of communicative rationality."

24. Hilary Putnam and Ruth Anna Putnam, "Education for Democracy," 361–76.

CHAPTER FIVE

FROM CRITICAL THEORY TO PRAGMATISM
Andrew Feenberg

1. This chapter was first published in *Philosophy of Technology: New Debates in the Democratization of Technology*, ed. Tyler Veek (Albany: State University of New York Press, 2006), 71–81.

2. See Joel Anderson, "The 'Third Generation' of the Frankfurt School," in *Intellectual History Newsletter* 22 (2000), http://www.phil.uu.nl/%7Ejoel/research/publications/3rdGeneration.htm.

3. Andrew Feenberg, *Questioning Technology* (London: Routledge, 1999), 136. Hereinafter in text and in notes as QT. Feenberg devotes about a half page to Dewey, but dismisses his view as exhibiting a "rather uncritical confidence in science and technology."

4. Since Horkheimer and Adorno identify technology with instrumental rationality, they see an unbridgeable gulf between technology and the values of the human sciences. The same is true for Heidegger and Habermas. Marcuse's version of this position was considerably more flexible. He thought that scientific technology might be reformed under the proper conditions. A necessary condition for such reform would be the reform of political life.

5. Anderson, "The 'Third Generation' of the Frankfurt School."

6. QT, xiii, 9. See also Andrew Feenberg, "Subversive Rationalization: Technology, Power, and Democracy," in *Technology and the Politics of Knowledge*, ed. Andrew Feenberg and Alastar Hannay (Bloomington: Indiana University Press, 1995), 4.

7. Don Idhe's quote comes from Don Idhe, *Technology and the Lifeworld* (Bloomington and Indianapolis: Indiana University Press, 1990), 128.

8. See Melvin Kranzberg, "The Information Age," in *Computers in the Human Context: Information Technology, Productivity and People*," ed. Tom Forester (London: Blackwell, 1989), 30.

9. Feenberg, "Subversive Rationalization," 4.

10. Ibid., 10.

11. Ibid.

1. An earlier version of this chapter was presented at the Workshop on Technology and the Character of Contemporary Life, in Jasper National Park, Alberta, Canada, September 1995, as "Devices, Focal Concerns, and the Reform of Technology: A Pragmatist Looks at Albert Borgmann's *Technology and the Character of Contemporary Life*." A revised version of that presentation was presented at the Meeting of the Central Division of the American Philosophical Association, New Orleans, Louisiana, May 8, 1999, as "Opening Borgmann's Black Box."

2. Langdon Winner, *Autonomous Technology* (Cambridge, Mass.: MIT Press, 1977), 228.

3. Albert Borgmann, *Technology and the Character of Contemporary Life* (Chicago: The University of Chicago Press, 1984), 197.

4. Ibid., 178.

5. Ibid., 179.

6. Ibid., 220.

7. Ibid.

8. Ibid., 221.

9. Ibid., 198.

10. Ibid., 141.

11. Larry A. Hickman, "Technology, Final Structures, and Focal Things," Review of *Technology and the Character of Contemporary Life*, by Albert Borgmann, *Research in Philosophy and Technology* 12 (1992): 337–45.

12. Albert Borgmann, "Reply to Larry Hickman," *Research in Philosophy and Technology* 12 (1992): 346.

13. Borgmann, *Technology and the Character of Contemporary Life*, 9.

14. Ibid., 10.

15. Ibid., 30.

16. Ibid., 11.

17. Ibid.

18. Larry A. Hickman, *John Dewey's Pragmatic Technology* (Bloomington: Indiana University Press, 1990).

19. Borgmann, "Reply to Larry Hickman," 345–47.

20. Borgmann, "Reply to Larry Hickman," 346.

21. Ibid.

22. Ibid., 347.

23. Ibid.

24. Borgmann, *Technology and the Character of Contemporary Life*, 219.

25. Ibid.

26. Ibid.

CHAPTER SEVEN

DOING AND MAKING IN A DEMOCRACY
John Dewey

1. Earlier versions of this chapter were published as "Doing and Making in a Democracy: John Dewey's Experience of Technology," in *Philosophy of Technology: Practical, Historical and Other Dimensions, Philosophy and Technology*, ed. Paul T. Durbin (Dordrecht: Kluwer Academic Publishers, 1989), 5: 97–111; and in *Philosophy of Technology*, ed. Robert C. Scharff and Val Dusek (Cambridge, Mass.: Blackwell, 2003), 369–77.

2. Dewey devoted no single work to his analysis of technology. His treatment of the subject is diffused throughout the thirty-seven volumes of his published work. For this and other reasons, the secondary literature of this field is scant. One of the first essays to call attention to this strain in his work was Webster F. Hood's, "Dewey and Technology," in *Research in Philosophy and Technology*, ed. Paul T. Durbin (Greenwich, Conn.: JAI Press, 1982), 5.189–207.

3. As Hannah Arendt pointed out in her classic essay "The *Vita Activa* in the Modern Age," in *The Human Condition* (Chicago: University of Chicago Press, 1958), 7–11, Aristotle's *Metaphysics* had placed the sciences of fabrication above the practical sciences but below the theoretical ones. She thought that this was so because for the Greeks the contemplation of the theoretical sciences was thought to be an inherent element in fabrication, that is, what allowed the craftsman to judge the finished product. The point of Dewey's critique of the Greeks was not that they did not give *techne* some of its due, but that they thought it secondary to grander technical forces, viz., supernature for Plato, and nature for Aristotle.

4. Plato, *Timaeus and Critias*, trans. Desmond Lee (New York: Penguin, 1983), 18.

5. Plato, *Timaeus and Critias*, 19.

6. Daniel Boorstin, *The Discoverers* (New York: Random House, 1983), 318.

7. Paolo Rossi, *Philosophy, Technology and the Arts in the Early Modern Era* (New York: Harper and Row, 1970), 35.

8. Stuart Hampshire, "Morality and Pessimism," in *The Philosophy of Society,* ed. R. Beehler and A. Drengson (London: Methuen, 1978), 32.

9. L. J. Beck, *The Method of Descartes* (Oxford: Clarendon Press, 1952), 261–262.

10. Don Ihde, *Existential Technics* (Albany: State University of New York Press, 1983), 25–46.

11. Martin Heidegger, *The Question Concerning Technology and Other Essays,* trans. and ed. William Lovitt (New York: Harper and Row, 1977), 12.

12. Heidegger, *The Question,* 13.

13. This quotation is from Bertrand Russell, *Religion and Science* (New York: Henry Holt, 1935), 12. Although the statement serves Dewey's purpose in this essay, there remains an underlying disagreement with Russell. There is something of the "mental mirror" in Russell's epistemology. Dewey rejects this view out of hand.

CHAPTER EIGHT

NATURE AS CULTURE

John Dewey and Aldo Leopold

1. This is a revised version of an essay by the same name published in *Environmental Pragmatism,* ed. Andrew Light and Eric Katz (London: Routledge, 1996), 50–72.

2. Dewey's British critics, including Bertrand Russell, and his German critics, including Theodor Adorno and Max Horkheimer read, or more properly misread, him in this way. Even George Santayana took up the refrain when he characterized Dewey as "the devoted spokesman of the spirit of enterprise, of experiment, of modern industry" and claimed that his philosophy was "calculated to justify all the assumptions of American society." See George Santayana, "Dewey's Naturalistic Metaphysics," in *The Philosophy of John Dewey,* ed. P. A. Schilpp and L. E. Hahn, 3rd ed. (La Salle, Ill.: Open Court, 1989), 247.'

3. George Santayana, "Dewey's Naturalistic Metaphysics," 251.

4. John Dewey, "Experience, Knowledge and Value," in *The Philosophy of John Dewey,* ed. P. A. Schilpp and L. E. Hahn, 3rd ed. (La Salle, Ill.: Open Court, 1989), 532.

5. John Dewey, "Experience, Knowledge and Value," 532–33.

6. John Dewey, "Experience, Knowledge and Value," 534. The term "emanates" was Santayana's. Dewey allowed its usage in connection with his

own view, provided that the *"aura* that clings to the word" be eliminated. See LW 14.19.

7. This is Frederic L. Bender's reading of James Lovelock. See Frederic L. Bender, "The Gaia Hypothesis: Philosophical Implications," in *Technology and Ecology*, ed. Larry A. Hickman and Elizabeth F. Porter (Carbondale, Ill.: Society for Philosophy and Technology Press, 1993), 64–81.

8. See Carolyn Merchant, *The Death of Nature* (San Francisco: Harper and Row, 1980), 293.

9. Paul W. Taylor, *Respect for Nature: A Theory of Environmental Ethics* (Princeton, N.J.: Princeton University Press, 1986), 75. Taylor does not base his biocentrism on the rights of individual nonhuman organisms, but rather on their status as "teleological centers of life." (Taylor, *Respect for Nature*, 122) He does allow that human beings have the right to destroy predatory organisms, such as the smallpox virus, on grounds of self defense. (Taylor, *Respect for Nature*, 264.)

10. Taylor, *Respect for Nature*, 99.

11. Dewey freely admits his debt to William James's for his notion of radical empiricism. "Long ago I learned from William James that there are immediate experiences of the connections linguistically expressed by conjunctions and prepositions. My doctrinal position is but a generalization of what is involved in this fact" (LW 14.18, note 16). Dewey's own term for this was "immediate empiricism," but I use James's term here to emphasize the provenance of the idea.

12. Max Oelschlaeger, *The Idea of Wilderness* (New Haven, Conn.: Yale University Press, 1991).

13. Ibid., 206.

14. Ibid., 216. See Bryan G. Norton, *Toward Unity among Environmentalists* (New York: Oxford University Press, 1991), especially 39–60, for an account of Leopold's development that differs slightly from that of Oelschlaeger. Norton thinks that Leopold's position was better integrated than Oelschlaeger and I believe it to have been. Norton does, however, make an interesting comment that relates to the notion of "nature-as-culture" that I am attempting to develop in this essay. He sees Leopold's work as "guiding the search for a *culturally* defined value in nature" (Norton, *Toward Unity among Environmentalists*, 58).

15. Oelschlaeger, *The Idea of Wilderness*, 228.

16. Aldo Leopold, "Some Fundamentals of Conservation in the Southwest," in *The River of the Mother of God and Other Essays*, ed. Susan L. Flader and J. Baird Callicott (Madison: University of Wisconsin Press, 1991), 95.

17. Leopold withheld "Some Fundamentals of Conservation in the Southwest" from publication during his lifetime.

18. Aldo Leopold, "Game and Wild Life Conservation," in *The River of the Mother of God and Other Essays*, ed. Susan L. Flader and J. Baird Callicott (Madison: University of Wisconsin Press, 1991), 166.

19. Aldo Leopold, *Game Management* (New York: Scribner, 1936).

20. Oelschlaeger, *The Idea of Wilderness*, 227.

21. Nathaniel T. Wheelwright, "Enduring Reasons to Preserve Threatened Species," *The Chronicle of Higher Education*, June 1, 1994, B2.

22. Aldo Leopold, "The Conservation Ethic," in *The River of the Mother of God and Other Essays*, ed. Susan L. Flader and J. Baird Callicott (Madison: University of Wisconsin Press, 1991), 183.

23. Thomas H. Huxley, *Evolution and Ethics and Other Essays* (New York: D. Appleton, 1896), 81–83, *et passim*. Quoted in EW 5.36.

24. See, however, the argument of Bob Pepperman Taylor that Dewey's view of nature represents no advance over that of Locke. Bob Pepperman Taylor, "John Dewey and Environmental Thought," in *Environmental Ethics* 12, no. 2, (Summer 1990): 183. Dewey was in fact quite critical of Locke's view of nature. Locke, Dewey writes, "was completely under the domination of the ruling idea of his time: namely, that *Nature* is the norm of truth." Further, "Nature is both beneficent and truthful in its work; it retains all the properties of the Supreme Being whose vice-regent it is" (MW 8.59). The irony here is that if Dewey's reading of Locke is correct, then his (Locke's) view of nature is much closer to that of the idealistic environmentalists such as Paul Taylor than it is to Dewey's view. This is a point that Bob Pepperman Taylor apparently misses.

25. See Oelschlaeger, *The Idea of Wilderness*, 226 for an account of this.

26. Ibid., 228.

27. Dewey apparently did not know of Koehler's work with apes, and so he denies choice to nonhuman animals. Since self-reflexive communication is the basis of his account of responsible action, however, he might well have wished to have included nonhuman animals, such as chimps who have learned sign language and entered into communication with themselves and humans by its means, as moral agents and thereby the bearers of rights. In any case, Dewey was enough of an evolutionist that he was acutely aware of transitions within nature, and that the history of evolutionary development is more or less continuous, if not in the temporal sense, then at least in the functional sense. For more on Koehler, see W. Koehler, *Mentality of Apes* (London: Kegan, 1924).

28. The question of legal (as opposed to moral) rights is, of course, a different matter. Legislators have in fact given legal rights to entities that are not moral agents. But legal rights are normally extended on the basis of human interests, and not on the basis of some putative status independent of human interests.

29. This tension is clear in Leopold's 1933 essay "The Conservation Ethic," where he writes of ethics as "possibly a kind of advanced social instinct." Whereas Leopold seems to think that there is already an ethics at work at the level of the aesthetic, Dewey would have argued that the primitive aesthetic response furnishes a platform for working out an ethical response to nonhuman nature. In the next paragraph, however, Leopold takes another tack. He suggests that the ethical dimensions of the human relation to the land is still in the formative stage, and that "science cannot escape its part in forming them." Dewey would have argued that if a robust land ethic is to be developed at all, then science will have to play a part. See Aldo Leopold, "The Conservation Ethic," 182.

30. See Frederic L. Bender, "The Gaia Hypothesis: Philosophical Implications," 68–71.

31. Eric Katz, "The Big Lie: Human Restoration of Nature," *Research in Philosophy and Technology* 12 (1992): 240.

32. See William R. Jordan III, " 'Sunflower Forest': Ecological Restoration as the Basis for a New Environmental Paradigm," in *Beyond Preservation: Restoring and Inventing Landscapes*, ed. A. Dwight Baldwin Jr., Judith De Luce and Carl Pletsch (Minneapolis: University of Minnesota Press, 1994), 17–34.

33. Ibid., 21.

34. Ibid., 24.

35. Ibid.

36. Ibid., 31.

37. Aldo Leopold, *A Sand County Almanac* (New York: Oxford University Press, 1966), 251.

CHAPTER NINE

GREEN PRAGMATISM
Reals without Realism, Ideals without Idealism

1. This is a slightly revised version of an essay by the same name published in *Research in Philosophy and Technology* 18 (1999): 39–56.

2. "America's Philosopher Attains an Alert 90," *New York Times Magazine*, October 16, 1949, 17, 74–75.

3. Larry A. Hickman, *John Dewey's Pragmatic Technology* (Bloomington: Indiana University Press, 1990).

4. Robert B. Westbrook, *John Dewey and American Democracy* (Ithaca, N.Y.: Cornell University Press, 1991), 75. STL, 330 refers to MW 2.330.

5. J. Baird Callicott, "On the Intrinsic Value of Nonhuman Species," in *The Preservation of Species*, ed. Bryan G. Norton (Princeton, N.J.: Princeton University Press, 1986), 142.

6. Ibid., 143.

7. Ibid., 142.

8. Decisions concerning which of two invaluable goods to sacrifice under conditions in which they become incompatible can precipitate profound personality disorders. Just such a case is presented in William Styron's novel *Sophie's Choice*.

9. Callicott, "On the Intrinsic Value of Nonhuman Species," 161.

10. J. Baird Callicott, "Intrinsic Value in Nature: A Metaethical Analysis," *Electronic Journal of Analytical Philosophy* 3 (Spring 1995): 59. Emphasis added.

11. J. Baird Callicott, "The Pragmatic Power and Promise of Theoretical Environmental Ethics: Forging a New Discourse," *Environmental Values* 11, no. 1 (Fall 2002): 17.

12. Ibid., 21.

13. Ibid., 22.

14. Brian G. Norton, "Environmental Ethics and Weak Anthropocentrism," *Environmental Ethics* 6 (Summer 1984): 134.

15. Ibid.

16. Ibid.

17. This is ironic, of course, because one of the great antagonists of the idealists of this period was G. E. Moore. "Eaton," Dewey's name for the character who presents the Pragmatist position, is also significant. It is probably a reference to the fact that we must eat to live.

18. Michael E. Zimmerman, "Quantum Theory, Intrinsic Value, and Panentheism," *Environmental Ethics* 10 (Spring 1988): 27.

19. Michael E. Zimmerman, "What Can Continental Philosophy Contribute to Environmentalism?" in *Rethinking Nature*, ed. Bruce V. Foltz and Robert Frodeman (Bloomington: Indiana University Press, 2004): 222.

20. Holmes Rolston III, "Values Gone Wild," *Inquiry* 26 (June 1983), 183. Emphasis on last two words added.

21. Ibid.

22. Ibid., 187.

23. Ibid., 197.

24. Ibid., 198.

25. Holmes Rolston III, *Philosophy Gone Wild: Essays in Environmental Ethics* (Buffalo: Prometheus Books, 1986), 44.

26. Ibid.

27. Rolston, "Values Gone Wild," 197.

28. Ibid.

29. Ibid.

30. Ibid.

31. Aldo Leopold, "Some Fundamentals of Conservation in the Southwest," in *The River of the Mother of God and Other Essays*, ed. Susan L. Flader and J. Baird Callicott (Madison: University of Wisconsin Press, 1991), 166.

CHAPTER TEN

WHAT WAS DEWEY'S MAGIC NUMBER?

1. This chapter was first published in *Contemporary Philosophy, Proceedings of the Twentieth World Congress of Philosophy*, ed. Daniel O. Dahlstrom (Bowling Green, Ohio: Philosophy Documentation Center, 2000), 8:221–31.

2. This observation is from a private correspondence with Michael Eldridge. I am grateful for his characteristically insightful analysis of an earlier version of this paper.

3. See volume 1, section 530 of Charles Sanders Peirce, *The Collected Papers of Charles Sanders Peirce*, vols. 1–6 ed. Charles Hartshorne and Paul Weiss, vols. 7 and 8 ed. Arthur W. Burks (Cambridge, Mass.: Harvard University Press, 1932–1960). Standard citation is by volume and section, rather than page number.

4. The term "mediation" is ambiguous in Peirce's work. In the context of his theory of inquiry, mediation is associated with the "middle" phase of deliberation that succeeds doubt and precedes resolution. In the context of his semiotic, mediation is associated with something standing to some sign-user in some way, which is to say that it is associated with a Third.

CHAPTER ELEVEN

CULTIVATING A COMMON FAITH

John Dewey's Religion

1. An earlier version of this chapter was published as "Cultivating a Common Faith: John Dewey on Religion and Education," in the *Korean Journal of Religious Education* 18, no. 6 (2004): 59–77 (in English); 79–95 (in Korean).

2. Michael Eldridge, *Transforming Experience* (Nashville, Tenn.: Vanderbilt University Press, 1998), 141.

3. Charlene Haddock Seigfried, "Pragmatism" in *The Cambridge Dictionary of Philosophy*, ed. Robert Audi (New York: Cambridge University Press, 1999), 730.

4. Eldridge, *Transforming Experience*, 141.

CHAPTER TWELVE

BEYOND THE EPISTEMOLOGY INDUSTRY

Dewey's Theory of Inquiry

1. This chapter is a revision of "Dewey's Theory of Inquiry," in *Reading Dewey: Interpretations for a Postmodern Generation*, ed. Larry A. Hickman (Bloomington: Indiana University Press, 1998), 166–86.

2. There is a good deal more to say about this issue. Dewey discusses the "excluded middle" further in his 1930 essay "The Applicability of Logic to Existence" (LW 5.203–9). Here is Dewey, responding to Ernest Nagel: "Fixing context, defining a set of operations, is just the work of thought. Upon *its* product, then, the excluded middle can be directly brought to bear. This was my point. And as I explicitly pointed out, the resulting definition—the reflectively defined object—is of use or avail in *dealing* with actual existence. What was denied was that *apart* from this work of reflection in fixing context and defining meaning, the properties designated by the excluded middle characterize existence. Mr. Nagel has given a valuable explicit statement of what I called 'the ideational and ideal character of "open" and "shut" ' " (LW 5.205–6). Instead of the difficulty being due to "failure to define operationally" the ideas used, the reverse is true. This operational definition is precisely what constitutes the object of thought, and its absence from prior existence is just why the properties of excluded middle do not characterize, and may not be assigned to, the strictly existential door (LW 5.205–6).

3. William James, *Pragmatism* (Cambridge, Mass.: Harvard University Press, 1975), 63–64.

4. See, for example, Alonzo Church, *Introduction to Mathematical Logic*, vol. 1 (Princeton, N.J.: Princeton University Press, 1956), 26–27.

CHAPTER THIRTEEN

THE *HOMO FABER* DEBATE IN DEWEY AND MAX SCHELER

1. An earlier version of this chapter was presented at the annual meeting of the Society for the Advancement of American Philosophy, Philadelphia, Pennsylvania, March 1987.

2. Sidney Hook, *The Metaphysics of Pragmatism* (Chicago: Open Court, 1927).

3. Ibid., 7.

4. Henri Bergson, *Creative Evolution* (New York: Henry Holt, 1911), 139.

5. Bergson, *Creative Evolution*, 23.

6. Ibid., 138–39.

7. Ibid., 138.

8. Ibid.

9. Hook, *The Metaphysics of Pragmatism*, 7.

10. Max Scheler, "Mensch und Geschichte," in *Philosophische Weltanschauung* (Bern: Francke Verlag, 1954).

11. Max Scheler, *Man's Place in Nature* (New York: Noonday, 1961).

12. Scheler, "Mensch und Geschichte," 73–74.

13. Scheler, *Man's Place in Nature*, 35.

14. Ibid.

15. Scheler, "Mensch und Geschichte," 67.

16. Scheler, *Man's Place in Nature*, 36.

17. Ibid., 36n.

18. Ibid., 36.

19. What I offer as key to the different accounts of human uniqueness in Scheler and Dewey is that Scheler was ultimately a religious thinker who, despite his prescient attempts to devise a phenomenology of experience, found it impossible to break with the traditional language of transcendent Being which, he thought, gives meaning to the human project. In *Man's Place in Nature* he wrote of "Being, absolute in itself, that transcends all finite contents of experience and the central being of man himself, and that commands an awe-inspiring holiness." Scheler, *Man's Place in Nature*, 89. These remarks stand in stark contrast to those of Dewey six years later in his 1934 book *A Common Faith*. He there rejected supernaturalism and transcendent entities of all types, especially for explanatory purposes. He characterized religion as a class of activities that is internally inconsistent, and he suggested, quite consistently with Scheler's phenomenological project, that religious experience is not *an experience* in itself, but rather a quality of many types of experience.

20. Scheler, *Man's Place in Nature*, 73.

21. Ibid., 74.

22. Ibid.

23. Ibid., 78.

24. Ibid., 80.

25. Ibid., 81.

CHAPTER FOURTEEN
HABITS AS ARTIFACTS IN DEWEY AND PEIRCE

1. This chapter is a revised version of "The Products of Pragmatism," in *Living Doubt: Essays Concerning the Epistemology of Charles Sanders Peirce*, ed. G. Debrock and M. Hulswit (Dordrecht: Kluwer Academic Publishers, 1994), 13–26.

2. Bertrand Russell, *An Inquiry into Meaning and Truth* (Baltimore: Penguin, 1969), 304.

3. Max Horkheimer, *Eclipse of Reason*, (New York: Seabury Press, 1974 [1947]), 42ff. "The core of this philosophy [Pragmatism] is the opinion that an idea, a concept, or a theory is nothing but a scheme or plan of action, and therefore truth is nothing but the successfulness of the idea."

4. Lewis Mumford, *The Golden Day* (New York: Dover, 1968), 137.

5. See volume 5, section 3 (5:3) of the *Collected Papers of Charles Sanders Peirce*, vols. 1–6, ed. Charles Hartshorne and Paul Weiss, vols. 7 and 8, ed. Arthur W. Burks (Cambridge, Mass.: Harvard University Press, 1931–58). In referring to the papers, I will follow the standard practice of using the volume and section number.

6. Richard Bernstein, *Praxis and Action* (Philadelphia: University of Pennsylvania Press, 1971), xiii.

7. Don Ihde, *Technics and Praxis* (Boston: D. Reidel, 1979), 117.

8. Heidegger, too, makes much of *poietike*, but his emphasis is quite different. For Heidegger it is as if language itself absorbs other forms of *poietike*, and language becomes actor instead of tool.

9. 5:512. "Every decent house dog has been taught beliefs that appear to have no application to the wild state of the dog."

10. Peirce explicitly rejects the view advanced by William James in *The Principles of Psychology* that the production of a habit must involve repetition. "[It] is noticeable that the iteration of the action is often said to be indispensable to the formation of a habit; but a very moderate exercise of observation suffices to refute this error. A single reading yesterday of a casual statement that the 'shtar chindis' means in Romany 'four shillings,' though it is unlikely to receive any reinforcement beyond the recalling of it, at this moment, is likely to produce the habit of thinking that 'four' in the Gypsy tongue is 'shtar,' that will last for months, if not for years, though I should never call it to mind in the interval. To be sure, there has been some iteration just now, while I dwelt on the matter long enough to write these sentences; but I do not believe any reminiscence like this was needed to create the habit; for such instances have been extremely numerous in acquiring different languages. There are, of course, other means than repetition of intensifying habit-changes. In particular, there is a peculiar kind of effort, which may

be likened to an imperative command addressed to the future self. I suppose the psychologists would call it an act of auto-suggestion" (5:477).

11. Larry A. Hickman, *Late Scholastic Theories of Higher Level Predicates* (Munich: Philosophia Verlag, 1980).

12. Larry A. Hickman, "Why Peirce Didn't Like Dewey's Logic," *Southwest Philosophy Review* 3 (1986): 178–89.

13. William James, *Psychology: Briefer Course* (Cambridge, Mass.: Harvard University Press, 1984), 132.

14. George Gentry, "Habit and the Logical Interpretant," in *Studies in the Philosophy of Charles Sanders Peirce*, ed. Philip P. Wiener and Frederic H. Young (Cambridge, Mass.: Harvard University Press, 1952), 75–90.

15. "I need not repeat that I do not say that it is the single deeds that constitute the habit. It is the single 'ways,' which are conditional propositions, each general" (5:510).

16. Gentry, "Habit and the Logical Interpretant," 78.

17. Charles S. Peirce, *The New Elements of Mathematics*, ed. Carolyn Eisele (Atlantic Highlands, N.J.: Humanities Press, 1976), 4: 142.

18. Ibid.

19. Ibid.

20. Ibid., 143.

Index

AMERICAN PHILOSOPHY SERIES
Douglas R. Anderson and Jude Jones, series editors

Kenneth Laine Ketner, ed., *Peirce and Contemporary Thought: Philosophical Inquiries.*

Max H. Fisch, ed., *Classic American Philosophers: Peirce, James, Royce, Santayana, Dewey, Whitehead,* second edition. Introduction by Nathan Houser.

John E. Smith, *Experience and God,* second edition.

Vincent G. Potter, *Peirce's Philosophical Perspectives.* Ed. by Vincent Colapietro.

Richard E. Hart and Douglas R. Anderson, eds., *Philosophy in Experience: American Philosophy in Transition.*

Vincent G. Potter, *Charles S. Peirce: On Norms and Ideals,* second edition. Introduction by Stanley M. Harrison.

Vincent M. Colapietro, ed., *Reason, Experience, and God: John E. Smith in Dialogue.* Introduction by Merold Westphal.

Robert J. O'Connell, S.J., *William James on the Courage to Believe,* second edition.

Elizabeth M. Kraus, *The Metaphysics of Experience: A Companion to Whitehead's "Process and Reality,"* second edition. Introduction by Robert C. Neville.

Kenneth Westphal, ed., *Pragmatism, Reason, and Norms: A Realistic Assessment—Essays in Critical Appreciation of Frederick L. Will.*

Beth J. Singer, *Pragmatism, Rights, and Democracy.*

Eugene Fontinell, *Self, God, and Immorality: A Jamesian Investigation.*

Roger Ward, *Conversion in American Philosophy: Exploring the Practice of Transformation.*

Michael Epperson, *Quantum Mechanics and the Philosophy of Alfred North Whitehead.*

Kory Sorrell, *Representative Practices: Peirce, Pragmatism, and Feminist Epistemology.*

Naoko Saito, *The Gleam of Light: Moral Perfectionism and Education in Dewey and Emerson.*

Josiah Royce, *The Basic Writings of Josiah Royce.*

Douglas R. Anderson, *Philosophy Americana: Making Philosophy at Home in American Culture.*

James Campbell and Richard E. Hart, eds., *Experience as Philosophy: On the World of John J. McDermott.*

John J. McDermott, *The Drama of Possibility: Experience as Philosophy of Culture.* Edited by Douglas R. Anderson